THE REALITY *of* BEING

The Fourth Way of Gurdjieff

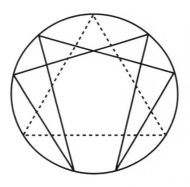

Jeanne de Salzmann

SHAMBHALA
Boston & London
2010

Shambhala Publications, Inc.
Horticultural Hall
300 Massachusetts Avenue
Boston, Massachusetts 02115
www.shambhala.com

9 8 7 6 5 4 3 2 1

First Edition
Printed in the United States of America

∞ This edition is printed on acid-free paper that meets
the American National Standards Institute z39.48 Standard.
♻ This book was printed on 30% postconsumer
recycled paper. For more information please visit
www.shambhala.com.

Distributed in the United States by Random House, Inc.,
and in Canada by Random House of Canada Ltd

Library of Congress Cataloging-in-Publication Data
Salzmann, Madame de (Jeanne), 1889?–1990.
The reality of being: to live the Fourth Way of Gurdjieff /
Jeanne de Salzmann.—1st ed.
p.   cm.
Includes index.
ISBN 978-1-59030-815-8 (hardcover: alk. paper)
1. Gurdjieff, Georges Ivanovitch, 1872–1949.   2. Fourth Way (Occultism)
3. Spiritual life.   I. Title.
BP605.G92S36   2010
299'.93—dc22
2010006464

Contents

Foreword

GEORGE IVANOVITCH GURDJIEFF (1866–1949) regarded knowledge of reality—what he called true "knowledge of being"—as a stream flowing from remote antiquity, passed on from age to age, from people to people, from race to race. He viewed this knowledge as the indispensable means to achieve inner freedom, liberation. For those who seek to understand the meaning of human life in the universe, he said, the aim of the search is to break through to this stream, to find it. Then there remains only "to know" in order "to be." But in order to know, he taught, it is necessary to find out "how to know."

Gurdjieff respected traditional religions and practices concerned with spiritual transformation, and pointed out that their different approaches could be subsumed under one of three categories: the "way of the fakir," which centers on mastery of the physical body; the "way of the monk," based on faith and religious feeling; and the "way of the yogi," which concentrates on developing the mind. He presented his teaching as a "Fourth Way" that requires work on all three aspects at the same time. Instead of discipline, faith or meditation, this way calls for the awakening of another intelligence—knowing and understanding. His personal wish, he once said, was to live and teach so that there should be a new conception of God in the world, a change in the very meaning of the word.

The first demand on the Fourth Way is "Know thyself," a principle that Gurdjieff reminded us is far more ancient than Socrates. Spiritual progress depends on understanding, which is determined by one's level of being. Change in being is possible through conscious effort toward a quality of thinking and feeling that brings a new capacity to see and to love. Although his teaching could be called "esoteric Christianity," Gurdjieff noted that the principles of true Christianity were developed thousands of years before Jesus Christ. In order to open to reality, to unity with everything in the universe, Gurdjieff called for living the wholeness of "Presence" in the experience of "I Am."

When Gurdjieff undertook to write *All and Everything*, his trilogy on the life of man, he envisioned the last book as the Third Series titled *Life Is Real Only Then, When "I Am."* His stated aim for this book was to bring the reader to a true vision of the "world existing in reality." Gurdjieff began work on it in November 1934 but stopped writing six months later and never completed the book. Before his death in 1949, he entrusted his writings to Jeanne de Salzmann, his closest pupil, and charged her with doing "everything possible—even impossible—in order that what I brought will have an action."

At the time of his death, Gurdjieff's followers were scattered across Europe and America. Mme. de Salzmann's first task was to call them to work together. The second was to give the teaching a form for practical work toward consciousness. In the forty years after Gurdjieff's death, she arranged for the publication of his books and the preservation of his dance exercises, called the Movements. She also established Gurdjieff centers in Paris, New York and London, as well as Caracas, Venezuela. In these centers she organized groups and Movements classes, whose participants referred to their collective engagement as "the Work." Today, through the efforts of these pupils and other followers of the teaching, Gurdjieff's ideas have spread throughout the world.

In the introduction that follows, Mme. de Salzmann reveals how she saw Gurdjieff as a spiritual "master" in the traditional sense—not as a teacher of doctrine but as one who by his very presence awakens and helps others in their search for consciousness. What she does not speak about is how she herself also taught by her presence. She had a quality of intelligence and, in her own words, an "attitude of vigilance" that she brought at all times and in all circumstances. For Madame, to live the teaching was a way of being.

The respective roles of Gurdjieff and Mme. de Salzmann were very different. As she notes, Gurdjieff created conditions for his pupils and was the dominant influence for each person. There was, however, no sense of an organized work together, and the seeds of knowledge that he planted in different people could not sustain a common endeavor. She called others to see, with the master gone, that their real guide was the teaching he left behind and their only possibility was to live it together. Her constant demand was that they understand the teaching and share the experience of a conscious relation. She returned again and again to the practice necessary to have a new perception of reality and a more stable Presence as an independent life within the body. To live the teaching would be to awake, to die to identification with one's ordinary level of functioning, and to be reborn to the experience of another dimension, another world.

A fundamental principle of the Fourth Way is that it is in life and through life. Mme. de Salzmann speaks of this in the introduction, exploring what it means that Gurdjieff came to bring a spiritual "way." The transmission of esoteric knowledge requires an engagement with others, a work undertaken together in what Gurdjieff termed a "school." Esoteric schools share the common aim of seeing reality, but they differ in their approach, their "way." When Gurdjieff brought a teaching of a way, he brought not only ideas but a particular approach— a certain "life to be lived."

Mme. de Salzmann's general concept of a "school" can be discerned from the operation of the centers that she organized. It is important to understand that she is talking about a collective practice of the teaching rather than an institution for acquiring conceptual knowledge. These centers are not exclusive and have no formal admission requirements or grades of achievement. Indeed, there are no teachers. For a certain time, participants work in a group with a leader who answers questions. Later, in more senior groups, they exchange among themselves. The Fourth Way is a way of understanding, not of faith or obedience to a charismatic leader. As Mme. de Salzmann wrote, "The teaching is the guide, and only he who questions more deeply can be responsible to serve."

Mme. de Salzmann was constantly reflecting on the reality of being and writing down her thoughts in her notebooks. This deep questioning was basic to her approach to others, in which every encounter was to be lived as wholly as possible. She carefully prepared by pondering and writing down what she wished to bring to meetings. She kept these notebooks, like diaries, up to her last years. Taken together, they provide a forty-year chronicle of her life's work reflecting on reality and bringing Gurdjieff's teaching to others. At ninety-one she remarked:

> I am writing a book on how to be in life, on the path to take in order to live on two levels. It will show how to find a balance, to go from one to the other, or rather to find the way in between. We have to see beyond, and through, our ordinary thinking in order to open to another mind. Otherwise, we remain at the threshold in front of the door, and the door does not open.

When she died ten years later, she left the notebooks intact, carefully preserved. To those closest to her, this was a clear sign of the legacy she intended for this material: to help complete Gurdjieff's writing on a true vision of reality and fulfill his mission to bring a lost system of knowledge to the modern world.

Mme. de Salzmann was wholehearted in her devotion to Gurdjieff and his work, dedicating her own contributions as "in homage" to him. She was also unrelenting in her call to others to live the teaching. These qualities are reflected in this book. She often echoed, and sometimes repeated, his exact words. Examples include the text on the octave in section 85, which she said came from him, and the exercise of divided attention in section 92, which is as he wrote it in the Third Series. She brought the teaching using his terms but with her own insight. For example, "conscious work" for her required simultaneous participation of the separate brains or "centers" governing the thinking, feeling and moving functions in order to experience a unified Presence; this required a certain "struggle" that was not directed *against* automatic functioning as much as it was *for* the positive aim of remaining present; it was important to maintain an inner "look," to "stay in front" in an "act of seeing"; and one had to experience Presence as a "second body" in order to have a stability and independence that could be free from outside influences.

At the same time, Mme. de Salzmann developed her own language and way of speaking, strong and direct. Like Gurdjieff, she cared little about conventions of grammar and vocabulary, much less metaphoric consistency. She also was unconcerned about conforming to accepted concepts of science. For her, the paramount concern was clarity of meaning in the experience of consciousness, even where it was necessary to be imprecise.

Readers should be forewarned about certain unusual characteristics of this book. There is almost no description or explanation of either the reality of being or Gurdjieff's teaching on how to live it. Indeed, like him in his later years, Mme. de Salzmann consistently refused to discuss the teaching in terms of ideas. When asked a theoretical question, she would invariably demur, saying "You have to see for yourself." For her the idea alone, the concept without experience, was not enough—truth could not be thought. Indeed, the knowledge of the thinking mind, especially thoughts about "who we are," was an obstacle, a veil hiding reality. So, instead of presenting a vision of the ultimate destination, this book is more like an account of an actual journey, including routes traveled and landmarks encountered along the way.

Jeanne de Salzmann had her own way of speaking, and not only her distinctive choice of words and capacity to shock. Listening to her, one had the impression that she knew precisely what she wished to say and how she would say it. This is confirmed by the notebooks, which show a remarkable clarity and consistency in her thinking over forty years. Yet what she expressed in the moment was more than mere words.

Mme. de Salzmann says in her introduction that Gurdjieff taught by his Presence, and later writes that knowledge of a higher level can be passed on through ideas and words only by one who knows from his own experience and can express the life contained in them. This expression required speaking from a conscious state—in effect, showing the direction in the moment for those who could follow. This way of teaching was highly concentrated, as reflected in this book. It would have been impossible to take in more than one of these texts at a time, or even to listen to one presentation after the other.

Like every experiential account, the inner journey Mme. de Salzmann describes can really be understood only to the extent the reader himself can live the experience—that is, has eyes to see and ears to hear. In this respect this book follows in the line of Gurdjieff's Third Series, which he foretold would be accessible only to those capable of understanding it. Nevertheless, each person reading or hearing these texts will be able to recognize what he or she knows and, perhaps more important, what he or she does not know, thereby opening to a sense of the *unknown* that Mme. de Salzmann would call the threshold to reality.

This book was edited by a small group of Jeanne de Salzmann's family and followers. Its contents are entirely from her notebooks except a few passages from other, recorded statements. No attempt has been made to identify isolated excerpts taken by her from Gurdjieff or other writers. The chapters have been compiled according to themes that emerged from the material, and arranged in an order corresponding generally to stages of inner work. Although the sequence is not chronological, most of the material in chapters I–IV originated from the first decade after Gurdjieff's death. Then and later, listeners would have already been familiar with his ideas from reading the published works listed in the biographical note at the back of this book, including the Law of Three and the Law of Seven summarized in the note.

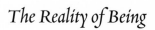

The Reality of Being

In homage to

George Ivanovitch Gurdjieff

Introduction

WHEN I MET George Ivanovitch Gurdjieff I was thirty years old and living in the Caucasus mountain region of what was then southern Russia. At the time I had a deep need to understand the meaning of life but was dissatisfied with explanations that seemed theoretical, not really useful. The first impression of Gurdjieff was very strong, unforgettable. He had an expression I had never seen, and an intelligence, a force, that was different, not the usual intelligence of the thinking mind but a vision that could see everything. He was, at the same time, both kind and very, very demanding. You felt he would see you and show you what you were in a way you would never forget in your whole life.

It was impossible really to know Gurdjieff. The impression he gave of himself was never the same. With some people who did not know him, he played the role of a spiritual master, behaving as they expected, and then let them go away. But if he saw they were looking for something higher, he might take them to dinner and speak about interesting subjects, amuse them, make them laugh. This behavior seemed to be more spontaneous, more "free." But was it really freer, or did it only seem so because he intended to appear like that? You might think you knew Gurdjieff very well, but then he would act quite differently and you would see that you did not really know him. He was like an irresistible force, not dependent on any one form but continually giving birth to forms.

Gurdjieff brought us a knowledge of consciousness, a science that shows what we are and our potential capacity, what needs to be developed. It is a real understanding of the energies in us, of their relation in ourselves and with everything around us. He came to bring a teaching, show a way toward consciousness. What is a *"way"*? And what is a *teaching* of a way?

Esoteric knowledge is the science of man's relation with God and the universe. Its transmission requires an engagement with others—so-called "schools"—because a certain energy can only be produced in conditions where people work together. Schools may differ in their knowledge and their approach—their way—but they have the same aim in common: to see reality. The knowledge is passed on theoretically and through direct experience, that is, by living a drama which follows the particular way of the school. This creates a relation, the link without which it would not be possible to live in two worlds of different levels at the same time.

Gurdjieff's teaching speaks to contemporary man, that is, to someone who no longer knows how to recognize the truth revealed in different forms since earliest times, someone with a deep sense of dissatisfaction, who feels isolated, meaningless. But how to awaken an intelligence that can distinguish the real from the illusory?

According to Gurdjieff, the truth can be approached only if all the parts that make up the human being—the thought, the feeling and the body—are touched with the same force and in the particular way appropriate to each of them. Otherwise, development will inevitably be one-sided and, sooner or later, come to a stop. Without an effective understanding of this principle, all work on oneself is certain to deviate from the aim. The essential conditions will be wrongly understood, and there will be a mechanical repetition of forms of effort that never go beyond a quite ordinary level.

Gurdjieff knew how to make use of every life circumstance to have people feel the truth. I saw him at work, attentive to the possibilities of understanding in his different groups and also to the subjective difficulties of each pupil. I saw him deliberately putting the accent on a particular aspect of knowing, then on another aspect, according to a very definite plan. He worked at times with a thought that stimulated the intellect and opened up an entirely new vision, at times with a feeling that required giving up all artifice in favor of an immediate and complete sincerity, at times with the awakening and putting in motion of a body that responded freely to whatever it was asked to serve.

It was a way that did not isolate his pupils from life but engaged them through life, a way that took into account the *yes* and the *no,* the oppositions, all the contrary forces, a way that made them understand the necessity of struggling to rise above the battle while at the same time taking part in it. One was brought to a threshold to be crossed, and for the first time one felt that complete sincerity was required. Passing over might appear to be difficult, but what was being left behind no longer had the old attraction. In front of certain hesitations, the picture Gurdjieff gave of himself provided a measure of what it was necessary to give and of what had to be given up in order not to take a wrong turn. Then it was no longer the teaching of doctrine but the incarnate action of knowledge—the action of a master. In Gurdjieff's own Presence, and because of his Presence, one knew a moment of truth and was capable of sacrificing everything for it. This was like a miracle. It was a miracle. It was a miracle—something of a force from a dimension above what we know.

What Gurdjieff brought us was the possibility of approaching a higher level of being. By his words, by the relations he established with us, by his Presence alone, he made us feel human qualities that awakened in us the wish to go in this direction. He drew us toward him, toward another level. At the same time, he made us suffer terribly by making us see our actual state, the way we really were. Most of the misunderstandings and disagreements about Gurdjieff's methods and behavior come from the fact that he worked at the same time on our two natures.

On the one hand, Gurdjieff worked on our essence. He listened to our inner need with tireless patience and kindness, which hurt because we always felt unworthy. He took an interest in our difficulties. He gave practical help to take the next step. With unbelievable exactness he indicated the definite inner act that each had to carry out at the given moment to free himself further from his automatism. Here there was on Gurdjieff's part never any acting, and no pressure. This was truly a gift from above, which left the impression of love and of compassion for the human condition. He made us feel our possibilities, our potential and, with the means he gave, he brought the hope of seeing them grow.

On the other hand, Gurdjieff worked on our functions in a relentless way—continual pressure, greater and greater demands, putting us in horrible situations, shocks of all kinds. Not only did he not attract us but, in pushing us to extreme limits, he forced us to resist him, to react against him. And he did this without mercy. By his Presence he obliged us to come to a decision, to know what we wanted. One could always refuse and go away.

Here was the grandeur of Gurdjieff. The first way, work on our essence, was outside life, wholly concentrated on inner action. The second, work on our functions, was in life itself and through life. With one hand he called us; with the other he beat us, showing us our slavery to our functions. Very few people had the chance to experience both sides. Yet it is impossible to understand Gurdjieff's methods or behavior without having received material of both these aspects of his work.

Without Gurdjieff, the master, we do not have the possibility of working in those special conditions. Yet his teaching remains—to develop our inner being. For this, we have to understand the teaching and submit to its principles. And this we cannot do alone. We cannot come to anything alone. Our way is to live these ideas in order to understand them, and to pass on the teaching to others if and to the extent we are able to live it with them. Sowing ideas without living them is sowing ideas that are empty. Gurdjieff left us not only words and ideas to be transmitted, but a certain life to be lived, a drama to be played out with others around us, without which the work will remain imaginary.

We have therefore a responsibility. Ideas have been brought by Gurdjieff as part of a science that we need to know well. But the idea alone is not enough. If it is not lived by all the parts of myself, I will remain as I am—passive and wholly at the disposition of surrounding forces. On a cosmic scale, man plays an important role on the earth. Without him certain forces cannot act and cannot maintain an equilibrium. But we do not see this, we do not know it and consequently we do not produce the force that could create a relation with other cosmic energies in ourselves.

What is necessary, in us and around us, is the creation of a certain level of energy, an attention that resists surrounding influences and does not let itself deteriorate. Then it has to receive a force that is more active, that will allow it not only to resist but to have an action and find a stable place between two currents of different levels. This possibility of equilibrium is the continuing challenge, the interval to be faced at every moment in the work for consciousness.

I

A CALL TO CONSCIOUSNESS

The child wants **to have**, *the adult wants* **to be**.

The wish **to be** *is behind all my manifestations.*

To learn to see is the first initiation into self-knowledge.

We struggle not **against** *something, we struggle* **for**
  something.

*I believe I need to pay attention when, in fact, I need to
  see and know my inattention.*

When I begin to see, I begin to love what I see.

Where our attention is, God is.

I AM ASLEEP

1. A nostalgia for Being

Man remains a mystery to himself. He has a nostalgia for Being, a longing for duration, for permanence, for absoluteness—a longing *to be*. Yet everything that constitutes his life is temporary, ephemeral, limited. He aspires to another order, another life, a world that is beyond him. He senses that he is meant to participate in it.

He searches for an idea, an inspiration, that could move him in this direction. It arises as a question: "Who am I—who am I in this world?" If this question becomes sufficiently alive, it could direct the course of his life. He cannot answer. He has nothing with which to answer—no knowledge of himself to face this question, no knowledge of his own. But he feels he must welcome it. He asks himself what he is. This is the first step on the way. He wants to open his eyes. He wants to wake up, to awaken.

2. The life force

We wish to live, to be in life. From the moment we are born, something in us seeks to affirm itself in the outside world. I want to be heard and seen, to devour the world. At the same time, I do not want to be devoured. I want to be first, always. But all too soon I encounter the resistance of the world, and the basic impulse of self-affirmation has to take others into account. My affirming often assumes curious, even though common, forms such as self-pity or a refusal to express oneself.

I wish to live, I agree with life. I do everything to live, and this same force maintains the life of my body. I wish for something or to do something, and when the wish appears, this force is here. It impels me toward manifestation. Throughout my life, in everything I do, I seek to affirm this force. There is no act, however small, that is not an affirmation. If I speak to someone or write a letter, I affirm this force, I affirm my intelligence. Even if I merely look at someone, it is this force. If I hang up my coat, it is this force. Behind this unbridled affirmation, there is surely something true. This force in me is irrepressible. At the same time, I do not know what the affirmation is based on. I believe I am affirming myself. I identify with this force. Yet even though it is in me, this force is not mine. And in affirming it as my own, I do not see that I separate myself from it. In wanting to attribute its power to myself, I cut off its action. I create an inner world that is deprived of the action of this life force. My sense of "I," of my self, is heavy and inert.

We need to see our childishness in relating to the life force, always wishing to have more. The child wants *to have*, the adult wants *to be*. The constant desire for "having" creates fear and a need to be reassured. We need to develop an attention in us that would relate the whole of ourselves to a higher force.

There is only one source of energy. As soon as my energy is called in one direction or another, a force appears. Force is energy in movement. There are different directions, but the source is the same. The life force, the force of manifestation, is always in movement. It has to flow. And I am entirely taken by it, I am swept along. I begin to suspect that I will always be taken if I do not also turn toward another, unknown part of myself.

3. *I do not know myself*

Who am I? I need to know. If I do not know, what meaning does my life have? And what in me responds to life? So, I must try to answer, to see who I am. First, my thought steps back and brings suggestions about myself: I am a man or woman who can do this, who has done that, who possesses this and that. My thinking volunteers possible answers from all that it knows. But it does not know what I am, does not really know me in this moment. Then I turn to my feeling. It is among the centers most capable of knowing. Can it answer? My feeling is not free. It has to obey the "me" who wants to be the greatest, the most powerful and who suffers all the time from not being first. So, my feeling does not dare. It is afraid, or doubts. How can it know? Then, of course, there is my body, the capacity to sense my body. But am I my body?

In fact, I do not know myself. I do not know what I am. I know neither my possibilities nor my limitations. I exist, yet I do not know how I am existing. I believe my actions are affirming my own existence. Yet I am always responding to life with only one part of myself. I react either emotionally or intellectually or physically. And it is never really "I" who responds. I also believe I am moving in the direction I want to go and that I can "do." But in fact I am acted upon, moved by forces that I know nothing about. Everything in me takes place, everything happens. The strings are pulled without my knowing. I do not see that I am like a puppet, a machine set in motion by influences from outside.

At the same time, I sense my life passing as if it were the life of another person. I vaguely see myself being agitated, hoping, regretting, afraid, bored . . . all without feeling that I am taking part. Most of the time I act without knowing it and realize only afterward that I said this or did that. It is as though my life unfolds without my conscious participation. It unfolds while I sleep. From time to time jolts or shocks awaken me for an instant. In the middle of an angry outburst, or grief or danger, I suddenly open my eyes—"What ? . . . It's *me*, here, in this situation, living this." But after the shock, I go back to sleep, and a long time can pass before a new shock awakens me.

As my life passes, I may begin to suspect that I am not what I believe. I am a being who is asleep, a being with no consciousness of himself. In this sleep I confuse intellect—the thought functioning independently from feeling—with intelligence, which includes the capacity to feel what is being reasoned. My functions—my thoughts, feelings and movements—work without direction, subject to random shocks and habits. It is the lowest state of being for man. I live in my own narrow, limited world commanded by associations from all my subjective impressions. This is a prison to which I always return—my prison.

The search for myself begins with questioning where "*I*" am. I have to feel the absence, the habitual absence, of "I." I must know the feeling of emptiness and see the lie in always affirming an image of myself, the false "I." We are all the time saying "I," though we do not really believe in it. In fact, we have nothing else in which we can believe. It is the wish *to be* that pushes me to say "I." It is behind all my manifestations. But this is not a conscious impulse. Usually I look to the attitude of others in order to be convinced of my being. If they reject or ignore me, I doubt myself. If they accept me, I believe in myself.

Am I only this image that I affirm? Is there really no "I" who could be present? In order to respond, I need to know myself, to have a direct experience of knowing myself. First, I have to see the obstacles that stand in the way. I must see that I believe in my mind, my thinking—I believe it is I. "*I*" wish to know, "*I*" have read, "*I*" have understood. All this is the expression of the false "I," my ordinary "I." It is my ego that prevents me from opening to consciousness, from seeing "*what is*" and what "*I am.*"

My effort to awaken cannot be forced. We are afraid of emptiness, afraid to be nothing, and so we make an effort to be otherwise. But who makes this effort? I must see that this too comes from my ordinary "I." All forcing comes from the ego. I must no longer be fooled by an image or an ideal that is imposed by the mind. I need to accept emptiness, accept to be nothing, accept "what is." In this state, the possibility of a new perception of myself appears.

4. "I" am not here

Real "I" comes from essence. Its development depends on the wish of essence—a wish *to be* and then a wish to become *able to be*. Essence is formed from impressions that are assimilated in early childhood, usually up to the age of five or six when a fissure appears between essence and personality. In order to develop further, essence must become active in spite of resistance from the pressure of personality. We need to "remember ourselves" for our essence to receive impressions. Only in a conscious state can we see the difference between essence and personality.

Ordinarily impressions are received in a mechanical way. They are received by our personality, which reacts with automatic thoughts and feelings that depend on its conditioning. We do not assimilate impressions because personality itself cannot be alive—it is dead. In order to be assimilated and transformed, impressions have to be received by essence. This requires a conscious effort at the moment of the impression. And it requires a definite feeling, a feeling of love for being, for being present. We must respond to impressions no longer from the vantage point of personality but from love for being present. This will transform our whole way of thinking and feeling.

The first necessity is to have an impression of myself. This begins with a shock when the question "Who am I?" arises. For an instant there is a stop, an interval that allows my energy, my attention, to change direction. It turns back toward me, and the question now touches me. This energy brings a vibration, a note that did not sound until now. It is subtle, very fine, but nevertheless communicates. I feel it. It is an impression I receive, an impression of a life in me. All my possibilities are here. What follows—whether I will open to the experience of Presence—depends on the way I receive this impression.

We do not understand the moment of receiving an impression and why it is so important. We need to be present because it is the shock of the impression that drives us. If there is nobody here at the moment an impression is received, I react automatically, blindly, passively, and I am lost in the reaction. I refuse the impression of myself as I am. In thinking, in reacting, in interposing my ordinary "I" in the reception of this impression, I close myself. I am imagining what "I" am. I do not know the reality. I am the prisoner of this imagination, the lie of my false "I." Usually I try to awake by forcing, but it does not work. I can and must learn to awake by opening consciously to the impression of myself and seeing what I am at the very moment. This will be a shock that awakens me, a shock brought by an impression that I receive. It requires a freedom to be in movement, not to stop the movement.

In order to wish to be present, I must see that I am asleep. "I" am not here. I am enclosed in a circle of petty interests and avidity in which my "I" is lost. And it will remain lost unless I can relate to something higher. The first condition is to know in myself a different quality, higher than what I ordinarily am. Then my life will take on new meaning. Without this condition there can be no work. I must remember there is another life and at the same time experience the life that I am leading. This is awakening. I awake to these two realities.

I need to understand that by myself, without a relation with something higher, I am nothing, I can do nothing. By myself alone, I can only remain lost in this circle of interests, I have no quality that allows me to escape. I can escape only if I feel my absolute nothingness and begin to feel the need for help. I must feel the need to relate myself to something higher, to open to another quality.

TO REMEMBER ONESELF

🪶 *5. Where our attention is*

I wish to be conscious of myself. Yet, as I am at this moment, can I know myself, can I be conscious of myself? I cannot. I am too scattered. I feel nothing. But I see that I am asleep, and I see the symptoms of this sleep. I have forgotten the sense of my existence, I have forgotten myself. And at this moment I receive a shock: I am awaking, I want to wake up. Then, having scarcely felt the shock, I feel myself taken again, held back by the elements of my sleep—associations that turn around, emotions that take me, unconscious sensations. I feel myself fall back into forgetfulness.

We do not realize how passive we are, always pulled along by events, people and things. We begin an activity with great interest, fully aware of our aim. But after a certain time the impulse weakens, overcome by inertia. Our understanding diminishes, and we feel the need for something new that will restore the interest, the life. Our inner work progresses like this in stages, and always depends on new forces. It is determined by laws. We must get rid of the idea that progress is continuous in a straight line. There are stages where the intensity diminishes and, if we wish not to fall back, a force must appear that is more active.

The passive "man" in us, the only one we know, is the one we trust. But as long as we remain passive, nothing new can appear. We must become active in relation to our inertia, the passive work of our functions. If we wish to change, we must look for the new "man" in ourselves, the one who is hidden. This is the one who remembers, who has a force that can only be brought by our wish, our will, and must grow degree by degree. It is necessary to see that a more active state, a greater intensity, is possible.

I need to recognize that in my usual state my attention is undivided. When I open to the outside, I am naturally interested in it. My attention goes there. I cannot prevent myself. If my force of attention is entirely taken, I am lost in life, identified, asleep. All my capacity to be present is lost. I lose myself, the feeling of myself. My existence loses its meaning. So, the first step is a separation in which my attention is divided.

Our effort must always be clear—to be present, that is, to begin to remember myself. With the attention divided, I am present in two directions, as present as I can be. My attention is engaged in two opposite directions, and I am at the center. This is the act of self-remembering. I wish to keep part of my attention on the awareness of belonging to a higher level and, under this influence, try to open to the outer world. I must make an effort to remain related, an effort of attention. I try to know truly what I am. I struggle to stay present, at the same time with a feeling of "I" turned toward a better quality and with an ordinary feeling tied to my self, my person. I wish to see and not forget that I belong to these two levels.

We must see where our attention is. Where is our attention when we remember ourselves? Where is our attention in life? Order can be born in us only if we enter into direct contact with disorder. We are not in the disorder. We *are* the state of disorder. If I look at what I really am, I see the disorder. And where there is a direct contact, there is an immediate action. I begin to realize that my Presence is where my attention is.

6. The first initiation

Behind all my manifestations, there is a wish to know myself, to know that I exist and how I exist. But in my contacts with the world, an image of "I" is formed at the same time as the contact. I am attached to this image because I take it as being me. I try to affirm and protect it. I am the slave of this image. Being so attached and taken in these reactions, I have no attention left to know that I am also something else.

As I am, I recognize nothing above me, either outside or inside myself. Theoretically perhaps, but not actually. So I have no reference with which to measure myself, and live exclusively according to "I like" or "I don't like." I value only myself and live passively according to what pleases me. This valuing of my ordinary "I" blinds me. It is the biggest obstacle to a new life. The first requirement for self-knowledge is a change in my opinion of myself, which can only come from actually seeing things in myself that I have not seen before. And in order to see, I must *learn to see.* This is the first initiation into self-knowledge.

I try to see how I am in a state of identification, to experience how I am when I am identified. I need to know the enormous power of the force behind identification and its irresistible movement. This force, which sustains us in life, does not want self-remembering. It drives us toward manifestation and refuses the movement inward.

To see myself in identification is to see what I am in life. But each time I remember my higher possibilities, I go away, I refuse what I am in life. And this refusal prevents me from knowing it. I must be clever in order to catch myself without changing anything, without changing my wish to manifest. I need to see myself as a machine driven by the processes that appear—thoughts, desires, movements. I need to know myself as a machine—to be present while I function as a machine. Who am I in life? I must experience it, have a more conscious impression of it.

In order to face the force of identification, there must be something present that attends—an attention that is stable, free and related to another level. I wish to be present to what is taking place, to remain conscious of myself and not lose myself. My effort is made with something that does not belong to my ordinary means. I need a certain will and desire unknown to my ordinary self. My ordinary "I" must give up its place. Through maintaining the attention and not forgetting to look, perhaps one day I will be able to see. If I see one time, I can see a second time, and if this repeats I will no longer be able not to see.

In order to observe, I have to struggle. My ordinary nature refuses self-observation. I need to prepare, to organize a struggle against the obstacle, to withdraw a little from my identification—speaking, imagining, expressing negative emotions. Conscious struggle requires choice and acceptance. It must not be my state that dictates the choice. I must choose the struggle to be present and accept that suffering will appear. There is no struggle without suffering. Struggle is unacceptable to our lower nature; struggle upsets it. This is why it is so important always to remember what we wish—the meaning of our work and our Presence. In going against a habit, for example, like eating or sitting in a certain way, we are not struggling to change the habit. Or in trying not to express negative emotions, we are not struggling against the emotions themselves or struggling to do away with their expression. It is a struggle with our identification, to allow the energy otherwise wasted to serve the work. We struggle not *against* something, we struggle *for* something.

7. Can we become conscious?

The work to be present is in the direction of consciousness—that is, a special kind of perception independent of the activity of the intellectual mind, a perception of oneself: who one is, where one is and then what one knows and does not know. In the moment of consciousness there is the immediate impression of a direct perception. This is quite different from what we usually call "consciousness," which operates more like a reflection faithfully accompanying what I experience and representing it in my mind. When this consciousness reflects the fact that I think or feel something, this is a second action that, like a shadow, follows the first. Without this shadow I am unconscious of and ignore the original thought or feeling. If, for example, I am angry and beside myself, I only see it as long as I am aware of the reflection which, like a witness, tells me in a whisper that I am angry. The whisper follows so closely upon the preceding feeling that I believe they are one and the same. But it is not really like that.

Can we become conscious? It is all a question of energies and their relation, with each energy always controlled by a finer one that is more active, more animating, like a magnet. The energy used in our functions—our thoughts, our emotions, our sensations—is passive, inert. Spent in movements toward the outside, this energy suffices in quality for our life as higher animals, but is not fine enough for an inner act of perception, of consciousness. Nevertheless, we do have some power of attention, at least on the surface, some capacity to point the attention in a desired direction and hold it there. Although it is fragile, this seed or bud of attention is consciousness emerging from deep within us. For it to grow, we need to learn to concentrate, to develop this capacity indispensable for preparing the ground. This is the first thing that we do ourselves, not dependent on anyone else.

The practice of being present is self-remembering. Instead of being taken outward, the attention of the functions is turned toward the inside for a moment of consciousness. I need to recognize that I can understand nothing if I cannot remember myself. This means remembering my highest possibilities, that is, remembering what I open to when I come back to myself alone. To remember myself also means to be present to my situation—to the place, the conditions, the way I am taken by life. There is no room for dreaming.

Perhaps I will not come to a state that is satisfying. It does not matter. What is important is the effort to be present. We cannot always find a better state that brings a feeling of something new. We feel unable and conclude that there is nothing permanent in us on which we can rely. But it is not true. There is something. In a better state, we can see that we have in us all the elements necessary to come to it. The elements are already here. This means the possibilities are always here in us.

What is too often missing is knowing what I want. And it is this that undermines my will to work. Without knowing what I want, I will not make any effort. I will sleep. Without wishing for a different quality in myself, to turn toward my higher possibilities, I will have nothing to lean on, nothing to support work. I must always, again and again, come back to this question: What do I wish? It must become the most important question of my life. Yet this wish for a different quality has no force at all if it comes from my ordinary "I." It must be related to something completely different from my ordinary "I" and free from the desire for a result. I must not forget *why* I wish. This must be for me really a question of life or death—I wish *to be,* to live in a certain way.

8. *The watchman*

We do not see our state of sleep. In this state we think of working; we think, "I wish to be present." But the effort to be present is something very different from thinking. It is an effort in the direction of consciousness. We must come to know whether we are conscious at a given moment, and all the degrees of this consciousness. Its presence or absence can thus be proved by an inner act of observing.

I am in front of something I do not know. I am in front of a mystery, the mystery of my Presence. I must recognize that I cannot know this mystery with my ordinary means of knowing. But I must understand, at least intellectually, what it would mean to be present—that is, to be present not only with my head, my sensation or my feeling, but with all these elements of my Presence together. Maybe then I still will not be truly present, but at least I will search for a common direction.

Who is present—who is seeing? And whom? The whole problem is here.

In order to observe ourselves we need an attention that is different from our ordinary attention. We undertake the struggle to be vigilant, to watch—the struggle of the watchman. We seek to have a watchman in us who is stable. The one who watches is the one who is present. Only the watchman is active. The rest of me is passive. The watchman must take an impression of the inner state while trying to see everything at the same time and have a sense of the whole. We must learn to distinguish between the real "I," which is nowhere to be seen, and the personality, which takes over and believes it is the only one who exists.

One has power over the other. The necessity is to reverse the roles. The danger is that we do not see the roles change back again. I believe I need to pay attention when, in fact, I need to see and know my inattention.

Observation of myself shows me how better to concentrate and strengthens the attention. It makes me see that I do not remember myself, that I do not see my state of sleep. I am fragmented, my attention is dispersed, and there is no force that is available to see. When I awaken, I make an effort to disengage enough attention to oppose this dispersion, and to see it. This is a state that is more voluntary. Now there is a watchman, and this watchman is a different state of consciousness. I must always remember that I do not know what I am, that the whole problem is *who* is present. Self-observation by my usual thought, with its separation between the observer and what is observed, will only strengthen the illusion of my ordinary "I."

At a certain moment we come to see two aspects, two natures, in ourselves—a higher nature related to one world and a lower nature related to another, a different world. What are we? We are neither one nor the other—neither God nor animal. We participate in life with both a divine nature and an animal nature. Man is double; he is not one. And as such, he is only a promise of man until he can live with both natures present in himself and not withdraw into one or the other. If he withdraws into the higher part, he is distant from his manifestations and can no longer evaluate them; he no longer knows or experiences his animal nature. If he slides into the other nature, he forgets everything that is not animal, and there is nothing to resist it; he is animal . . . not man. The animal always refuses the angel. The angel turns away from the animal.

A conscious man is one who is always vigilant, always watchful, who remembers himself in both directions and has his two natures always confronted.

THE NEED TO KNOW

~~~ *9. New knowledge is necessary*

Gurdjieff brought a teaching of the Fourth Way that calls for conscious work rather than obedience. A fundamental idea is that in our ordinary state everything takes place in sleep. And in sleep we can see nothing. We cannot direct our lives by our own will. We are entirely dependent on influences from outside and enslaved by the automatic reactions of our functioning. It is complete slavery. There is no higher principle, no conscious principle.

Man has the possibility to awaken from this sleep, to awaken to the higher, *to be*. The means is the attention. In sleep the attention is taken. It must be freed and turned in another direction. This is the separation of "*I*" and "*me*." It is the active force opposed to the passive, the struggle between the *yes* and the *no*. This mobilization of the attention is the first step toward the possibility of self-remembering. Without a different attention, we are obliged to be automatic. With an attention that is voluntarily directed, we go toward consciousness.

Dividing the attention makes it possible to begin the observation of oneself. Self-observation must always be related to the idea of centers and of their automatic functioning, in particular, the lack of a common direction. Our three centers—mind, body and feeling—work with different energies, and their disposition determines the influences that reach us. We can receive more subtle, higher influences only if our centers are disposed in a certain way. When we are wholly under the power of lower influences, the higher cannot reach us. Everything depends on the quality of the influences that we obey, higher or lower. As we are, each influence produces a kind of reaction that corresponds to it. Negative emotions are a negation on a very low level. If our reactions are on a low level, what we receive is on a low level. We need to learn to obey the law governing higher forces, consciously to submit our will to the higher. The moment of consciousness is a moment of will.

New knowledge is necessary, a knowledge that can lead to a new understanding of man and to a change in being, that is, to evolution. The science underlying the Fourth Way is ancient, although it has been forgotten. It is a science that studies man not just as he is but as he can become. It regards man as having a possibility of evolving, and studies the facts, the principles and the laws of this evolution. This is an evolution of certain qualities that cannot develop by themselves. It cannot be mechanical. This evolution calls for conscious effort and for seeing. Knowledge is knowledge of the whole. Yet we can only receive it in fragments. Afterward we must connect them ourselves in order to find their place in an understanding of the whole.

The Fourth Way is to be lived. In the work to be present I need first to find each day a certain quality of coming back to myself. Then I must become able to observe my identification with the life force and find a place in myself in which at certain moments my attention can hold itself between the two. For this, it is necessary to work with others.

10. Self-observation

If I wish to understand myself, I must above all have a mind that is capable of observing without distortion. This requires my full attention, which appears only when there is a real need to know, when the mind turns everything away in order to observe. I never observe myself in action. I never see myself functioning mechanically, nor see that I like to function mechanically. I need to be convinced of the detours—experiences and knowledge—that prevent me from observing myself. This kind of observation is the beginning of self-knowledge.

I wish to experience each thought and each feeling in myself, but my attention always wanders. No thought is ever completed, no feeling is ever concluded. The feeling swings from one thing to another, ordered here and there like a slave. With this continual movement, I cannot discover the profound meaning of these thoughts or these feelings. My reactions have to slow down. But how? This cannot be imposed. It would create conflict and undermine the effort. Yet, when I concentrate in order to see, by itself this act slows down the speed of the reaction. If the attention is free of any image or word, free of knowledge, my feeling slows down. There is an instant before the reaction appears, in which I can see my thoughts and feelings arise. I see them as facts. For the first time I understand what a "fact" is—something that I cannot change, that I cannot avoid, something *which is*. This is true! As my only interest is to see, I do not intervene and the real significance of these thoughts and feelings is revealed. Truth becomes all-powerful to me. In this state my knowing has stopped; the search alone exists. How can I know a living thing? By following it. To know the Self I must be with the Self. I must follow it.

Gurdjieff taught the necessity of self-observation, but this practice has been mostly misunderstood. Usually when I try to observe, there is a point from which the observation is made, and my mind projects the idea of observing, of an observer separate from the object observed. But the idea of observing is not the observing. Seeing is not an idea. It is an act, the act of seeing. Here the object is me, a living being that needs to be recognized in order to live a certain life. This observation is not that of a fixed observer looking at an object. It is one complete act, an experience that can take place only if there is no separation between what sees and what is seen, no point from which the observation is made. Then there is a feeling of a special kind, a *wish to know*. It is an affection that embraces everything that I see and is indifferent to nothing. I need to see. When I begin to see, I begin to love what I see. No longer separate, I am in contact with it, intensely, completely. I *know*, and this knowing is the result of this new condition. I wake up to what I am and touch the source of true love, a quality of being.

The truth of what I am can only be seen by a fine energy, an intelligence in me that sees. This requires a precise relation between my usual thinking and this seeing. One must submit to the other, or I will be taken by the material of the thought. There can be no contradiction, however small, in myself. Otherwise, I cannot see. A contradiction means on one side the need to know what I am, and on the other a head that functions for itself alone, an emotion that feels for itself alone, and tensions that cut me off from sensation. When I see myself lost in the dark, I feel the need for clarity, for vision. I feel the necessity to see, a completely different feeling from wishing to change because yesterday I had a better state. Then, little by little, the tensions in the body let go by themselves. The mind sees without seeking a result, and the body opens to a different quality. The energy becomes free and an inner reality appears. There is no more contradiction. I see, just that . . . I only see.

To observe without contradiction is like following a fast current, a torrent, anticipating the rushing water with one's look, seeing the movement of each little wave. There is no time to formulate, to name or to judge. There is no more thinking. My mind becomes quiet and sensitive—very alive but quiet. It sees without distortion. Silent observation gives birth to understanding, but this truth must be seen. Order is born from understanding disorder. To be disorder and, at the same time, present to the disorder brings the knowing of a different possibility, a different order of things.

11. Conscious effort

Why do I begin to work? In order to know what moves me to make an effort, I need a more conscious attention. This attention cannot be mechanical, because it must be constantly adjusted in order to last. There has to be someone vigilant who watches, and that watchman will be a different state of consciousness.

When I withdraw from life to open to what I am, a moment sometimes comes when I feel myself belonging to a new order, a cosmic order. I receive this impression, I become conscious of it. This impression could now become part of my Presence. It is here to help me, and it can help me if I connect it to other similar impressions. By associating it with these other impressions, I can make it appear consciously. I must watch with a voluntary attention to keep the conscious impression of myself as long as possible.

We can have accidental moments of remembering due to conscious and unconscious impressions. These impressions recur in us, we know not how. But they escape and are lost because they are not connected, not associated voluntarily. We have no voluntary attitude when we experience them, and consequently they are bound to lead to blind reaction. I need to find an attitude that is more conscious with respect to them. When I see that I am not the same from one moment to the next, I feel the need to have a point of reference. I have to measure these differences in my state in relation to something that is always the same. All my work will then revolve around this point. For me this reference is my actual understanding of what it is to be a conscious being.

There must be a sacrifice to sustain the feeling of Presence I have at the moment of an effort. I have to accept voluntarily to give up my ordinary will, to make it serve. Everything depends on my active participation. In general, I put too much emphasis on not being taken, on not losing my state. I forget at what point I need help. I trust something that will never sustain me, and I do not pray for something higher, something in myself that is finer. So, nothing sustains me and I am deprived of what I need. It cannot be otherwise.

Feeling passes through phases that are linked to attention. In becoming active, the attention acquires a finer quality and becomes capable of grasping what is taking place on other levels, where vibrations have a different wavelength. When I have a feeling of my Presence, I am connected with higher forces. At the same time, I am connected with lower forces. I am in between. I cannot have a sense of myself without the participation of the lower forces that work in me. A conscious attention means something that is between two worlds.

What is difficult to understand is that without conscious effort, nothing is possible. Conscious effort is related to higher nature. My lower nature alone cannot lead me to consciousness. It is blind. But when I wake up and I feel that I belong to a higher world, this is only part of conscious effort. I become truly conscious only when I open to all my possibilities, higher and lower.

There is value only in conscious effort.

12. *The sacred manifests as inner consciousness*

We are seeking to approach the unknown, to open the door to what is hidden in us and pass beyond. It is necessary to submit entirely to an inner voice, to a feeling of the divine, of the sacred in us, but we can do it only in part. The sacred manifests as inner consciousness. The divine, God, must be found within. Truth, the only truth, is in consciousness.

Everything that exists is constituted of three forces. They can be represented as the Father, the active force; the Son, the passive force; and the Holy Spirit, the neutralizing force. The Father creates the Son. The Son returns to the Father. The force that descends is the one that wishes to return, to go back up.

In man it is the mind that is opposed to the body. The neutralizing force is the wish that unites them, connects them. Everything comes from the wish, the will. To represent God, it is necessary to represent these three forces. Where the three forces are reunited, God is. Where our attention is, God is. When two forces are opposed and a third unites them, God is here. We can say, "Lord, have mercy on me." We can ask for help, *to come to this in ourselves.* The only help is this. Our aim is this, to contain, to unite these three forces in us . . . *to Be.*

II

OPENING TO PRESENCE

The moment of receiving an impression is the moment of becoming conscious.

Consciousness is always consciousness of self.

I need to feel that this Presence forms itself in me.

It is only by working to be present that my attention will develop.

In each event of life there is a double movement of involution and evolution.

The effort I can make with my ordinary means, the only effort that is incumbent on me, is one of voluntary passivity—a conscious effort.

The attitude we take, our inner and outer posture, is at the same time our aim and our way.

IN A PASSIVE STATE

~~~ *13. My functions are passive*

Whatever the state in which I find myself at this moment, whatever the sense of the force I manifest, the highest possibilities are here, hidden by the thick screen of my passivity in believing in my self-sufficiency. My destiny begins when I feel the call of another force in me and respond to it voluntarily. This is my first voluntary act, becoming available to a reality that changes my purpose for living. I am here in order to hear this force, not to expect something from it or to appropriate it. I am here to understand the action that will create the possibility of a responsible life.

As I am today, I feel empty, living without meaning, without a real aim, without purpose. I am here simply because I have been created. And I feel my life go by without any sense of direction, all the while suggestible, subject to what I hope, what I expect, what I have to do, what all this means. My functions are passive, under the influence and at the mercy of everything that touches them. My thinking hears words it believes it understands, and immediately has associations. My feeling, on the lookout for what pleases or displeases me, is curious or refuses. And my body is heavy, digesting or lounging in its torpor. I feel myself passive. When I have to manifest, to express myself, I simply react to the impression received according to the way my centers have been educated. I only see forms—things and persons—never forces. I never respond from vision, from an understanding of reality. That in me which is more truly "I" does not appear. All inner and outer events seem like a dream because I do not feel truly touched. What is it that impressions do not reach? What is it in me that does not feel touched to the core?

I wish to see myself. But the energy of my looking, my seeing, is passive. I see what I look at only through an image, an idea. So I do not really see, I am not in direct contact with what I see. Held passive by the idea, my attention is not free. I react to the image of what I see, and things repeat in the same way indefinitely. My thinking reacts automatically, making comparisons and obeying commands from all the material accumulated over time. Can I have a thinking that is more active and not continually occupied in drawing from its memory? Such thinking would hold itself in front of a fact, sensitive and receptive, without making any judgment or suggestion, without any thoughts. It would hold itself simply by an urgency to know the truth. This thinking would be like a light. It would be able to see.

My sensing is also passive. I sense myself as a familiar form to which I return again and again, a form that corresponds to my usual way of thinking. Can I have a sensing that is more active, awakened entirely to the energy it receives? This sensing, like this thinking, would be without any motive to possess.

When I experience this more active thinking and sensing together, I discover a new wish, a feeling of urgency to be like this. It is only at the moment this intensity appears—of wishing to see, of wishing to know *what is*—that I awake to myself and to what I am as a whole. I awake not in order to change but to know the true, the real. What has changed is my attitude. It is more conscious. And I see that if this active wishing is not here, I will fall back into my dream.

My wishing to know and understand takes precedence over everything. It is not just an idea in my head, or a particular sensation or emotion. It asks everything of me all at once. Can I learn to listen to it?

14. I need impressions of myself

In my state of being today there is no stability, no "I." I do not know myself. I begin to feel I must come to a moment of Presence that is more complete. What I need above all is to have an impression—as deep as possible—of myself. I never have a deep impression. My impressions are superficial. They just produce associations at the surface, which leave no memory and change nothing, transform nothing. Gurdjieff spoke of impressions as food, but we do not understand what it means to feed ourselves or its significance for our being.

I am poor in the material of impressions of myself. What I have is so little, it has no weight. If I really want to know something, to be sure of something, I first need to be "impressed" by the knowledge. I need this new knowledge. I must be "impressed" by it so strongly that I will at this moment *know* it with all of myself, my whole being, not merely *think* it with my head. If I do not have enough impressions, enough of this being-knowledge, I can have no conviction. Without this knowledge, without material, how will I value things? How will I work? There is nothing to provide an impulse in one direction or another. There is no possibility to act consciously. So, the very first thing I need for conscious action is impressions of myself, both in quiet conditions when I am more open to what I am, and in the midst of life when I try to see myself being lost. Until I have a certain quantity of impressions, I cannot see further, I cannot understand more.

We think of impressions as lifeless, fixed like a photograph. But with every impression we receive a certain amount of energy, something alive that acts on us, that animates us. I can feel this when I have a new impression of myself, an impression entirely different from the way I usually experience myself. I suddenly know something real in myself in quite a new way, and I receive an energy by which I am animated. But then I lose it, I do not retain it. It goes as if taken by a thief. And when I need it most, when I wish to be present in front of my life, there is no support to help me and I lose myself. I begin to see that impressions of myself are food, that they bring an energy which must be received and must be retained.

We need to see what is in the way, and we need to understand why receiving an impression is so difficult. It is not because I do not wish to receive it. It is because I am not able. I am always closed, whatever the circumstances of life. At times, maybe for a flash I am open to an impression. But almost immediately I react. The impression is automatically associated with other things and the reaction comes. The button is pushed and this or that thought, emotion or gesture must follow. I cannot help it, first of all because I do not see it. My reaction cuts me off from the impression, as well as from the reality it represents. This is the barrier, the wall. In reacting, I close.

What I do not see is that I lose all contact with reality when my habitual functions take charge. Now, for example, I turn to my body and sense that my body is here. I sense my left arm—that is, I have an impression of my left arm. As soon as this impression reaches me, it provokes my thought, which says, "arm . . . left arm." And at the moment I say this to myself, I lose the impression. In thinking of the arm, I believe I know it. I have more trust in the thought than in the fact, the real existence of the arm. But the thought of the arm is not the fact. And it is the same with my own reality. I have the impression of life in myself, but as soon as I think "It is me," I *lose* it. I take my thought to be the fact itself and believe I know it. With this credulity, this blind belief in my thought, I no longer have any question or any interest in receiving the impression.

I am unable to take in impressions consciously. Therefore, I do not know myself. At the same time I need this more than anything else. If I cannot receive an impression of myself, I will never be able to remember myself and know what I am. The moment of receiving an impression is the moment of becoming conscious. It is the act of seeing.

15. *Hypnotized by my mind*

An inattentive mind is filled with thoughts. In a passive state it is constantly creating images and applying them to what I observe. The images provoke pleasure or pain, which is recorded in my memory, and illusions form around desires for satisfaction. In observing from a fixed vantage point, this mind creates a kind of separation, an opposition, a judge that reacts to everything with a preconception based on what has been learned. This inner disposition is one of the greatest obstacles to receiving impressions, any impression—judging oneself, judging another, judging others, judging . . . no matter what. In truth, our entire life is colored, even directed, by this tendency, which is stronger than we are. Whenever and wherever it arises, this judging shows that our ordinary "I" is involved. There is not a moment in the day when we stop judging, even when we are alone. It keeps us in ferocious slavery, enslaved by what we believe we know and what we believe ourselves to be.

There is in me an essential energy that is the basis of all that exists. I do not feel it because my attention is occupied by everything contained in my memory—thoughts, images, desires, disappointments, physical impressions. I do not know what I am. It seems that I am nothing. Yet something tells me to look, to listen, to seek seriously and truly. When I try to listen, I see that I am stopped by thoughts and feelings of all kinds. I listen poorly; I am not quiet enough to hear, to feel. What I wish to know is more subtle. I do not have the attention that is required.

I have not yet seen the difference between a fixed attention coming from only one part of myself and a free attention attached to nothing, held back by nothing, which involves all the centers at the same time. My usual attention is caught in one part and remains taken by the movement, the functioning of this part. For example, I think about what I am feeling, and my thought responds in place of me. It answers with a knowledge that is not true, not an immediate knowing. My thoughts are merely the expression of what is stored in my memory, not revelations of something new. This thinking is enclosed in a narrow space within myself. Always preoccupied, it holds back my attention in this space, isolated from the rest of me, from my body and feeling. With my attention continually projected from one thought to another, from one image to another in a flowing current, I am hypno-tized by my mind. These thoughts—and all my desires, affections, fears—are connected only by habits or attachments, which link each one to the next. My attention is caught in this current because I have never fully realized that it was given to me for another purpose.

Could my mind be silent in its perception? Could it perceive with-out recognizing and naming, that is, without separating to be someone who looks, judges and knows? For this, I would need an attention I do not know, an attention never separated from what it observes, allow-ing a total experience without excluding anything. It is only when I exclude nothing that I am free to observe and understand myself. When my brain can be active, sensitive, alive in a state of attentive im-mobility, there is a movement of an extraordinary quality that does not belong just to the thinking, the sensation or the emotion. It is a wholly different movement that leads to truth, to what we cannot name. The attention is total, without any distraction. . . . In this state I wish to see if I am capable of "not knowing," of not putting a name on what I perceive. I have a sensation of myself, which my habitual thought calls "body," but I do not know what it is, I have no name for what is here. I am aware of tensions, even the smallest, but I do not know what tension is. Then I feel breathing, which I do not know . . . in a body that I do not know, surrounded by people I do not know. . . . My mind becomes quiet.

I begin to see that real knowing is possible only in the moment when my attention is full, when consciousness fills everything. Then there are no distinctions—one thing is not more than another. There is pure existence. The creative act is the vision of what takes place. I learn to watch.

16. What is up to me

One feels a greater wish to know oneself. But we do not feel enough demand, we do not feel the necessity for a conscious effort. We know there is something to do, an effort to be made. But what effort? The question is not experienced. As soon as it appears, we either dismiss it or try to answer with our ordinary means. I do not see that to face the question I need to prepare myself. I have to gather all my force, to remember myself.

As I try to remember myself, I see where my wish comes from. It is from my ordinary "I." So long as the impulse comes from the possessiveness at the core of my personality, it will not bring the freedom necessary for a perception that is direct. When I see this . . . I have the impression of being a little freer. . . . But I wish to keep this freedom, and the way I wish comes again from possessiveness. It is like finding freedom from the influence only to fall back under it again, as though following a movement inward toward the more real and then a movement outward away from the real. If I am able to observe and live this, I will see that these two movements are not separate. They are one and the same process. And I need to feel them like the ebb and flow of a tide, with a keen attention that does not let itself be carried away and that, by its vision, keeps a balance.

Am I capable of distinguishing in myself a passive state from an active state? At this moment my force is here without direction, at the mercy of whatever may take it. It is not entirely occupied in moving toward a desired goal. I listen, and I look in myself, but I am not active. The energy being used to observe is not intense. My attention is not in contact with myself, with *what is*. It does not have a quality of perception that can liberate, that can change my state. So, I am passive. My body obeys nothing and my feeling is indifferent. My thought is traversed by ideas and images, and has no reason to free itself from them. In this passive state my centers are not related, they have no common direction. I am empty. . . . Yet, as I feel a need to be present, I see that when my thought is more voluntarily turned toward myself, a sensation appears—a sensation of myself. I experience it. . . . And then, I let my thought wander, and I see that the sensation diminishes and disappears. . . . But I come back to myself, quietly, very attentive, . . . and the sensation reappears. I see that the intensity of one depends on the intensity of the other. And this calls forth a feeling for this relation. The three parts of me are engaged in the same aim, that is, to be present. But their relation is unstable. They do not know how to listen to each other or what it would mean to be attuned.

What is most important today is to open to this new state that I cannot describe, to an experience of . . . Presence on which I can put no name. When I am quiet I feel this action on me. I do nothing myself. But my feeling is touched. There is an unknown feeling, which is not linked to an attachment to my person. It is a feeling that knows directly. When it is here, nothing in me is isolated. I feel the wholeness of Presence. But it only appears when my thinking is free, capable of being here without words. When the thinking changes, the feeling changes. The body also needs to adapt, to be attuned. I do not know how the relation comes about. When it is established, it always seems to be miraculous, and I see it as not depending on me. But to establish it depends very much on me. I must see what is up to me.

I need to learn first to render each part passive so as to receive a more active force. Everything is a question of forces. Our existence, our Presence here below, is also a question of forces. Nothing belongs to us, nothing is ours. We are here either to transmit forces or to transform them if we understand how. It is necessary first to feel these forces in a distinct way, to feel each in itself, and then to feel them together in order to create a new force able to confront the others, able to last, able to be.

AN EXPERIENCE OF PRESENCE

✑ *17. The awareness of "being here"*

There is in me something very real, the self, but I am always closed to it, demanding that everything outside prove it to me. I am always on the surface, turned toward the outside in order to take something or to defend myself. Yet there is perhaps another attitude, another disposition, in which I have nothing to take, I have only to receive. I need to receive an impression that nothing outside can give me—an impression of being, of my self having a sense, a meaning. The movement of knowing is a movement of abandon. It is necessary to open one's hands.

In moments of greater attention, I have an awareness of "being here"—a look, a light, a consciousness that knows. Consciousness is here. I cannot doubt it. And yet I do not trust it, I do not feel it as "I," as my essential nature. I believe I can look for consciousness, see consciousness, know it. We take consciousness as an object of observation. But we cannot see consciousness. It is consciousness that sees and that knows. I realize this if I experience it as coming from behind my body or from above. There is no observer, there is a knowing. Yet if I experience consciousness as in my body, it seems that the "I" is the body and consciousness an attribute of the body.

I begin to feel what it means to be true, that is, the moment when my thought knows itself *as it is* and my feeling knows itself *as it is*.

Another kind of thinking appears—immobile, without words, capable of containing my usual thought—and there is a feeling of my essence, a feeling that is not of my form but that can contain the form. I have then a new thinking and a new feeling that see the fact, that see *what is*.

So, the only reality for me today is in my effort to be present to myself. Nothing else is real. Everything is distorted by the veil of my mind, which prevents me from being in contact with the nature of things. I must first go toward my own nature, awake to the consciousness of "I," and be attentive only to this. Consciousness is always consciousness of self. We can call the Self whatever we wish—the seat of consciousness, even God. The point is that it is the center, the very core of our being, without which there is nothing.

I have to learn to concentrate my attention toward this center and stay here. I need to understand this act of Presence, this active movement of Presence, which is always threatened by a passive movement in the opposite direction. I am aware of a reality that I cannot possess. It is myself, what I am in the depth of my being. Yet I feel that to recognize it requires something of me . . . I know not what. This reality belongs to a level of perception I have never explored. My avidity separates me from it and prevents me from understanding my true place. I always want to get or take what is due to me, without feeling the respect that alone will allow an unconditional opening.

I begin to realize that what I am trying to approach is not only mine, not only in me, but immense and much more essential. In front of this, my tensions let go one after the other until the moment I feel, as a gift of unity, a collected Presence. This brings with it a question—a question of existence. It is in doubt at each moment, never certain, never assured, always so unknowable that it requires everything of me. Now I exist with a sense of a mysterious force that cannot be named, which has led me to this unity. To what influence am I opening? . . . I wish to know. I am here. I am not closed, imprisoned in one part of my being. I am conscious of being a whole.

18. Conscious of inner being

I exist without knowing how. My existence itself is a question to which I am obliged to respond, whether or not I so wish. My response is in the way I exist at the very moment, and the kind of action in which I am engaged. At every degree of awareness my response is strictly conditioned by my state of being. The challenge in the question is always new. It is the response that is old, creating a separation from the question. This is because in the response the ordinary "I" is in play.

What does it mean to "remember oneself"? It is not to remember the person I represent—my body, my position in life, my obligations. It is to become conscious of my inner being. I wish to be whole, unified, *one,* what I essentially am. When I feel this wish, it is as though my whole orientation changes. In all the parts of myself, freely and without my doing anything, a movement takes place toward a certain Presence. For this movement to follow its course I have to obey and be wholly attuned. Its force depends entirely on the tranquillity of all my centers and on the freedom of my attention. I need to feel that this Presence forms itself in me.

In looking, I begin to see that I have to be in contact with all my centers at the same time. Sometimes in one part, sometimes in another, the flow of energy is too strong or too weak. If I am too much in my head, the movement does not take place. Too much in my feeling or too much in my body, it is the same. There must be a corresponding intensity everywhere. What is important is a conscious attention, of a kind that I do not know. I can feel this only in quietness, in a tranquillity that is greater and greater. The Presence which is here acts on me, takes charge of me. But I must wish it, will it. This is the presence of "I."

I learn to purify my power of seeing, not by dismissing what is undesirable or turning away and settling on the agreeable. I learn to see everything without refusing the details. I learn to see clearly. I see that all things have the same importance, and I accept failure as good for me. I begin again a thousand times. Everything depends on this seeing.

I am not trying to find or to do something. But I feel the weight of the imagination of myself, the weight of this image that I feel compelled to sustain all the time in a violent battle to preserve its continuity. And behind it, I am aware of emptiness, a void. . . . I do not know who I am. Yet I cannot know the emptiness because the place is occupied. When I see this, the wish *to know* arises in me—not to know a specific thing, but to know who is here, what I am at this very moment. The place is taken. I feel it in the tensions, in the ideas that cross my mind without stopping, in the waves of emotions that respond. I do not try to resist, nor to withdraw or distract myself. This is the way I am. I accept it. And in living it, I see it *as it is*, as if I see further, through it, becoming more and more free. I see my inattention. I realize that my being depends on this power of seeing, and that I am free not to take one part of myself for the whole, free not to be isolated in one part.

I need to develop an attention that is pure and sufficiently intense not to be diverted by subjective reactions. I return tirelessly to the root of my perception. In this movement my attention purifies itself and little by little eliminates the elements foreign to a direct perception. Only the impression of reality remains.

19. *An echo of "I"*

A right effort to be present requires a force that is conscious of the direction it wishes to take and that has the will to act. The attention coming from the different centers must be here in a right proportion and remain engaged as a conscious Presence. But it is constantly threatened by what draws it outside. We need to become conscious of this attraction. There is a wish to move, a desire to create, to act. There is also a wish to be moved, to be drawn, to obey. These two forces are constantly here, in us. To confront them voluntarily at a given point can produce a concentration of energy that has its own independent life. It is in the friction between these forces that the quality which re-unites them can appear.

Behind all the vicissitudes of life, behind all my cares, sorrows and joys, there is something that is greater, something I can feel that gives me meaning. I feel I exist in relation to this greatness. It is outside me, but also in me. And it is in me that I know it—this life, this vibration so fine that I feel its grandeur because I feel its purity. I feel it as an echo, as a feeling of "I" in the contact between my thought and my sensation. This relation reveals that I am a unity, a whole, and that I can exist as a whole. The echo is what I can know today of another nature in myself, coming from another world through my higher centers. I feel it reso-nate in the form of a fine vibration, to which I try to attune all the parts of myself. This calls for a quality of attention that will allow it to go toward this vibration and sustain a contact with it. I need an energy of a very special kind, an intense energy that is active enough to remain alive in front of my thoughts and feelings. This energy does not let itself go down or be influenced by anything. My wish to be present to myself includes this activity.

My thoughts and emotions are animated by energy of a different level. In order to understand their nature, I need to see and know them as facts. They come from another source, an influence of inertia that holds me in its tempo. I must place myself under a more active influ-ence if I wish to be free. That is, I have to find in myself an energy of attention that is strong and sensitive enough to hold the movements of inertia under its look. I must not lose sight of them; I have to live with them. These movements are here and they are a constant attraction. If I do not see them as they are, I give them another value. I trust them and give myself to them, depriving them and myself of all meaning. Therefore, in order to know myself, I must agree to enter the field of search.

It is only by working to be present that my attention will develop. When it has a better quality, I struggle to keep it from weakening, I try to prevent its being taken. I try but cannot, and I try again. I begin to understand what this requires from me even if I cannot do it. In the struggle where I come back and then go again toward manifestation, I see that when my attention is completely taken, it is entirely lost to me. But if it does not go too far, it can be pulled back, as by a magnet. In that movement of my attention, I learn something of its nature. I will have to go toward manifestation, and I will always lose myself unless my attention goes both toward life and toward the inside.

We think it is one attention divided equally, but in fact the parts are not equal, not the same. There is a great difference that I need to experience. If I cannot center my effort in a certain way, I am bound to lose myself. I must see that I cannot do it because I do not have the quality of attention that is required. Here is my effort, here is what I have to exercise. This is the only thing that matters.

20. Two currents

What we are in our essence—our highest possibilities—we do not know. What we are in our person—the implacable conditioning that defines us—we also do not know. We identify with our person, ignorant of the relation that should exist between it and our essence. Yet inner development begins with the capacity to know myself, to understand my entire self.

I have to know that I have a double nature, that there are two forces in me: the descending force of manifestation and an ascending force returning to the source. I have to experience them here at the same time in order to know myself as a whole. There must be some reason why I am here, something that is needed for a relation between the two. This is the meaning of my Presence.

In each event in life—whether family, professional or inner life—there is a double movement of involution and evolution. The action is directed toward an aim, toward manifestation, but behind it is something that has no aim, that does not project itself but returns to the source. These two currents are indispensable to each other.

We know in theory that the two currents exist, but we are not really conscious of them. I do not know enough the ascending current. I do not have in myself, at the time I wish, the elements that would allow me to feel its life, to feel my life. The other current I do not know either, because I am blindly immersed in it. Yet without the vision of the two currents, the wish to be present at a given place and a given time has no sense. I need a constant vision of them in order to see the point of application of the attention and of the will, the will not to lose myself.

With my attention today I cannot be aware at the same time of two movements going in opposite directions. I am taken by one movement and ignore or oppose the other. Nevertheless, I have to accept that the two currents determine my life, and that I have two natures in myself. I must learn to see the lower nature and at the same time remember the higher. The struggle is in living the two together. I need to have a conscious impression of these two aspects of myself, at first independently of each other, then simultaneously. One nature must serve the other. But what does it mean to serve? I must find my real place and accept it. It is I who is called to be here. I must see that if I am not present, I serve only my ordinary self and go toward the destruction of what I truly am. So between these two currents then there is nothing, there is nobody.

What is important is that the two currents be established in me, having a definite relation that is maintained. Until now the descending current alone has been the master of my Presence, without being confronted. The ascending current has its source in the will *to be*—not "will" in the usual sense but in the sense of the "wish *to be*." It is necessary above all to disengage this will, to make room for it. I must accept being passive, really passive in order that an active vibration can be perceived by my feeling. The effort I can make with my ordinary means, the only effort that is incumbent on me, is one of voluntary passivity—a conscious effort.

A MOVEMENT OF AVAILABILITY

❧   *21. A new way of functioning*

The state of my being today is conditioned by my way of thinking, feeling and sensing, which takes all my attention and restricts me to a narrow part of myself. In order for me to go beyond this, there must appear in me a new way of functioning. I have to discover the total ineffectiveness, the insufficiency, of my thoughts and feelings as a means to approach the true nature of myself. The automatic functioning of my thought and feeling comes between the world as it is—what I really am—and the perception I have of it. The state in which I live is without order, vision or aim. I am here without knowing why or what I serve.

Each of my functions responds to impressions as though it were alone, from its point of view based on what it knows. But the functions cannot separately perceive reality, which includes a much higher energy. Their force is too passive. For understanding in the light of consciousness, the functions must all be attuned and united in a single movement of availability. If there is any distance between them, the common aim is lost and the blind function acts according to its habit. Thus the first thing to understand is this availability of my thought, my body and my feeling to receive together, at the same time, an impression that they cannot know in advance. Everything they know is not the immediate perception of what is here, now, when they are quiet. And I must pass through the disappointment of seeing that their intervention, in which I always believe, only brings images of the known instead of direct experience. Then perhaps I will begin to understand why this teaching places such importance on the fact that our centers work without any relation with each other. So long as a relation is not made, I cannot go beyond my habitual state of consciousness.

Can this relation be made? Do I feel as a fact, in a real way, that there is a lack of relation? Do I feel at this very moment my lack of intelligence to know my own truth and the truth of what is in front of me? Do I see that I am held back by words, ideas and emotions, full of doubt, belief and fear? I need to realize by experience what this disconnection of my centers means. I have a certain sensation of myself, and my thought is on the sensation. But one or the other is always stronger. I am not one, not a unity.

This accord of my centers of energy and their functioning cannot be brought about by forcing. There must be a quieting, a letting go of their movement, in order for a balance of energy to appear between them. But something is missing. I feel I am always too passive. So the need for an energy appears, an attention that will stay free and not become fixed on anything. It is an attention that will contain everything and refuse nothing, that will not take sides or demand anything. It will be without possessiveness, without avidity, but always with a sincerity that comes from the need to remain free in order to know.

22. *Awakening to a new force*

We wish to become conscious of the state and movement of energy in ourselves. This can only be done in the present moment. I need to be more active inside. I practice trying to be present, to awake. But every activity that I have not yet mastered provokes tension. I wish, and I am not capable. So I tense, and in this way create an obstacle to realizing my aim. I come up against this obstacle again and again until I become convinced of the falseness of my conception of effort—that is, as a movement toward a result. Then I feel relieved, a letting go that is a clear sign of my own Presence.

The practice of observation is not easy to understand. Usually I wish to see and know myself as an object. I am separated from what I am observing. I try to know it with my different centers. I see myself trying to use one function, then another. I have an awareness of their efforts, each one separate, and their agitation. And then I see that all these efforts are fruitless. I am trying to know, to see, with a passive energy, with a quality of attention that is not more active than what is perceived. It provides insufficient power to know. I am trying to know one center with another center, both of the same quality. This inevitably brings conflict. So I cannot observe. I see nothing. I have an impression of dispersion and disorder.

But where, then, does knowledge come from? How can I see myself? I do not know. . . . And since I do not know, I become still. There is a movement of availability, an awakening of a new force in me. It appears only when I see that all the other impulses are useless and do not relate me with real fact, with what I am. I want to become conscious of the reality of life. There is in me something mysterious that nothing is able to grasp, something that no thought or feeling can help me know. It appears only when I am not caught in the web of my thoughts and emotions. It is the unknown, which cannot be grasped with what I know.

In order to come to the total stillness in which I will be free to know, I must abandon both the pretension that I am able and my belief in what I know. I must see myself blindly believing, again and again, in what my thinking or my emotion tells me. I need to see myself always fooled until I feel the uselessness of it all, until I feel how poor I really am. Then a calm appears and perhaps I learn something new. In any case, it is like a door opening. All I can do is leave it open. What will follow I cannot foresee.

The quality of influence that reaches me depends on the quality of my Presence. And the quality of my Presence depends on the relation of my thought, my feeling and my sensation. In order to be attuned to a more subtle force, the attention of each part needs to concentrate, to become charged with a new meaning and power to relate voluntarily. In this way the thinking purifies itself, as do the feeling and the sensation. Each plays its own role and functions in concert with the others for the same goal of being attuned with a more subtle Presence. This Presence needs to shine, to animate my body. It has an intelligence, a vision that is like a light in the darkness and thickness of my sleep.

As I am today, directed by my ego, I cannot know the very essence of my Being. I am not prepared for this. A greater abandon, a greater magnetization toward my real "I," toward my "divine" nature, must take place. I feel the need for it, and I awaken to this wish, this life. I feel this intelligence awaken.

23. *The attitude we take*

The attitude we take, our inner and outer posture, is at the same time our aim and our way.

At any moment we each have a particular posture, an attitude we cannot avoid. The postures assumed by the body are always the same and provoke corresponding postures or attitudes in the mind and the feeling that are also the same. I am enclosed in a subjective world of habitual attitudes. But I do not see this. I am not even aware of which parts are tense or relaxed. The body has its repertoire of postures that imprison me. I have to find a position, inner and outer, that will free me from my attitudes and allow me to emerge from sleep, to open to another dimension, another world.

In the work in the quiet, the position of the body is very important. It must be precise in order to allow a field of energy to be established. At the same time, I must feel an ease, a well-being, a kind of stability that allows my mind to come to a state of total availability, to empty itself in a natural way, to let go of the agitation of thoughts. With a right posture my centers come together and can be related. This requires close and continual cooperation between my thought, my feeling and my body. As soon as they separate, the posture is no longer held.

We are seeking stability. What is always essential is the position of the spine, which should be at the same time free and straight. When it is not straight, there cannot be a right relation between sensation and thought, or thought and feeling. Each part remains isolated without a real connection with the others. But if the spine is straight, we feel that the energy contained in the body has an action on the body. Its density changes. There is no longer a form and a Presence—they are one and the same.

My posture will be more stable if I am seated on the floor, on a cushion so that the knees are lower than the hips. One foot is placed, if possible, on the thigh or calf of the other leg. Crossing the legs checks the active impulse and allows the deepest level of quietude. The hands rest in the lap, the favored hand supporting the other, with palms up and thumbs touching. I sit absolutely straight, with the ears and shoulders in a vertical line. The eyes are slightly open or may be closed. If unable to sit on the floor, I can use a stool or chair provided I sit straight, with the knees lower than the hips. Maintaining the spine vertical frees pressure so that the upper part of the body feels no weight.

When beginning the work in the quiet, I try to find the exact position for the pelvis that does not draw my body either forward or backward. If my spine is vertical, like an axis, this also maintains my head in a right position. Then a letting go comes by itself. As tensions fall away, I feel a movement of energy toward the abdomen and, at the same time, a movement toward the higher. The rigor in my attitude comes exclusively from one imperative necessity—not to impede at any point the movement toward unity that is required for opening to the higher centers. This attitude is not easy to come to. It is not to be taken once and for all, but has to be renewed from moment to moment. This calls for an intelligence that must always remain present. Without a voluntary attention, my spine will not maintain its position and the whole meaning of this attitude in front of life will be lost. I need to see that, as soon as the effort stops, my attitude can be an immediate hindrance to consciousness. And the effort lasts only for a flash.

24. Coming together

Attention is the conscious force, the force of consciousness. It is a divine force. The search is for contact with an energy coming from the higher parts of our centers. At times we have an intuition of it that is less strong or more strong. This intuition is the action on us of higher centers from which we are separated by our attachment to our functions. When this action is felt, it affects the body which then receives more subtle and alive sensations. It affects the thought, which becomes capable of holding under its look what is immediately present. It affects the emotions, giving rise to a new feeling.

But this action, coming from the higher centers, is not to be sought from outside or brought about forcibly by some function of the lower centers. In order for this action to be felt by my body, mind and feeling, there must be a certain state of availability. Here is the obstacle, the barrier. The quality of energy of the lower centers must correspond to the vibrations of the higher centers. Otherwise, the relation is not made and the lower centers do not express the action of the higher on the level of life. They do not serve as intermediaries, they are not called to serve. As a result, they do not have any conscious activity and do not feel any need to be purified.

Why does this relation with the higher centers not appear? Is it so difficult? The reason is that between the lower centers there is no relation, no common aim, no common interest. They do not feel any need for coming together. This is because we do not see, and we do not experience, their isolation and what it means. Nevertheless, in order for transformation to take place, there must be a total attention, that is, an attention coming from all the parts of me. In order for a certain blending to occur, my thinking, my feeling and my sensation must be together.

At the beginning, in the Absolute, there are three forces that come together to know each other and form a whole. They remain united and never separate. It is in this coming together that something new can appear. From the Absolute, however, there is a projection that, without unity, creates mechanical movements and division. In man everything is separate, isolated. We exist as a machine. Nevertheless, we have the possibility to exist unified as a Presence. When a relative unity can be felt, it is possible to say "I—I am." To maintain this unity, there must be a sustained movement, and it is this movement that I lose all the time.

The laws governing the universe are here and act in us. The aim is that all the forces, which are within ourselves, turn toward a center and again form a whole. It is this movement in an ascending direction that we must learn. But everything that is below holds us back. It must all be purified. In this coming together, the energy acquires a different quality. The aim of this reuniting is the power *to be*.

III

IN A COMMON
DIRECTION

Am I convinced of the uselessness of everything I believe I know?

Truth cannot be thought.

Not knowing, discarding everything, is the highest form of thinking.

Sensation is an instrument of knowledge, of contact with myself.

I need to feel the presence of the spiritual in me. The spirit penetrates matter and transforms it. I need this act itself, to be spiritualized.

Relation is contact, a direct contact on the same level with the same intensity.

Feeling is the essential instrument of knowing.

A FREE THOUGHT

🖋️ *25. The functioning of the mind*

What does it mean to be present, to be here now? I have the sensation that I am present. I think it, I feel it. The three centers are present with the same force, with an intensity that comes from the same degree of activity. I feel an energy that circulates more freely between them, which is not held more in one place than another. This energy is nourished voluntarily by the three parts. There is a common direction, bringing the possibility of a conscious action in which the impulse comes from the three centers at the same time. I wish *to know* with all the parts of myself.

In order to be present, I must understand the working of my thinking mind, that its function is to situate and explain, but not to experience. Thought is made up of accumulated knowledge in the form of images and associations, and it seizes an experience only to make it fit into categories of the known. Although it can entertain the new when it is quiet, the thinking immediately transforms it into something old, with an image that has already been the object of an experience. The image awakens an immediate reaction. This always repeats, so that there is never anything new.

Can I say today that I know what I am? Does the attitude of my mind allow me to truly confront this question? This is more important than I think. Am I convinced of my ignorance and of the uselessness of everything I believe I know? I may say so, but do not really feel it. I value my knowledge, and I always want to bring an answer or reach a conclusion. I am conditioned by this. Everything I know limits my perception and conditions my mind. All that I know is a mass of memories that impel me to accumulate, repeating the same kind of experiences.

I need to see that my mind is always moved by the demands of my ordinary "I," by its associations and reactions. This corrupts it. A thought that is moved by associations is not free. The pathways it travels are strewn with obstacles in the form of images, fixed ideas and experiences. They immobilize it or change its course while all the time giving an impression of continuity. Yet continuity resides, not in the material that occupies the thought but in the energy itself. Believing in the material holds the energy imprisoned in the circle of thoughts. The energy loses all its mobility and acuity, and becomes more and more feeble; the thought becomes petty and narrow-minded. We notice this in the constant tensions in the head, face and neck.

A mind that is subject to the ordinary "I" cannot be still. But tranquillity, a quiet mind, will not come by turning away or struggling against the condition. This will not lead to liberation. Freeing myself from this conditioning can come only by seeing it, without ignoring or denying it, thereby creating a new conditioning. I need to see and to understand the functioning of the mind. The mind is the source and center of my ordinary "I," the ego. This "I" seeks security. It is afraid and identifies in order to find security. This is a perpetual battle. My usual consciousness consists entirely in judging—in accepting or refusing. This is not real consciousness. Indeed, in this state, without a quiet mind, nothing real can be revealed to me.

26. Not knowing

To see myself as I am would be to perceive what is real, a direct perception that is possible only in a state free of all conditioning. I believe that I search. But I do not see that my very search is paralyzed by what motivates it. I am seeking a way not to be confined by the conditioning of my thought, of my memory, of what I believe I know. I seek to go beyond it. I try: I make efforts to work, to be present. But in this I am taken—I am taken all along, during the entire course of my effort. The first thought that impedes me is that "I work." I do not see who is working, I do not see that the mind is an obstacle. I put a word or idea on what I am seeking, and so I project an image and set out from a feeling of lack to go toward the objective. I believe it is necessary to know what I am looking for. The representation becomes more important than the search for the truth.

My relation with my thinking mind must change. I have to see its conditioning and lose all illusion of its capacity to perceive directly what is beyond its functioning. Truth simply cannot be thought. It cannot be looked for by the thinking alone, or by the wish to acquire or to become. Truth does not become—it *is*. I need to see that my thought is held back by the stubbornness of an idea or the attachment to a form. In the very moment I see this, the mind is freed from the idea or form, and a new perception can take place. To have a direct perception would mean to discover something entirely new, something unknown that my mind can never bring.

Why is it that my mind never discovers anything new? I am a prisoner of all the impressions deposited in me. I am conditioned by the reservoir of my memory, the result engraved in me of the influences that have touched me. It is all that I have to answer with in life. Little by little, I unconsciously accept this state of conditioning, and the energy of my mind deteriorates. My mind is sapped in its vitality and strength. It simply accumulates more and more information. I can discipline my mind, polish my knowledge. It can even become brilliant. But I remain in the realm of the known. How could I go beyond this way of thinking so that something new could appear?

I need to be free enough to discard everything and to question without expecting an answer. I understand that not knowing, discarding everything, is the highest form of thinking, and that if an answer comes, it will be false. I have to stay without answering and learn to see, to see without judging, without a thought, without a word. To see is an extraordinary act which requires an attention that is unknown to me. This is the factor that liberates, that brings a new thought, a new mind. Attention is the essential energy in man. And this energy can only appear when one is constantly occupied in seeing, in listening, in questioning—never in knowing with my thinking mind. We must give our complete attention to the question in front of us. The attention will not be total if we seek an answer. Total attention is the process of meditation.

By vigilance and meditation, the nature of thought may be revealed to me, the way it acts. If I recognize with all of myself that "I do not know," I am no longer relying on my memory to find an answer. At this moment, and only at this moment, I become free of my conditioning, the prison of my memory, and can have a direct perception of what is beyond it. I see the role of the thought as a factor for remembering, only a factor for remembering.

27. A new thinking

Our thoughts and emotions constitute a subjective world, a world that enslaves us. Like cowards, we accept being dominated by the currents of low quality in which we bathe. And it will be like this so long as we do not feel nostalgia for another current.

I take my thinking, my thought, as being "I" in the same way I take my body as "I." I am always ready to be the victim of my thoughts because I have never disassociated myself from them. I have still not realized what an enormous obstacle they are to the consciousness I seek. I must understand that I am not my thinking and that I do not have to welcome whatever thought arises in me and expect something from it.

I have to see that the thought "I" is the greatest obstacle to consciousness of myself. Everything I know through my senses has a name. I am encumbered by names, which become more important than the things themselves. I name myself "I," and in doing it as if I knew myself, I am accepting a thought that keeps me in ignorance. If I learn to separate myself from names, from thoughts, little by little I will come to know the nature of the mind and lift the veil it casts over me. I will see both what it means to be enslaved by the thinking and the possibility of being free from this tyrant.

At the same time, my mind must not turn away, because wishing to turn away creates fear; not facing the fact creates fear. My mind needs to see itself, to see its functioning and not be taken by words. This requires an extraordinary precision of thought, an attention that does not deviate. When the words have disappeared, what remains? One comes to the door of perception. The mind understands that it is alone. Then it approaches the meaning, the importance of a word— whether a word creates feeling. In seeing the word as a fact, the mind will be free of its influence.

I need to see that my thought is almost never directed on knowing myself as I am in this moment . . . and again in this moment. It is difficult for the thought to remain on *what is,* because it is based on memory and is constantly visualizing the possibility of *becoming.* How to resist the desire to *become* in favor of simply *what is?* It is difficult for my thought to stay in front of the unknown. This means abandoning belief in everything it knows, even the trace of the preceding moment.

To stay in front of the unknown, my mind must be profoundly silent. This is a silence that is not obtained by suppressing or by sacrifice. I do not make the silence. It appears, when the mind sees that by itself alone, it cannot be in contact with something it cannot measure, something higher. Then the mind no longer seeks, it does not try to become.

I need to see that there is never any stillness and that all this thinking of the known prevents me from having an experience of reality. Then stillness and silence take on meaning for me. There is the possibility of a quiet mind. I no longer seek the known. I no longer seek security or to become. I feel myself freer, more open. The thought becomes free, moment after moment, and there is then an understanding of truth at each moment. This is the only way to know. True thinking has no conclusion. It always begins anew.

28. *Beyond our usual consciousness*

We seek something that is beyond the world of our usual consciousness, our usual thoughts and feelings. We think of truth, of reality, as if it were fixed, a point that we should find a way to approach. But reality is not fixed. It is alive. It cannot be measured by anything we know. It can be approached only by a thought that is entirely free—free of everything, every expectation, every fear—a thought without movement, completely silent, a thought that knows only itself. The thought that knows only itself lives in the present moment. In this moment, here, now, it has nothing to expect, nothing to lose. It is "consciousness of being"—not being like this or like that—only of being. It *is*.

Here we discover the source of thinking. We see that the division between the observer and the observed is at the origin of our thought. The observer is grounded in memory, that which knows from past experience. It looks, thinks and acts from memory. This separation into observer and observed does not touch reality, it consolidates the ego. But when the observer is the observed—when the thinking is the experience—then there is no more thought. There is a state of tranquillity in which an impression can be received as new, as with little children. The eyes clearly receive the image from outside, but there is no observer perceiving, no mental processing.

In order to experience this unified state without an observer, it is necessary to pass through my usual state and to see that it is not enough. So long as my thought tracks what I am doing and experiencing, judging it in one way or another, I remain in the realm of my limited consciousness. I remain under the influence of my ordinary "I." What is important is to see this division between observer and observed, to see the thought creating the separation. It is in seeing this that I become free of its authority and open to another reality.

Who am I? The question eludes me because I am separate from it. It is in front of me, but outside. So long as it is separate and I am not completely united with it, the question remains beyond understanding. To see the impossibility of understanding brings a suffering. When this suffering is real, there is no more separation and the thinking subsides. Only silence remains.

Yet the moment of being present is short. As soon as I come back to myself, the impression makes me think, and in thinking I become separate again. I go away from myself and no longer live in the present. Then, if I see it, the impression of being lost brings me back to myself. This coming back and going away is a normal movement that I need to accept. The feeling of living, of existing, depends on it. My thoughts never stop. When one has passed, another is here, followed by another. I am attached to all of them. But if for a moment a space appears in the thinking, then there is nothing for me to be attached to. I am free. In the silence, the mind can be conscious of each movement of the thinking. This perception is free from reaction, and the energy that results is not mechanical, not the product of thought. It is the energy that spiritual seekers have been looking for throughout the ages.

AN INNER SENSATION

~~~ *29. An instrument of contact*

I wish to experience the fact that I exist, not merely as a body, an animal, or as a machine, but as a human being. My thoughts and feelings are on the level of an animal. When I do turn my attention toward myself, I find I am never aware, never awake. I do not know that I exist or how I exist. I just forget about it. All my life passes without my experiencing the most important thing.

By attempting to turn my attention toward myself, I see that it is difficult, and in fact I almost never even try. My attention always goes to something that is not *me*. Everything is important except *me*. I can think about the world but not about *me*, about who I am. So the first step is to think "I exist," the fact of existing. Without this thought, I will never remember my existence. Yet this thought alone is insufficient, it is not an experience. Only my thought is present. In order to remember my existing, I also have to wish. But I have no wish, I do not care. I have no interest in the fact that I exist. If I really see this, it is a shock. I begin to understand that my feeling does not obey me. I have absolutely no power over it.

I take my existing for granted, but I do not *know* it. I do not know what it means to exist as a human being. Yet unless I realize that I exist, I will never know why, and I will never know how, I exist. I have to experience it, to know it—my existing has to be a conscious existence or it has no sense. What does it mean *to know,* to experience? I have to see that my thinking is not enough, that I will never experience something by thinking about it. I have to bring more into my Presence. But how?

I need to see that what is lacking is a connection with my body. Without a connection I am caught in thoughts or changing emotions that give way to fantasy. And my body is either my master, a tyrant demanding satisfaction of its appetites, or my enemy, obliged to pay for all my thoughts and feelings. Yet my body could be the greatest support for experiencing my existence. It is on the level of the earth and draws its strength from it. The action of our life is on this level, this sphere, not somewhere up in the air. I have to feel the body on the earth, the ground. I do this by sensation—sensing its weight, its mass, and, more important, sensing that there is a force inside, an energy. Through sensation I need to feel a connection with my body so deep it becomes like a communion.

We will see later that there are sensations and sensations. But for now I need to recognize that sensation is an instrument of knowledge, an instrument of contact with myself. If I wish to know that I exist, I have to feel the force and energy in me by contact. If, for example, I wish to know the quality of my thinking, I have to come into touch with it through a certain sensation. It is the same with the energy of the body and the energy of the feeling. I need to have a sensation, not merely of the flesh, of tensions, but an inner sensation of the energy, a sensation that my body is alive.

It is difficult to have a voluntary sensation. In life nothing brings an inner sensation except a rare blow like great sorrow or danger. If nothing forces me, I have no sensation of my existence. When there is no pain in it, I forget I have a stomach. But in order to know the state of energies in myself, I have to have a sensation that is voluntary. A conscious man would have a permanent sensation of himself and always know how he was inside. So our first aim is to develop an inner sensation.

30. *Obeying the attraction of the earth*

The body obeys the attraction of the earth, from which it draws its energy. The subtle force, a finer energy in me, obeys another attraction. When the body conforms to the attraction of the earth, the subtle force is freer, as if the two movements complement each other. This is what allows man to hold himself upright. Always and in all circumstances, I must accept this law from which my equilibrium comes, and let these forces act freely in me. When I obey the earth's attraction in a conscious way, the subtle force is liberated and my ordinary "I," my ego, finds its place, its purpose. The poles are related. I obey this law and find my place in a world of forces that has made me what I am. But thinking it does not help. I must live it.

Tension and relaxation have great importance for the way in which we manifest and relate to the world around us. We tense toward life in order to take, to oppose, to master. All our affirmation is in tensions. But these tensions separate us from a subtle energy, a more essential reality. We are imprisoned by tensions, and our possibilities are not developed. Our attention can never have an action if there is a tense resistance in the body. It is retained on the surface, unable to penetrate deeper levels in ourselves.

I have access to myself only through sensation. But there are different kinds of sensation. The one we usually know comes from uncontrolled tension, however slight, which appears when my thought is directed on one part of my body. It is a sensation that is static, fixed on a particular part; it can be studied only if we stop moving. This sensation awakens an energy that is superficial. There is a depth that is not attained. In order for me to receive a deeper sensation, a sensation of reality, there must be a letting go in which I am entirely free and available. Instead of seeking sensation, I need to open and receive the impression of a finer vibration. For this a new feeling needs to appear that allows the vibration to spread. This is why Gurdjieff had us say, "Lord, have mercy," which opens us to a feeling of our nothingness and awakens a deeper energy.

The quality of my sensation depends on the state of my body. In being attentive to my usual state, I discover that relaxing and tensing are a constant action. Either there is an exaggerated tension where I affirm myself with violence, with pride, or there is a letting go where I give up out of weakness. When I see that this action is directed by my ego, I begin to feel the need to dissolve its hard coating so that life can spread in me. Then I may experience a descending movement, a letting go of the force held in my tensions. Once in movement, this force by itself submits to the attraction of the earth and obeys. At the same time, I feel an ascending force appear that allows all the centers to be integrated in a whole Presence.

The possibility of receiving a more subtle vibration arises only at the moment when I know my incapacity and my refusal. Because I know it, there is an opening to vibrations of a different density, as if passing a threshold. By an action that comes from an immediate understanding of being insufficient, the body as a whole lets go in order to be attuned to this Presence. I begin to see that there are infinite degrees of sensation which represent an unknown world.

I need stillness and great sensitivity to have a sensation of a Presence in my body. This sensation comes not from tension but from a contact that is revealed to me. My body is centered, not tensing in any direction. It does not tend upward; this is not its nature. It does not pull me. I do not pull it. There is no tension. I feel free. My totality is no longer threatened. I see that sensation is like an act of obedience to this Presence. The need to open is what we call prayer.

31. A global sensation

It will be a long time before I understand the significance of my tensions. But I can see that they are here and that the energy in me is not free. Thoughts are tensions, emotions also. The energy is stopped by vibrations of inertia, which keep me in the lower parts of my being. I am held by my tensions, as though attached, engaged in satisfying the specific needs of one part without taking account of the whole. My energy is not free to pursue the unobstructed movement that is the life of a whole. I need, above all, to experience an energy that is liberated.

Usually I experience the energy in myself in a degraded form that is not contained. Nevertheless, I can perhaps know it in a form that is more pure, more still, and thus experience what I am. For this I must agree to have no tension. I must be able to remain without judging, without expecting anything, without hoping, entirely in the awareness of *what is*. I will then perhaps come to the perception of a living Presence in me, a global sensation of the life of the whole. My vision embraces my entire body, it sees the movements of the whole. Although I can intentionally put the accent on one part, on an arm or leg or the head, I must not lose the sense of the whole. As soon as I am stopped by the idea of a part, my sensation is distorted and my vision loses its meaning.

Seeking a balance between tension and relaxation opens me to the struggle with the ordinary "I." When I am relaxed and have a sensation of all of myself, I am not separated from my inner being. I am one. In my true being, already *I am,* and I am free. I can live this as long as I keep a right attitude, a right inner posture, a balance of tension and relaxation. I feel centered, with a global sensation of myself. And yet I see the tendency again to become partial, to return toward tensions that are always the same and that preserve my ordinary "I." I feel the need for a letting go that liberates me from them.

This is the struggle to be what I am, a struggle between the subjective "I" incarnate in my tensions and the unknown life in me. Either I am imprisoned by my ordinary sense of "I," which prevents any contact with my real self, or I have a nostalgia for the "divine" that I feel at the root of my being, which shows me what I must serve. My entire life is shaped by this struggle, and I must understand it if I wish this life to be conscious. My tensions form the web of my life. They are always here, my mind drawn toward an aim and my body tensed toward what the mind imposes upon me. Even when I have no pressing aim, there are tensions crystallized in me. And in each tension, the whole of me is engaged.

In seeking to open to a sensation of myself, I see that I am still filled with tensions. The only sensation I have is of these contractions, like a wall that separates me from myself. My attention does not reach the Presence in me that lives another life. I feel the lack. The sense of this lack is the greatest truth I can approach today, the star that shows me the way. As long as I am conscious of this lack, purely attentive without interference from my thought or feeling, I see the limits of the world of the known, of form, which I have to abandon in order to face the unknown.

32. To be spiritualized

Today the forces that move us have limited power to vivify. Their waves, their vibrations, quickly diminish. These are vibrations of inertia. The energy put in movement is little charged with will, with a "will *to be*," and is incapable of transmitting this will.

A call from the depths of oneself is always here. It becomes more and more insistent, as if a different energy were wanting to be heard, seeking a relation. In a state of immobility, in stillness, the relation can be better established, but this requires opening to a different inner density, to another quality of vibration. Sensation is the perception of this new quality. I need to feel the Presence of the spiritual in me. The spirit penetrates matter and transforms it. I need this act itself, to be spiritualized.

The creative action of the life force appears only where there is no tension, that is, only in the void. If I wish to develop my being, I must come to this point of no tension, which I feel as a void, as unknown. It is void of my ego . . . something I do not know—my essence. I perceive emptiness because the fineness of vibrations is beyond the density in myself that I usually know. At this moment I touch on the wish *to be*, the will to be what I am beyond form and time. I become conscious of the void by the change in my sensation, which becomes finer as tensions are dissolved.

I begin to understand what is meant by a pure sensation, which appears when my thought is free, seeing without any image. Under this vision my body lets go. Relaxation comes by itself, progressing with the clarity of my seeing. This sensation is the first sign of obedience to something greater. It can be conscious only if I am voluntarily passive. It is not my ordinary "I" that does this, it is not this "I" that seeks to manifest its force. My force is of another kind. If this is not true for me— if I do not sincerely know it at the moment I work—I will not be able to liberate myself. I need to recognize a higher force, a master, and feel its authority. This recognition comes when the ordinary "I," the ego, ceases to create its own movements. Then an energy of a very special quality appears, which is irresistible, all-powerful, as long as it is recognized and obeyed. It is this energy to which, along with all the traditions, we could give the name "love" if we knew what love meant. Conscious sensation is the first step toward this force.

To go toward a conscious sensation, a sensation of *what is,* I need a new thinking, a thought that is free of all knowing and believing, free even of past experience. This thought sees at once all the contradictions and disorder, and at the same time is able to remain absolutely still, tranquil. Then I may feel my body entirely passive, as though it no longer existed. To maintain this state of passivity is my first power over the body. It indicates that a new energy participates in my Presence. I no longer let myself be taken by any tension—any contraction, thought or feeling. I have only one aim in which all my centers participate: to perceive the fine vibrations to the extent I am able to discern their quality.

A conscious sensation of ourselves signifies and is proper to incarnation, in which the spirit materializes and takes on a definite density, becomes flesh. Experiencing a pure sensation within the physical body can lead to a spiritual experience. We penetrate the world of vibrations, of fine substances. Here is my body and here is energy, a life that is in me. Yet I feel them as one and the same. Is it possible? In front of this question, I can neither deny nor affirm, and there arises a feeling of truth, of the real.

A NEW FEELING

🖋 *33. I blindly trust my feelings*

In facing life, I am driven by the force of my ordinary "I," whose very possibility of existing depends on the world that surrounds it. This "I" has a deep fear of being nothing and is afraid of not having security, power, possessions. It is thin-skinned and easily wounded, always eager to be recognized, easily discouraged, rebellious against others, full of self-pity. There is almost constant fear—not a particular but a general fear—of being insecure or incapable, or some other vulnerability. And there is always avidity. I want to obtain, I want to change, I want to become.

My usual emotional state is negative, always reacting to people and events from my selfish, ego-centered point of view—what pleases or displeases *me*, what *I* like or what *I* do not like. There is a perpetual closing, in which I harden, imprisoned in an ego that cries "I." The being, the whole being, is forgotten. At the same time there is a need to give, to love. But I cannot love outside consciousness. Love is a quality of consciousness.

If I wish to know *what is,* I have to realize that neither words nor the feelings that accompany them are perceptions of reality. The word is not the fact, the feeling is not the fact. They are both the reaction of my conditioning to impressions, to everything that impresses me. But

I blindly trust my feelings. I never doubt them. I believe they express a pure vision and do not see that they really reflect implacable conditioning. Because of this I do not see the absolute necessity to observe them—that is, to remain in front of them without reacting, to be merciless toward my desire to react. My wish to know my feelings must be stronger, without either excusing or rejecting them. My thought has to be keen and precise in order to be free from their effect, and my attention must not weaken or deviate if I am to see their meaning and the extent of their influence on my life. I need, at the very moment, to be able to open to the intelligence of silence, in which alone understanding could appear.

In order to enter into this search, I have to observe a feeling that generally occupies a great part of my attention—fear, for example, or anger or envy. I always avoid looking at these feelings. But if I wish to see them, I have to face them, living with them from moment to moment. I am entirely attentive with my whole Presence to the movements of my feeling. The attention is pure, with no subjective ambitious aim, and has to remain pure in order to see. It is a higher energy, more powerful and intelligent than the feelings that agitate me. Only by working in this way will I measure the strength of my attachment to them.

I need to experience what keeps my thought and my feeling in a certain sphere—the repeated contacts with an order of ideas to which the thought submits. I need to see the hypnosis of this contact. In order to aspire to other contacts, to other impressions, I become more sensitive to a finer energy belonging to a more rarefied level. More frequent contact with this energy brings new possibilities.

34. *Feeling allows relation*

All the possibilities are in me, but I can pass my life without any real change. The highest energy, which gives birth to all others, is in me. It is part of me. The question is not to make it appear but to allow it to appear, to submit to its action. The more I try, the more the way is

restricted . . . nothing gets through. I must learn to submit voluntarily
to its influence. The active force and the passive force are always present in us. But two forces alone are not enough. They are not related. A
third, reconciling force needs to appear, a certain feeling that allows a
relation and thus transforms everything.

If we could see the action of this law of forces, we would understand better why it is so difficult to be present to oneself and to remain
here. I need to be present to two parts of myself at the same time, and
to experience the necessity of a reconciling force between them. A new
feeling must then appear—a feeling of "I" that is turned toward a
greater reality in which I participate and, at the same time, drawn by
the world in which I live. The call of these two worlds requires me to
be present, understanding that they cannot exist without each other
and that one should be spiritualized by the other. A conscious relation
must appear.

Relation is contact, a direct contact on the same level with the
same intensity. There are different kinds of contact: one time I feel,
another time I have a sensation, at another moment I see. When the
intensity is the same in all three centers, there is consciousness. But a
conscious relation cannot come from the old thinking, which clings to
words and images. It has no power to see the unknown. Another dimension cannot appear as long as the old thinking is active.

I begin to discover that the highest energy in me is not free, that
my thought fashions the state in which I find myself. When I see my
suggestibility to the least of my thoughts, my interest awakens. But I
must go much further, to the source, and see the thoughts arise. With
precaution, without presupposing or taking anything for granted, I silently observe the motives and reactions of my thought. It is a difficult
effort, requiring patience. It leads me to discard everything. With a
deep wish to know, to know truth—whatever it may be, though not
what I expect—I discover something new. In the quality of attention
that is here to face the fact as it is, there is a light, an intelligence—I
hesitate to say a "feeling," because we think we know what feeling is.
It is an entirely new quality that has the capacity to know. When it

appears, my thought abandons its authority, and my body, released from this influence, relaxes. The liberated energy finds its own movement, and my body submits in order to find a right relation toward it. This feeling for what I am brings together what is seen and what sees. There is no longer an object and an observer. I am both the one who sees and the one who is seen.

When I open entirely to my Presence, when "I Am," I enter a different world where neither time nor space exists. I am one, a whole. Thoughts cease and reason disappears. I *feel* the "I." Feeling is the essential instrument of knowing.

35. I feel "I am"

Do you see that the problem before us is a question of feeling? We begin to see the poverty of all our feelings and the need for a feeling that is more pure, more penetrating. But we do not reach the depth in ourselves where a transformation could take place. I do not abandon my idols. A wish arises to be more myself, to open to a very high part of myself and experience an emotional force that knows. I need to hear it. For this it is necessary to reach a depth of silence where my feeling is no longer attached to my usual egoism. Only in silence is this possible.

I wish to be present, to remain present. But I feel powerless, that I cannot wish, cannot be. I do not have a strong desire, a strong will. I need help, a force of another quality. Help appears in the form of a more active feeling, with more conviction, a feeling that comes from the higher emotional center. In this moment I know a new possibility of being present which situates me differently in relation to what surrounds me and gives meaning to my Presence.

But I only receive this help if I feel a compelling need for it. The call comes from the vision, the experience of my powerlessness as I am. Then there is something right, true in my awareness of my situation, and I can wish for the help of this force, for another possibility of being.

Wishing to submit to its law, I make room for this force, attentive so that the attitude of all my parts conforms to receive it. So long as the force is primary for me, I can receive its help. But this feeling of power-lessness is too fleeting. Again I believe that I can "do," as I am, and return to my imagination of "I," to my blindness.

How to understand the experience of feeling? We know what sensing is, an inner touch. Feeling requires another quality. It has nothing to do with "like" or "dislike," and yet it is emotion. I *feel* sorrow or joy. Feeling is always rising up. Like fire it flares up, then dies away. And I *feel* "I am." Pure feeling has no object. I can understand it only if I am capable of seeing without an idea, word or image, able to be in contact with *what is*.

I begin to see that the world in which I live is a world of fictions. It is not real. The vision I have of myself is not a vision of my own reality. I see myself through the thinking, lost in my imagination of "I." For short moments only, I touch on something real in myself—I have a feeling *"I am."* The feeling I have of myself makes me know my reality. At this moment, and only at this moment, I know that I am. I am at the source. I now have a measure of my reality, which is reality itself rather than my usual state with my ordinary perception. This reality is always here. It needs to become the center of attraction for my feeling.

Gurdjieff gave us the exercise "I am" to work on feeling. In a collected state I come to the feeling "I." I direct it into my right arm—"*I*"—and then have a sensation in my right leg—"*am*." Thereafter, I have a feeling, right leg; sensing, left leg; feeling, left leg; sensing, left arm; feeling, left arm; sensing, right arm. I do this three times, each time feeling "*I*" and sensing "*am*." Then when I have done it three times, I feel the whole body —"*I*"—and sense the whole body—"*am*." I experience "*I*" always as feeling, "*am*" as sensing. Feeling is a more intense quality of sensing. This exercise can also be practiced beginning successively with the right leg, left leg and so on. The words "I am" can be replaced by the words "Lord . . . have mercy."

✎   36. Love of being

If I feel the energy that animates my body, there is a link between my mind and body, but it is not enough. A kind of balance is established, but so long as my feeling does not open, it is not truly alive.

I begin to have a wish to be and to feel myself as a whole, but I am all the time confronted by the force of my automatism. On one side there is a movement of unity that opens me to new perception, and on the other an inexorable movement of dispersion. This confrontation calls forth in me a force that I did not suspect, an attention that otherwise would never need to appear.

The attention that leads to the moment of consciousness is the fire which brings about a blending of forces, a transformation. To become conscious simultaneously of both these movements requires a greater activity of my attention. The effort *awakens* it, awakens a force that was asleep. My attention is entirely mobilized, including at the same time the higher centers and the lower centers, the functioning of my whole Presence. This depends on a new feeling that appears, the feeling of *being*. Remembering oneself is above all remembering this other possibility, the search for a force in myself that is more active. I wish to know, I wish *to be*.

I need to understand what is required for a change in being, and to understand that without the help of the higher centers I can come to nothing. In our usual state we have recourse only to our ordinary mind, which does not have the necessary energy. We would understand more if we could be more emotional about our state, about the fact that we do not hear the call of the higher centers, we do not listen to it. In order for my being to change, I must understand my state emotionally.

I think I understand my state, but my feeling is not touched. This thinking is passive, and does not see. There is no vision that could penetrate and allow a perception of the real fact, no energy capable of coming in contact with it. So, either I try to avoid my thoughts and emotions, or I go against what imprisons me without being able to escape. I do not understand my reality as a whole, and the fact has no action on me. I think, I feel, I sense, or, instead, my attention abruptly withdraws and I am calm, reassured. But I do not realize I have become passive. What follows comes not from the act of knowing but from the desire to hold on to what I feel and what I affirm or deny. I do not see the need for an energy that is uncontaminated by my thought and feeling, an energy capable of penetrating the nature of what opposes it.

The only force that could change something appears when the need becomes conscious. I am dissatisfied, I have nothing in myself that knows. It is not an anxiety but a fact that I see: the lack of accord between my centers. I am touched by this fact. I have a new feeling, a sense of urgency, a caring, a love of *being*. I engage myself—to see— and in this act of seeing, an energy appears. It belongs to the act of seeing and is here as long as the act is pure. It is the appearance of "I."

To be conscious of self is to be conscious of the impression that is received. In the moment of this consciousness, that which sees and that which is seen blend into a single entity. The whole being is changed. A pure feeling is born, an uncontaminated energy that is absolutely necessary for me to go further. Without it I will never know what is true, never enter a world entirely new.

IV

THE WORK TO
BE PRESENT

What do I understand today, and what do I need to understand?

Understanding depends on my state of being, on my state of Presence.

It is absurd to pretend in my sleep that I wish to work, while all the time dreaming that I can.

Our efforts to work in life are, first of all, to discover how far we are from our highest possibilities.

At the center of our work is the wish to live in a more real way.

My lie is affirming myself without having the taste of truth, the taste of reality.

We can be either an unconscious slave or a conscious servant.

IN A QUIET STATE

✎ *37. A way of understanding*

The Fourth Way is a way of understanding that is to be lived. How we exist, our way of living, is a fact that reflects in exact measure our understanding. I cannot say that I understand what it is to be present. This simply is not true, because I do not live it. When I live without being present, it means there is something I do not understand as I am. And I will never, as I am, understand unless a question about it arises in me.

What is the effort that we call "working"? What are we trying to obtain? What do I understand today, and what do I need to understand? We always wish to change something in ourselves because we do not like it. This is not the right starting point. It is not based on understanding. It does not come from understanding and cannot be trusted. I am able to commit myself only to the extent of my understanding.

Understanding is based on conscious impressions and depends on my state of being, on my state of Presence. What I know in a moment of awareness is what I understand. As soon as my state changes and consciousness diminishes, this understanding is lost. It is immediately taken by the associative thinking and automatic feeling, my ordinary means, which steal it and pretend it belongs to them. We have to know this tendency as a fact, so that we are not fooled. Understanding is a precious treasure that must enter as a living element in my effort. If it enters with clarity, it can give an impetus that will be right and will lead to a conscious impression, a new understanding. We have to be careful not to allow this new impression to be defiled by our ordinary means and to be accompanied by undesirable associations.

In our usual state of sleep, of identification, we can know nothing. When I am wholly identified, I am completely absent. There is nobody here to see, to know. There is not one particle of attention free to see. In my state of sleep I wish to work, and I try in one way or another. But this is impossible. It is absurd to pretend in my sleep that I wish to work, while all the time dreaming that I can. I need to put in doubt my illusion of myself, my habitual affirmation. The first effort is to awake, in order to see.

We do not give enough importance to the moment of awaking, the moment we see ourselves as we are in our sleep. We believe that to awake is to enter into an entirely different life, which will have nothing in common with the one we lead. But, in fact, awaking means, above all, to awake to ourselves as we are, to see and feel the sleep, the identification. The moment itself when we emerge and see the identification is *the only moment* from which an impetus could come. Only then do I have a chance to wake up. Afterward, in the next instant, I justify, I lie. During the moment of the impression, I realize that the level of my state is very low. I am concerned and wish to get free. Then I wish to be present. In seeing myself taken by my imagination, suddenly I am awakened, as though by a light. I wake up by becoming aware of my dream. I recognize a great possibility: I can awake when I am not entirely taken.

Although we could wake up, most of the time we refuse this possibility. We could awake to our own Presence but do not. And when we do, we see that we cannot remain present. I was awake, now I find myself asleep. I was present, and again I am not here. Most of the time I am absent but do not know it. And if I do not discover the way I am taken, I will remain caught in a circle with no way out. To see, to know, becomes the most important aim. It is necessary to understand that I can be able and I can wish, that I can work to be present. I need to wish to stay present and to be able to stay present.

The way in which I question myself, in which I try to know what I need, is very important. I can no longer begin from a vague wish that I take for granted. I have to know why I work and what effort I am making.

38. Each day

We need constantly to redefine our aim. This is because the very sense of our work, of a right effort, gets lost along the way. We forget that what is necessary is to recognize and relate two different levels in ourselves. We do not see the simultaneous movements outward toward manifestation and inward toward a reality at the source, two kinds of vibrations. Always I nourish the feeling of my ordinary "I," clinging blindly to the first movement, the vibration that draws me outward. I am taken by my activity of the moment, and believe that in this vibration lies the affirmation of myself. In this identification I am lost in one or another part of myself, unconscious of the whole. So, my effort is to remember myself.

We are subject to identification under the laws of this world, but because we do not recognize it and do not know another possibility, we submit and are taken by it. We cannot escape unless we see that it is a state of sleep and we awake to another life in ourselves, a higher reality in ourselves. For this we must first know a state that is of a different quality than what we experience all the time. This is possible only in work in the quiet, in conditions that are free from the demands of outer life.

In order to concentrate, my thought engages solely with the question of "I," and all my parts are attentive to knowing my existence. Only one thing counts: "I exist." I know I exist. I can exist, I wish to exist. Nothing else matters. Because I know I exist, I know that everything around me exists. Everything rises and falls, appears and disappears. Yet behind these movements something remains still, unchanging. I must become conscious of it, not staying on the surface but concentrating as deeply as possible at a level I can hardly penetrate, much less remain. I wish for this knowledge, I have a wish for what I can know here. It is stronger than everything else. It is a conscious wish to hear the sound that is "I," to hear it resonate in myself.

Each day I have to give as much time as it takes—sometimes more, sometimes less—to come to a clear perception of an inner Presence, a life in me that is much higher than my body. I need to know this Presence as something really existing, not merely a possibility that I sometimes touch. I can come to it if I am actively passive, quiet enough for an energy of another quality to appear, to be contained in me. This is a state of deep letting go where the functions are maintained in passivity. I let my functions come into my Presence. I do not go into them; they come into me. Only the attention is active, an attention coming from all the centers. I need to find this Presence again and again until I know it as a reality that I cannot doubt.

This certain reality will become the foundation on which I can base my work. If I return each day to something absolutely sure, which I understand and of which I am convinced, I will see the way, the direction that will allow me to know how I am living. I will see myself enclosed in the narrow circle of my wishes and interests, taken by life. Yet by experiencing myself each day in another state, outside this circle, I will recognize that in reality I can escape, and I may even see that the circle does not exist.

39. The way up

What is required to come to an inner sensation, an inner feeling of reality? We need to know the way, the process, accepting that as we are today we have no means to open to reality amid the activity of life. I must know the road I am traveling—the way up and the way down. I learn first to withdraw from activity in order to find this Presence, something real in me. Afterward, I will again go toward manifestation.

In turning toward the perception of another quality, I see that my usual thinking, feeling and sensation cannot help, and I give up my ordinary attitude and my illusion about myself. I can "do" nothing. Nevertheless, I can become conscious of how things take place in me, and I can find an attitude, an inner posture, that will allow opening to a higher energy. To be conscious would mean that all the parts of myself have this knowledge. Going toward this opening would require each part to become passive, available to receive this energy, in a conscious movement of remembering myself. The opening would depend on the attention being of equal intensity in all the centers, as though all the parts were attuned. It would be like forming a world in which each part voluntarily took its place.

The principal obstacle to consciousness is the wandering mind. Everything that distracts from my concentration is my enemy. Yet I do not have to fight the distractions. I need to ignore them and not nourish them with my energy, my attention. My thinking is too unstable, moved by every shock because I naively expect something from it. This thinking is agitated by ever-present thoughts, by their vibrations, which invade my brain. Nevertheless, my mind has the capacity to concentrate on certain thoughts that, in communicating their vibration, can prevent other thoughts from passing through the door of consciousness. Thus the mind can be the cause of my slavery or a factor for liberation.

In working in the quiet, I learn to separate myself from the multitude of thoughts and come to the sole vibration of a single question: "Who am I?" As I try to attune myself to it, a silent, continuing perception of "I" appears behind the waves of thoughts. Then I am no longer agitated by their vibrations, and remain indifferent, expecting nothing from them. Who am I? I stay with the shock of the question until all other thoughts come to submission. It is not easy, but I do not allow myself to be discouraged or afraid. Nor do I cling to the idea of becoming conscious of myself. The aim of concentrating on this one question is to lead me to consciousness. Any other idea which is added—even that of consciousness—is useless, harmful. If another thought comes, I recognize it for what it is and do not entertain it. My mind becomes still and takes on strength, with a power to know without participation of the thought.

Because my mind is still, the sensation of a more subtle energy appears, of a living Presence in me. I feel it comes from my head, a vibration behind my associations, and circulates in my body—a current of energy within the muscles. The current required for an intense sensation of myself is highly charged as compared with the current for manifestation. I extend the reach of my attention so that it penetrates everywhere, becoming like a net or filter that can accumulate the higher current in its mesh. The innermost, smallest muscles are relaxed but only up to a certain point. They keep the precise tautness required to hold the current—neither too much, which cuts me off from my body, nor too little, which allows the current to escape. The larger muscles are supple and without tension, ready to be animated by the other current necessary for manifestation. Regulating the balance between tension and relaxation, the overall "tonus," affects the arising of thoughts, the rhythm, and as a result can bring a kind of mastery over the associations. I feel a stillness, an inner sense of reality.

Remembering oneself begins to be more complete as my attention is divided and feeling participates. When I am concerned with both the mind and the body, it is impossible for the feeling not to come in—it cannot remain indifferent. My feeling has to be touched either by the quality of my state or by the lack of accord. The particular energy necessary for self-remembering can only be produced at a moment of strong feeling. Before this, it is only preparation.

40. An exercise is a temporary aid

When I work in the quiet, I am not disturbed by influences that ordinarily act in my life and I can have a right attitude, an inner posture, that includes my two natures. It is otherwise in everyday life, where I am subject to influences that create very different conditions for my effort.

As I experience the difference between the sensation of tension and of letting go, I see that only in a very relaxed body can a sensation of another Presence appear. It is as though this Presence needs to establish its order in the body. I have to understand this new order and see that I am a part of it, that I wish for it, and that in it I am more essentially myself.

In coming back to myself, there are exercises that I may undertake to clarify the experience of Presence. An exercise is always a temporary aid, a means to help me take a step that I need to take, to see my situation better and to understand the effort I have to make. It can be a help only at the moment when I need it and understand its sense. Otherwise, an exercise will in no way help and, on the contrary, may prevent further understanding. This is why it is important never to experiment blindly with an exercise or do an exercise that was given for others.

In undertaking an exercise, I must first ask myself why I am doing it and if I really want to do it. Otherwise, the exercise will be done passively and, because passivity never brings understanding, it will not help me. In doing the exercise, I pay special attention to work always with three centers. If I see that I am working only with one or two, I can be sure that the effort is mechanical or merely half-conscious. There is real consciousness only when I work with the same intensity in all three parts. If the initiative comes from only one of them—for example, if the center of gravity is first in the head and then passes to the solar plexus—this is weakness, an imaginary work that can only lead to self-deception. And if I relax in a general way, this is also weakness. Without consciousness it has no value. In order to engage wholly, my head needs to be vigilant like a watchman, my body so sensitive to the energy filling it that there is no involuntary tension, and the feeling always aware of the truth of what I am living. Then, I can feel the presence of a fine energy that circulates in my body.

Because it is difficult to have a sensation of the whole—of what I really am—I may begin by sensing different parts of the body. I feel this energy more particularly in my right arm, alive and fluid. It circulates from my right arm to my right leg, then to my left leg and then to my left arm. And I go around the four limbs, beginning each time with the next limb in turn. Then I feel the energy alive in my back . . . in my head . . . in my solar plexus . . . in my body as a whole. "I am." I may intensify the exercise by counting with the sensation of each limb—for example, 1, 2, 3, 4 . . . 4, 3, 2, 1; 2, 3, 4, 5 . . . 5, 4, 3, 2; 3, 4, 5, 6 . . . 6, 5, 4, 3; . . . up to 9, 10, 11, 12 . . . 12, 11, 10, 9; recommencing at 1.

In doing an exercise, I try not to get carried away by the experience. It is a serious moment. I feel the gravity of it. My work depends on what I am going to know now. If each part maintains the initiative, the taste of truth is reinforced and the experience "I am" has a support, a vibration that comes from this conscious effort. But this will more or less quickly disappear. In order for it to remain longer, a certain voluntary thought is necessary. In the quiet state at the end of the exercise, I resolve to myself that something will remain with me until the next time, and that the next time it will be more.

IN THE ACTIVITY OF LIFE

꧁ *41. Only in everyday life*

I must be present to my life if I wish to know what I am. When I open to forces of a higher level, I am able to participate at that moment, but staying there is not my role, my place. I cannot maintain myself in this relation, and after a certain time I only imagine it. When I return to life, it is with my ordinary "I" that I respond. I fall back into my ordinary thinking and my ordinary feeling, and forget the other possibility that I had approached. It is far, very far from me—a huge distance. I no longer believe in it and in manifesting, no longer obey it. I obey the force of my reactions and am lost, identified in my subjective feelings. I believe that by myself I am something, that I need nothing more. I am deaf to the call of a higher force.

As I am, I cannot keep from being lost in life. This is because I do not believe that I become lost and do not see that I like being taken. I do not know what it means "to be taken." I do not see it because I do not see myself in my manifestations and do not really know either my *yes* or my *no*. I have no strong impressions to support my effort to be present. So, my first conscious act is to know my mechanicalness, to see myself blindly obeying an automatic force of attraction or repulsion, and to realize my own passivity, my inertia

in the face of it. My automatism is a prison. So long as I believe myself
free, I will not get out. In order to make the necessary effort, I must
understand that I am imprisoned. I have to see myself being a machine, to know myself as a machine, and to be here while functioning as a machine. My aim is to experience being mechanical and
never forget it.

What is put to the test at the moment of manifesting is the feeling
I have of myself. All our identifications are animated by an essential
force. It is this that we have to confront. The forms that the identification takes are nothing. They are not the heart of the problem. We have
to come back to this essential source, to see that it is behind each of our
masks. It is really our own force that is stolen from us by the affirmation of our individual self. We say "I" all day long. When we are alone,
when we speak with others, we say "I," "I," "I." We believe in our individuality, and this illusion supports our sense of existence. We are constantly striving to be something we are not, because we are afraid of
being nothing.

At the same time, we are bearers of higher possibilities. In better
moments we each feel ourselves as a particle of something greater. We
carry in us a seed of this greatness. This is our value as human beings.
We must become conscious of these possibilities in order to put them
in contact with our life force, to make them participate in our life force.
It is through this consciousness that my real self and my ordinary "I"
can come to know each other and establish a relation.

Ordinary life opposes my knowing higher possibilities hidden in
me. It does this in a natural and implacable manner, which subjects me
to being the way I am today. But when I see in myself the opposition of
two lives, two different levels subject to different laws, I feel the necessity of a way, a direction. Without this opposition I would not feel
it, and I would not learn to see myself as I am. Only in the conditions
of my everyday life can I study where my force and where my weakness lie. Afterward, when I know these, I will also know if it is necessary to change.

42. *The source of manifestation*

The life force is always present in us and is a continual source of manifestation. But we have no contact, no relation with it. We do not feel engaged. We do not know our life force. In order to know it, we have to be present to our identification. We must accept going toward manifestation, at the same time making an effort to see ourselves taken by the life force and to follow the changes that take place in our state. We must come to feel engaged voluntarily—a conscious engagement that we make by choice, by taking a decision.

We have to accept that a force in us will always be in activity, always wish to express itself, to manifest. My thought will always go on, my feeling will always go on, my body will always move. There is a hunger for activity, a kind of avidity, which will always be here. How do I participate in it? What is my relation to it? Here is the root of the problem—I do not see the ego behind all my manifestations, I do not know it. I do not see the impulse that provokes this avidity in myself—this thought "I," "I," "I," which arises with all my emotions, all my movements . . . this constant thought "I." This impulse is a part of me, I cannot deny it. But I do not know my relation to it, what place it should have. I do not even know what in it is good or bad, or what attitude I should have in the face of it. There is nothing conscious. I cannot even stay in front of it to try to understand.

In order to see my identification, I have to accept as a fact my powerlessness to remain present. I have to experience it, and seek again and again to know it. In order to know a force, I have to resist it. So I resist being identified in order to know the force with which I am identified. But what does it mean to "resist"? What is the work of consciously separating two forces in order to become conscious of them both? In the movement to free my attention, I see that attitude is important. In order to stay present, I need to see when my attitude changes and not give in to the force that takes me.

In my ordinary state of identification, I blindly adhere to the movement of manifestation. I am lost in one part of myself, taken in the activity of the moment, unconscious of the whole. This nourishes the feeling of my ordinary "I," which I believe to be the affirmation of myself. Nevertheless, there is in me a finer energy that is quicker, more intense. If I could become conscious of it, I would be able to affirm another quality of myself.

The moment of manifestation tests the feeling I have of myself. I know that the feeling of Presence is not strong. It quickly goes away. It is bound to go because I cannot sustain the effort. But I can repeat, and I can again find the same force, the same taste of something real. Then I struggle not to disappear so quickly in the activity, and I try to see what is required to be present. What do I sacrifice in a moment of work? What is needed for me to have "will"? Who wills, who wishes? If there is a feeling of self, of what self? Who is here? I have to see how I agree to disappear.

43. A measure from above

Our efforts to work in life are, first of all, to discover how far we are from our highest possibilities. Little by little we come to know the differences in our state; our knowledge is a knowledge of differences. There is a difference between the state we experience in the quiet and our state in the activity of life. The state in life is very changeable. We are not the same here as there, now and one hour later, or even five minutes later. Even when we see that our state changes, this has no meaning if we merely register the differences on one level. We have to measure them in relation to something higher which is always the same, that is, an inner seeing that never changes. We measure the lower with a higher part of ourselves.

At the center of our work is the wish to live in a more real way. But as soon as we begin, all the resistance is here, which makes us lie and deny our wish. We do not have a sensation of ourselves or a feeling of

ourselves. So, in saying and thinking "I," what we affirm is not something we recognize as real. Here is my lie—affirming myself without
having the taste of truth, the taste of reality. But I cannot hold on to a
lie and the truth at the same time. To know what I am, I have to make
room, to give up my lie for the feeling of truth. My struggle is a constant effort to be free of this lie and find again what is true at the center
of my work. For this I need to have a point of reference, a certain feeling in myself that is always here, always the same—my actual understanding of what it is to be a conscious being. Each time I work, I have
to make contact with this feeling. This contact, which may be less or
more, is a relation that depends on a voluntary attention. It is my measure, the measure both of my capacity and of the quality of my moment of work.

In order to come back to myself, I have to become free from words
and images, and from emotions, so that I may turn toward the sensation of a more subtle, higher energy. To receive it I must be present,
with all my centers available for an act of consciousness. If I find a balance, I may feel the presence of this different energy, the contact with
a force of another level. Nevertheless, to feel this contact with a higher
world is only one part of the conscious effort to know myself in life. In
this I only know one aspect of myself.

In a moment of work, I first take back part of the attention lost in
identification and relate it to the most intimate reality in myself. My
attention changes by virtue of being turned toward another possibility. But in order to be present, I have then to turn again toward life
with this new attention. One part of it remains aware of my reality,
the other is directed toward life with all the risks of identification.
There is a conscious effort to be related at the same time with both
higher forces and lower forces. I am in the middle, between two
worlds. My attention is entirely mobilized in two directions at the
same time, and remains active in order not to allow myself either to
be carried away or to withdraw from the action. I see the fluctuations
of my level of being.

44. *The way down*

I must know the road I am traveling—the way up and the way down. After withdrawing to find something real in myself, I learn to go more consciously toward manifestation, to open to reality amid the activity of life.

When I awaken in life by chance, I see that I am not prepared. My engagement is not by conscious choice and my attention is scattered. In order for me to be present, there must be a certain wish or will, a certain quality, that does not come from my ordinary person. My effort has to be made with something beyond my ordinary means, beyond my ordinary "I."

For this I have to take a decision. I decide to remember myself and to remain related in two directions at a predetermined moment in a specific circumstance. Usually, my moments of work are isolated and unconnected. When I remember myself alone in the quiet, I go away from what I am in life. I refuse what I am in life and cannot know it. Then, when I try in life, I have nothing prepared in advance, nothing on which my effort can be based. My effort is therefore weak, slack. So I need to connect the moments when I work in the quiet with the moments of work in life. I need to connect them consciously by a decision. Something of what I experience in life must enter my work apart, and something of my work apart must come into my work in life. In my work in the quiet, I try to find again the impression of what I am in life, feeling also the resistance. If I am then able to project a strong impression of both aspects of myself on a future moment of work, my decision to be present can be voluntary. The relation accepted ahead of time can be made at the desired moment, provided my effort is clear. But taking a decision to work is very difficult because the decision has to touch these two aspects of myself at the same time. My incapacity reflects my limited power *to do*.

Our entire Presence must be here at the moment of this decision, including our ordinary "I." Even if we regard it as illusory and disappointing from the point of view of consciousness, this "I" is the provisional center of initiative that supports our life. It must agree with the decision so that all the forces in me will be present when it is carried out. Of course, my "I" does not want this, is not interested in carrying out the decision. But it has to feel and accept that there is something more urgent, something greater. In taking the decision, it resists but at the same time accepts—it accepts the struggle. At the chosen moment of work, when we remember our decision, we need to have a feeling of obedience, of submission to something greater. My ordinary initiative accepts carrying out the decision in the name of something higher. Thus it is our life force, transformed, that is at the center of our action. I have to be shrewd in order to see what I am in life. I must not change in my desire to manifest. I have to catch myself by surprise and at the same moment divide my attention. It is almost impossible.

In taking a decision, we must "take our measure" in order to be able to make a right effort. This means to measure the forces. To conduct a more conscious struggle, I need to know my capacity—what I am able and what I am unable to do—and I need to anticipate the resistance. There are obstacles that I must understand, including both the illusion of my ordinary "I" and the recurring doubts about my capacity. My passivity does not wish to give up and is a very cunning beast. It will tell me that it cannot decide or carry out a decision. This is true—it cannot. But something else can. I need to listen to that, and not to the doubt brought by my passivity. At the same time, I cannot today be present in just any circumstance. It is important to choose an activity that corresponds to my measure, to my capacity to be present. I need to see that I am unable to open to Presence even in the simplest activity.

When I have achieved something, there is always the tendency to become satisfied and to stop working. I forget the strength of my inertia when there is a complete standstill, and how difficult it is to start again. I must learn how always to make new impulses for work, conditions that are hard enough, yet not too hard. If they are not hard enough, they will not serve as an impulse. If too hard, they will create such resistance that I cannot go on. Do not make a promise to yourself that you cannot be sure you are able to keep. If you undertake a task, you must feel it as a strong necessity from the beginning of the day. In order to bring a struggle, the demand must have the force of a strong identification.

STAYING IN FRONT

≈≈   *45. To "know myself"*

Two kinds of movement share my Presence: a movement toward the
source and a movement toward life. I need to see and remember that I
belong to two levels. I can become conscious only when I feel a reality
that is higher than myself, when I recognize that without it I am nothing and have no force to resist being taken by identification. Then I can
open to this reality and consciously receive its action, be nourished by
it. But this requires an attitude that I cannot maintain. Always I return
to the feeling of my ordinary "I," which does not understand that it
must serve. This "I" is blind. It believes itself free and always returns to
its slavery.

When I see my situation, I begin to understand this illusion of "I,"
which is fed by my life force, and to feel the need for a new attitude
toward myself. The initial effort is to free my attention from identification. But there is no solidity, no stability. I need to find the effort that
will allow the formation of a central core, a more stable center of gravity of my attention. In order for me to remain related to the two levels,
my attention must be entirely mobilized and maintained in two directions at the same time. The power of divided energy is my power of
attention.

We do not value enough the short moments when we are situated

94

between two forces. At each step in remembering ourselves, we encounter doubt. I doubt myself, I doubt a more real part of me, I doubt that I can find help—possibilities higher than what I know. It is here that I need to be true in the face of the lie present even in my best moments. I have to struggle with doubt until something gives up. Then help appears which calls me to remain true to maintaining the relation with a higher energy. It is not necessary to come always to an exalted state, only to a level at which I can stay present a little longer. Simply remaining above the level of sleep—a little higher but in a way that has some stability—is itself extraordinary. It constantly jars something in us that awakens. We need to know what we are—either an unconscious slave or a conscious servant.

Our attention has no center of gravity. It is not magnetized by a force that has some authority, some power over it, and continues to run wherever it is called. Perhaps here I see that I am not available because my attention is not available. I am unable to be more collected in myself, more inside, and at the same time to be more outside. So, what is required? The inner reality is the source of my life, but I have also an absolute need to project myself outside. If I can see this inner reality as acting like a magnet, I will see the outside as an opposing attraction, another magnet. Then maybe I will understand what attention means. It is an energy that connects me both with the source and with the outside world, and permits me to receive knowledge, that is, *to know*.

We use the word "know" so much that it does not mean anything. But when we say "I wish to know myself," we are not speaking about acquiring conceptual knowledge, something learned once and for all, then recalled passively. We are speaking of a very intense and active action. After the first shock of Presence, of awaking and coming back to myself, there is a struggle to stay in front of two movements, two levels in myself. With the need for this Presence to last, there is a second shock, the awakening of a new feeling, a new wish, a *will*. In order to continue knowing myself and not disappear, I *will* this Presence to last.

The result of effort is always foreordained. It is determined, has to come as a consequence of laws. What occurs is not always what we might expect. This means the effort was not as it should have been. With a right effort, the result will always come, in due course.

🌿 46. *Only contact, only relation*

There is something too passive in the way I try to be present to myself. I forget that my effort is to become conscious of how the forces sharing my Presence are related to each other, and to find my place in this relation. After trying for a short time, I experience no more than the form in which the effort is being attempted, and I tense in order to keep this form. I no longer see the necessity to know the relation of the forces. I forget that my role is to see and not abandon this vision. Passive, I cling to a form in which nothing more can take place.

There will always be an energy that exists in a state of intense concentration. And there will always be another energy, a dispersed energy that has less power and flows outward. The sense of my life is in the consciousness I have of these forces. This is not in order to prevent them from being what they are, but to know their relation. For this a purer attention is needed, so that I am not carried away by movements provoking tension toward the outside. This relation of forces, this constant awareness of forces, is the very sense of my effort of consciousness. But I forget this and believe it is sufficient to consider one force alone, for example, when I impose relaxation on my body and inwardly fall asleep. The form of the effort becomes the aim, as though to relax is to be present. I need to realize and guard against this constant danger. The sense of my search lies in questioning from moment to moment. The question "Who am I?" is always here—who am I in the middle of these forces that share my Presence?

To see requires an attention that is active, not simply one produced by the shock of an impression. We need to realize that our usual attention is not in contact with what it is perceiving, and as a result we do not really see. For this contact, the attention must become active. We need to face its passivity, to realize our insufficiency, our nothingness, and to stay in front. This brings the activation.

Everything always repeats. We need to stay in front of this repetition in order to go toward the new, the unknown. With our ordinary mind, we cannot. We always expect a result, and so our thought is never free. We delight in change, and do not truly want to know. In order to pass beyond this point, there must be an opening to consciousness beyond the usual functioning, to a consciousness that does not judge but sees. Is it better to wish to change what appears and have a passing experience? Or to stay in front, without leaving, in order to know what I am? I learn to see, and again to see, to remain in front of my lack of will, the lack of desire to face *what is*. To stay in front of what I do not know is a very great thing—and I am an unknown to myself. I begin to understand that only contact, only relation, brings real change, brings consciousness.

With my usual awareness, the higher centers cannot act on me. They are prevented by the dispersed and discordant state in which I constantly find myself. Here is a law: I can do nothing. Is it possible to see this dispersion, to understand it? Because so long as I have not seen it, nothing can change for me. There will be no new impulse, no change of direction or quality in the movement of my energy. The passage toward a better quality, coming from the higher centers, takes place through opening—that is, with the appearance of an attention that was not here before. This comes about at the moment when, incapable of understanding, of receiving, I stop. And in this stop the attention, which was engaged, captive, unconscious of itself, suddenly becomes free. Once free, it is able to stay in front, conscious of itself. This opening to another level puts in question what I am.

47. *The struggle for being*

When we are mechanical, we are acting with only one center, and our energy is spent without our seeing it, used up in associations, emotions and movements. We must see our mechanicalness, and we can only see it by resisting it. We resist being identified in order to know the force with which we identify. When we resist, a different quality of energy, of

Presence, appears with a different taste—a momentary center of gravity. But what does it mean to resist?

Where am I when I am not present? I need to see my complete submission to suggestions, my willing slavery. I like to obey, I accept being cowardly. I cannot even understand what it would mean to wish to free myself. I have never thought that the sense of an independent existence is to be found in the struggle to know my slavery. I have never tried to stay present in life by struggling not to give in so quickly.

My wish to struggle is not strong enough. Otherwise, I would watch. When I begin, I want to withdraw just enough to be able to struggle to stay present. But I forget my wish and prefer to withdraw completely. If I understood that my only possibility to be present is in the struggle, I would not seek to situate myself outside it or avoid it by withdrawing and escaping identification. Seeing my identification would be connected to the struggle. It would be part of my struggle. Conscious effort does not mean staying in one place without changing, but *continuing* the effort. We always dream of reaching a place in order to remain there permanently. Yet permanence can only be found in movement. We are not seeking something static, but the power of a mobile attention, a conscious attention that can follow the entire movement in manifestation, whatever the circumstance.

We need to remember that the struggle is *for* and not *against* something, particularly in relation to what we call "desire"—the wish for pleasure or some other satisfaction. The illusion of desire arises from images recorded in the memory with pleasure or pain. Although the desire leads to fragmentation, it is not getting satisfaction that is bad but the fact that I am absent, unable really to satisfy or not to satisfy it. At one moment, for example, I may experience a wish to indulge a pleasure like smoking or eating. Either I immediately give in to the idea and have no contact with the desire, or I refuse and create conflict, again without contact because I have dismissed the desire. And everything that arises in me proceeds like this. The desire is life itself in me, extraordinarily beautiful, but because I do not know it and do not understand it, I experience frustration, a certain pain, in giving in or in repressing it. So, the struggle is to live with the desire, not refusing it or losing myself in it, until the mechanism of the thinking no longer has an action on me, and the attention is free.

In this struggle, everything is in the attention. A single moment of inattention and all is lost. I must find in myself something real. It is always here. I need to put my trust in it. Without this, there is no support when I have to manifest. So inevitably I will be taken, I will be lost. This is why I have to return to this reality which I recognize in myself—which I belong to. I know that I will be able *to be* only when I can remember what is real for me at the moment and not forget it going into life. I must have this need, this feeling that I need it. This is my wish *to be.* I need it because without it I am nothing, I really am absolutely lost.

At the same time, I have to expect setbacks. The search for "I" is a lifelong journey. I take a step, I fall. I take two steps, I fall. In falling I come to know the obstacles, and when I begin again I am forewarned. I know one obstacle, then a second. We would like to ascend without falling but do not see the danger. It would be terrible if we were to reach the very next-to-last step, fall back to the bottom, and have no more time to climb again. So, we have to accept discontinuity. In evolution each step or note in the octave contains the obstacles of the one that preceded it.

48. *Playing a role*

To be present requires dividing the attention. Three-quarters must be kept inside and only one-quarter allowed to support the movement toward manifestation. This is a law that cannot be avoided. In order *to be,* we have to "play a role."

My need is to reconcile the aspiration toward the higher with the attraction to affirm myself in the functions. I want to unite both forces in order to be conscious of myself as a whole and to remain conscious of myself, actively present to my situation. If I do not remain present, I will be passive, taken by one or the other force. Here I need to see my limitation, to see that my centers are not related. My attention has to stay in front of this fact and not go away until the feeling of "I" appears. It is in trying to stay here longer that this feeling appears at the very heart of the struggle. I alone can resolve the issue . . . if I wish, if I *will*. But in order to *will*, it is necessary to continue staying in front with an active attention. This produces a force that acts on my passivity, and a change takes place in the relation between the centers.

When I see that my energy is entirely drawn outward, I feel a need to come to a different state. This requires an absolute quietness in which I can feel the disconnection between the centers and experience the need to have them in accord. I live this lack of connection, this fact, and see that the energies of the mind and the body are not related. As I stay in front, the two come to the same intensity. But I see that this is not enough. A new feeling must appear, the feeling of being. This is a new energy, a conscious force that needs to be present if I am not to be re-taken by my automatism.

We can be related to our inner reality when we withdraw into a quiet state, but everything disappears when we manifest in life. Our ordinary "I," our ego, takes over. We do not even see the change. The key to staying here is service, provided this "I" can serve our ideal. This is what Gurdjieff meant by "playing a role," a practice so often misunderstood. Inside we have to recognize our own nothingness and identify with nothing, and outside we play a role. One supports the other. If we do not outwardly play a role, it is impossible not to be identified. Without being strong inside, it is not possible to be strong outside. Without being strong outside, we cannot be strong inside. The aim is to obtain inner freedom by doing not what we like but what the other person likes. If he likes me to sit on his right, I do it. If at another moment he prefers the opposite, I do that. In this way I get used to carrying out obligations, a potential attribute of a free man. We have to submit to the forces we wish to serve and at the same time exercise will in our functions.

We seek to be present in everything we do. Ordinarily we live in our functions without consciousness or we withdraw toward consciousness without a relation with our functions. But if our effort is clear, we can also function with consciousness. For example, right now. If I am asleep in myself and I hand you this box, it is not really "I" who gives it. But if I am present in myself and *I wish, I will,* to give you the box, then I know what I am doing. I am here. "I" give you the box. I know, I am present.

We want to be true to ourselves, to not lose entirely our wish for the higher and yet be able to answer to life. It is my life that I will have to live. To be true would mean to ask myself how much I can face this situation. Always more than I think, more than I do. I can be more active. I can begin again and again.

V

WITH OTHERS

The Work is a special current sustained by a source of energy that can only be touched by a person who is whole.

Others are as necessary for us as the teaching itself.

Life is relation and working together, cooperation.

The work with others is a condition for living this teaching.

The teaching is the guide, and only he who questions more deeply can be responsible to serve.

A group creates a possibility of consciousness in which what we engage is more important than what we wish to take.

The Movements are a way of living the idea of Presence.

A SPECIAL CURRENT

49. We say we are "in the Work"

We say that we are "in the Work." What does it mean? The Work is a special current sustained by a source of energy that can only be touched by a person who is whole. This current consists of a certain energy of thought, of feeling, of action. Its life depends on the individuals entering it, who are each and all together responsible for what gives it quality, lucidity. A work together is necessary, cooperation to produce something—like a chain of beings seeking to be more conscious, whose efforts assist one another. Each person joining the chain has to find his place, a place that is determined by his usefulness. Then, by his attitude and actions, he either maintains and vivifies the chain at the place where he is the link, or he falls away and no longer participates in it.

The force of life is always here with its continuous action on me. The higher force is also here, but I am not ready to receive it. It is difficult by myself to sustain the effort needed to have the required intensity in the different centers. This is the reason a group is necessary. A common work is necessary in order to come to a greater intensity together. A concentration toward a higher level by a certain number of beings produces a common vibration. The life that comes from this vibration can be a center of attraction, a powerful magnet, which draws others to its movement. This is the force of monasteries and churches, temples and holy places. The more the concentration is conscious, the greater the force of attraction. But in a group, as in oneself, the elements that participate in this concentration must be of a quality that can come to a certain balance. Otherwise the center and the density will be weak, as will the resonance of the unifying shock.

Each action taken in the name of the Work adds or removes a possibility for the common undertaking. To be related to the Work means to be related to those who feel responsible in front of it. This relation brings an obligation. The first step is to recognize that there is no conscious relation among us and that we must go toward this relation. If we cannot come to relate ourselves consciously, there will be no Work, none at all. Each step we take now, however small, will either strengthen our relation or take us in the opposite direction. Until today we have received the fruits of the efforts and energy of those who came before. Now the life of the Work depends on us. The Work will not live without us, without our sharing in the responsibility. This requires a total engagement, with all our intelligence, all our willingness.

The Work could play its role in the world if we understood the way, the form that is needed to correspond to the state of things today. We will encounter resistance, inner and outer opposition, but we need this. Such resistance can help us find our place, our responsibility, at times in agreement, at times without any relation. Everything depends both on an essential movement in a certain number of people, a creative movement within oneself that opens new possibilities, and on another movement that allows an exchange with a larger group. The force and quality of the current we call the Work will depend on what can be lived and what can be received.

50. Why together?

Why do we come to work together? We feel that if we do not participate in certain conditions, we will be taken by habits and life circumstances in which we will be lost. Perhaps here, together, it will be possible to experience conditions in which a higher energy can appear in us and around us. We will then become responsible together to serve it.

We must understand the necessity of working with others, that others are as necessary for us as the teaching itself. At difficult moments we think it would be easier to work alone . . . not with these people here, not in these conditions. This shows a total lack of understanding of our way, of the need to see and free ourselves from our self-will, which has nothing to do with real will. We have to step out of the narrow circle of thoughts and feelings in which we are enclosed. We have to escape in order to have the possibility to approach another world and exist in a different way. For this, efforts are necessary.

We come together because we each feel the necessity to become conscious of ourselves. So long as I am what I am—that is, think as I think and feel as I feel—I will know nothing true, nothing real. I need to become conscious of my way of thinking and feeling, which conditions all my actions. Only the perception of truth unites. Real work together, cooperation, comes from a common understanding of truth, from the fact that we each see the truth and feel the necessity to put it into action together. The basis of this Work is not a special approach, a special method or special conditions. It lies, above all, in opening to another order in oneself and in others. Life is relation and working together, cooperation, seeing things together, feeling together, living together. This relation requires the same intensity at the same level and at the same time, or it is not "together."

Each of us is alone and in our self must be alone—alone in front of our understanding, in front of the call of the divine and the fact of our human person. I become linked with others when I begin to recognize my original nature and see that we all have the same difficulty realizing it with the whole of ourselves. This brings a special energy, which allows the action of a finer, more subtle nature. The energy has the power to call and to irresistibly attract. This represents the true help that we can bring to each other. It is the only help, the only true relation. Every other relation disappoints. But this relation has to be accepted and maintained. It requires sincerity and rigor at every moment. Everyone is dependent on one another, responsible for one another. What one brings of his work the others receive as help, and what another brings of his inertia or opposition pulls in another direction. I may understand the effort less than others, and some may be groping more than others, but it does not matter. The common direction in which we go is recognized.

On a deeper level, the work with others is a condition for living this teaching, for playing out the drama Gurdjieff left for us. The way toward inner rebirth requires vigilance, first of all to counteract the lie in the affirmation of ourselves. It is a decisive test. There must be no compromise with truth. This is why the most important condition, the necessary condition, is to work with others of comparable experience and understanding, who are capable of upending the completely false scale of values established by personality. We need to see that at the center of everything is this monstrous proliferation of our vanity and our egotism, which takes all the room. To work together sincerely would be to understand our nothingness and what a real human relation would be.

51. To organize

Our work needs to be organized. Efforts that are accidental and anarchical will lead to nothing. My efforts need to be disciplined and subject to rules, to laws of another order above the ordinary level. So long as I do not see the imperative necessity of submitting to this order, I believe in my ordinary "I" and do not really work, do not advance toward my aim. I have to recognize this necessity. I need to put myself to the test—put my ordinary "I" to the test—in a circle of life where the principal interest is to awaken. For this, at certain moments it is necessary to belong to an organization, to a center where people work in the same direction.

To organize means to create an organ, an organism with a prescribed aim. Like every organism, it has to contain in itself the cause for its appearance, and manifest this cause in the details of its organization and in all its results. The effects in all its branches, its centers should project something of the quality of its cause. He who understands the cause perceives it in all its traces. The organization must contain a sense of the sacred. This dimension should never be absent. Behind what is visible there must be an intensity that is not perceived from the outside. It is this that produces the miracle, and an organism from which the miracle is excluded is not a living organism.

The first requirement of a living organization is to come together, to unite. We can attain nothing unless the conditions of "coming together" are right. Without impatience, without intellectuality, without sentimentality, an event must take place. I need to be called and I need to call. The cause is the same. I need to listen and to hear the call, and I need to bring the call in a way that will be received. What is needed is a conscious relation sustained by vigilance and the giving up of my ordinary will in order to work together. I accept or I do not accept this relation with the others. At a certain point there are no leaders and no followers, only those who both question and listen. The teaching is the guide, and only he who questions more deeply can be responsible to serve. What each of us understands depends on his level of being. I must learn to know my own limitations and to recognize when others understand more.

When I think of myself and the rest, the others, I realize that others please me, make me afraid, threaten me. But I need them. It is by my reactions that I can see both myself and the others, not just me. In order to know what I really am, I must go from discovery to discovery. Liberation is not to be found in judging the "bad" or the "good." It is in the disappearance of the ego and the union with everything and everyone. The only bad is ignorance, the only good, awakening. Yet everyone wants to direct or be directed as he likes, to judge and criticize before seeking to understand. This attitude is fundamentally false. What we have to seek is not to impose an order, but to enter into an order, an order that existed long before us. It is the order that is important, not the organization.

We must understand that our organization exists in life on two levels. One level, which alone gives true meaning, is that of the work, our search, with all the conditions it requires. The other is the official or outer aspect, which is only a cover, nothing more, but which can help us pursue our work without disturbance. This distinction seems easy to understand but in fact is not. I have seen that this official side, organized to meet the image and routine required by life, always reclaims its rights and tends to impose its structure on the work, that is, to impose a form that responds in no way to its true order of values.

52. *A school of the Fourth Way*

A house of work is like a school based on the principles of this way, this teaching. It is here for a limited time during which certain things need to be accomplished. The house plays its role according to the level of the people who participate there. It may have those who understand that they are not what they should be, but are not convinced that they wish to change their being and do not yet understand the necessity of effort. The house may also have people who are already disappointed with themselves, who no longer believe in their ordinary "I," and know that their life will take on meaning only when they can make a precise effort to awaken and see their situation. And there can be houses where some have gone still further. Each time the role of the house in the whole of the Work is different, depending on the level of the people who participate. Yet we need to understand that the Work will never go very far without a center organized to bring the necessary conditions, without a life subject to the principles of the teaching we follow. A school requires both understanding of its principles of work and discipline based on them. We have to pay for what we receive.

This house is like a world within another world. I seek to know and to be what I am. For this my attention is always turned toward myself, toward the perception of my true nature, which is not the expression of my person, my ego. I see my ego expressing itself in my thoughts, my desires, my movements. And I try not to be taken by them. I measure myself constantly. Because of this, because I am always in question, I do not judge the others. I learn to see, to understand without judging. There is no "me" and "you." There is only manifestation. I learn to see the laws of the world in which we are living, the laws of manifestation.

A basic principle of this school is always to do more than what ordinarily we can do. Only this will lead to change. If we do merely what is possible, we stay as we are. It is necessary to do the impossible. This is the difference from ordinary life, in which one only does what is possible. Another principle is that we intentionally do not rely on a precise form given in advance, so that an active and more conscious search can take place. Our aim is to free ourselves from everything that keeps us attached to an activity, and to develop a kind of vigilance that will allow us to go further. When a form of work is brought, we first receive it as new but afterward repeat it as given. In this repetition we have less and less understanding of the principles that are behind the form. For a form to remain alive, we need always to return to the source, to the truth. Below the Absolute, at all levels, there is remembering and a thirst to turn toward the greater, toward *what is*. But, as we descend the ladder of involution, forgetting appears and becomes deeper and deeper.

Truth of another level can be brought through ideas. This requires knowledge and understanding based on being. There must be knowledge of the ideas, both of their overall structure and of the place of each idea within it. Equally important is to have understanding based on personal experience of the truth contained in the ideas. We have to ourselves be able to live the idea so that what is communicated is its life, not a dead form. The idea is the creator of everything. It has an extraordinary force that could live in us. We need to understand how to be awakened and enlivened by the ideas, and how to be responsible for the life that is lost when we let them die in us. We have received a lot of ideas, but we are very poor in ideas.

This Work is a school for developing a new center of gravity. Until now the center of gravity around which our life has turned—whether

we accept it or not—has been our ordinary "I." And it is still this "I"
that hopes, that evaluates, that judges . . . and all this even in the name
of the Work. So long as my entire psyche turns around this "I," everything that is manifested—whether I wish it or not—will reflect the
authority of this "I." Our aim in a school of the Fourth Way is to become different, to change our being from the level of man number
one, two, three to that of man number four with a new center of gravity, and from the level of man number four to that of man number five
with an indivisible "I."

EXCHANGE IN A GROUP

✎ *53. A special condition for exchange*

Our independent efforts, each by ourselves, are insufficient. A group is the beginning of everything, a group of people seeking to live in a more conscious way. A group can succeed better to maintain the effort. Some of us are more vigilant, more responsible. We help one another. But the appearance of this form has to be recognized, not imposed. We have to feel the need for coming together, to be present with others to share a relation of reciprocal attention. To have a basis for a conscious relation, each member must know and accept himself. Each must feel the need for the group, for a world traversed by a certain current of thought and feeling. He has to know that he needs it, and must not forget that he needs it.

We are, of course, speaking of a group formed for work on one-self that is not on the level of ordinary life. It is animated by thoughts that are different from those of ordinary life, and also by different feelings. Its existence has to be marked by events that are essentially different from those of ordinary life. The first event is the active and committed search for a center of gravity of vigilance in oneself. A centered attention may be drawn in different directions, but it always returns to the center. When we are dispersed we can learn nothing new. This is the "old man," the automaton who pretends to know, who mouths useless words about ideas that are supposedly understood. The one whose attention is centered seeks to express only the essential about his search and his observations. He is different, a "new man."

We are in a group because we need help to find a quality in ourselves, a state in which we can experience something real. We need higher influences that are inaccessible when we work alone with our ordinary means. Without the group we cannot come to the necessary intensity. The group is thus a special condition for exchange and a kind of conduit for higher influences, ideas from a higher level of life. But we must be wholly present. We receive these ideas in the exact measure that we are present.

What then is our responsibility? We have an obligation to exchange, and to accept and help each one to play his role in the group so that consciousness, the measure of our actual awareness, determines everything we do. In becoming conscious of ourselves as a group, we experience the truth of our work. It is not right if I only do what I wish in my own way, independent, unwilling to be tested. This shows I am incapable of confronting myself and of relating to the work of another. It means my work has stopped. If the group does not become conscious of itself as a group, it cannot know its place and obligations in the Work. It cannot serve, cannot play its role in the Work.

The group, the fact that we are together, creates a possibility of consciousness. What we engage, what we give, is more important than what we wish to take. Each time the possibility is renewed, we have the opportunity to engage our attention and to serve. This possibility is something great that we must strive to maintain. We have to look at it as precious, as sacred.

I am not alone in my work. When I decide something for myself, I have to feel my belonging to the group. Its life is greater than my own, and it represents something more on the scale of higher Being.

54. *I need to speak*

We always begin far away from the essential. Even if we repeat and repeat, we have to think of the meaning of what we are doing, of the meaning of our work and our Presence. It should never be forgotten, but we all the time forget. We lose the meaning and have to come back. We must not pretend and take for granted that the meaning is understood. It is not true. Each time we meet together, the meaning has to be again renewed for oneself. Each time has to be a moment of acute questioning. If I don't know for myself now what I am doing, what is at stake, what is in question—if I don't know it each time— something different will happen that goes in the opposite direction. My effort has to be clear, what I am looking for has to be clear. Every- one, together, has to make this Presence appear in himself at the same time. This Presence must become a reality, our common connection above the personal, a reality that we serve and obey.

The life of a group depends on our state and on our questions. We ask whatever we wish about our own work. What are my difficulties now? What do I need to understand, what do I wish to know? What seems important to speak about in my work? When we come together, I must be prepared to speak. I must constantly reflect on my work and not come in a passive state. If I come without being prepared, it has not much sense. If I have no definite aim, we have nothing to speak about. How can we have an exchange? It is impossible.

One of our greatest obstacles is our concept of question and an- swer, that is, of the transmission of knowledge sought and passed from one person to another. We think that the questioner is less knowledge- able and is in effect asking for an answer to dispel his ignorance. And in life, where everyone relies on what is known, it is like this. But in a group the direction is toward the unknown. The questioner is open- ing the door to the unknown, and the listener is called to an exchange that flows between them, a movement in two directions. Real change of understanding would mean that, with the listener also questioning and the questioner really listening, the level of both participants would change.

To begin with, if I am in the position of listener, a change is needed in my state. If I am searching for a more active attention, freer to listen, freer from associations and reactions, there can be a greater possibility to explore the question, to go into it more deeply without being caught in the outer formulation. If my attention is more actively engaged, there can be a participation that permits the exchange to flow in two directions and activates the "hearer" in both questioner and listener. But if this active attention is not being searched for, if I receive the question with my ordinary attention—that is, passively—I respond passively and nothing is exchanged, no matter how clever my words or how strong my emotional force. Instead of a new quality of attention and receptivity, permitting the flow of new knowledge in both directions, there is a one-sided relationship of dependence, already existing and now strengthened. This attitude of dependence, which is mutually harmful, will become more and more fixed, and will not allow the activity and freedom necessary for a real exchange. . . .

Once I have come to a more concentrated state, I need to speak about my work and my questions, to exchange, always working to be present. My thought is necessary, but only on what I am saying, not on something I have already said or something I will say. Only on what I say at the very moment.

55. Real exchange

The current practice of questions and answers is exterior, outside oneself, both for the questioner and the listener. It is, of course, necessary that a question appear, but also silence. The question is the opening to silence, the gateway to the unknown. What is the new inner condition brought by the question?

A false attitude develops in the groups between those who put questions and those who respond. This in effect becomes questions-with-answers or answers-to-questions, not a moment of presence together in pursuit of a new understanding, a new way of thinking and feeling. Here questioner and listener are relying on some knowledge, and there is an event that does not take place. This is not because nothing could take place—the elements are here—but because what is put forward is not the right material.

When I exchange in a group, I need to know to what I am calling the other person, to what participation. At the very moment of speaking, I may be awkward or insufficient. I do not know what to trust and I agree too easily to lie in affirming a false image of myself. Nevertheless, I need to know the nature of the cooperative effort in which I am engaged. How can I stay in front of what is in question? How can I understand the other, understand his question and relate it to my own in order to have a real exchange? The most important thing is for me to open to my question and to remain open. We wish to learn together, to open to the unknown.

There is an attitude that we must not allow in ourselves, which ruins our work and that of others. We are here with the others to see our nothingness, which otherwise is too difficult to perceive, and to open to the possibilities in ourselves and with others. This requires a desperate effort to find again our measure between these two things. Instead of this, either with our questions or in our responses, we affirm our ordinary "I" and even presume to teach the others.

Nobody can teach. We can only work. And before working we must have taken our measure in order to be convinced of the effort we have to make. Nobody can ask us to be more than we are. But we have no right in the name of the Work to pretend in front of others to something that is not true. Above all I need to work myself, to take my measure. When the others bring questions, it is I who must put a question to myself as well as to them. If I am able to respond a little to the question, it is to myself that I am responding.

We need to exchange what we have received in order that this material remain alive in us. If it is not exchanged, it will not live. But an exchange cannot be unilateral. At the moment of exchange, I need to be in question myself, open to my inquiry, truly living it, sensitive to all my own reactions and to those of the others sharing my experience. In this moment, thirsting to be free enough to obey the law of the highest force and aware of my incessant reactions, I know what I am. I know my weakness. Yet if I see that the sense of my life is here, only here, I have a constant direction for my effort, an effort to be a responsible individual. All the rest—for example, that I know more than others—is in the realm of dreams.

56. This form

We begin to understand better that this work requires certain conditions, depends on certain conditions. One of these is that we unite our efforts. We depend on other human beings who either feel the problem of existing more deeply than we do, or who are questioning on the same level as ourselves.

The need we each have depends on the truth of our work. In fact, we depend tremendously on one another. We can do nothing without one another. The exchange we can have together is more necessary than our daily bread. We make efforts alone—we struggle alone, suffer alone, respond alone. But a moment comes when exchange is indispensable, when we need to nourish one another with the fruits of our efforts. And without this exchange, we cannot go further. The more we value our existence, the more the question of relation appears.

Only in the beginning is it necessary to create groups artificially with a leader answering questions. For a definite time, a work of penetration can only take place in coming together in this way. Later the organism forms itself naturally among those of the same level who together feel the need. As we go further, the need for conscious exchange becomes more urgent. We may work separately, each making efforts alone. Yet at certain moments it is imperative to come together to verify and exchange, and in order, by a certain common effort, for truth to emerge more strongly.

There is a time for everything. I speak of the form that our work today has taken, of groups, and of the possibility that has been created.

If this possibility is not sufficiently realized, this form will degenerate by itself and will never give birth to a new, more inner form, with a new possibility. Forms do not invent themselves. They arise from the need to work together that certain elements feel is necessary to preserve their existence.

How much more time should this form last? This depends on the depth of work of a certain number of people, and the relation established between them—the quality of their exchange. I need to collaborate in a common effort of ascent. If I do not, whether or not I wish it, I am responsible for the stone I do not bring to the edifice. So, we have to reflect deeply on our work together, which little by little must manifest itself in our lives. We must reflect on our relation, on the form of our life together, and, above all, on our exchange.

WORK IN MOVEMENTS

❧ *57. A double aim*

In man, as in the universe, everything is in movement. Nothing stays still or remains the same. Nothing lasts forever or ends completely. All that lives evolves or declines in an endless movement of energy. The laws underlying this universal process were known to ancient science, which assigned man his proper place in the cosmic order. According to Gurdjieff, sacred dances, handed down over the centuries, embodied the principles of this knowledge, allowing it to be approached in a dynamic and direct way.

All the manifestations of life in man are expressed in forms by movements and attitudes, that is, postures. From the most ordinary to the highest level, each possible manifestation has its own movement and its own attitude. A thought has a movement and a form that is proper to it. A feeling has a movement and a form proper to it. For an action it is the same. Our entire education consists precisely in learning a whole repertoire of attitudes of thinking and feeling, and attitudes of moving. This repertoire constitutes our automatism. But we do not know it. And there is a language here that we do not understand.

We believe that we are conscious and that our movements are free. We do not see that each movement is a response, a response to the shock of an impression. Scarcely has the impression reached us than the answering movement is set off, usually long before we are aware of it. The awareness comes afterward. This whole event takes place suddenly, and nothing in us is quick or sensitive enough to perceive it at the very moment it happens. Whatever the answering movement may be, wherever it comes from, it has inevitably been conditioned by the automatism of our associations, by all the habits and clichés engraved in our memory. We have nothing else with which to respond. So our life is an endless repetition of accumulated memories. But as we remain unaware of this, our movements appear to us to be free.

In fact, we are prisoners of our attitudes of thinking, feeling and moving, as though caught in a magic circle from which we cannot escape. In order to get out, I would need to be able to take a new attitude—to think otherwise, to feel otherwise, to act otherwise, all at the same time. But, without my knowing it, these three are interconnected and, as soon as I try to change one, the others intervene and I cannot escape. My automatism keeps me on a very ordinary level of thinking and feeling.

The Gurdjieff Movements represent notes of an octave on a different level than that on which we live automatically. They lead the energy of our functions in an ascending direction, to a quality of vibrations of equal intensity in all the centers. A certain succession of movements has been foreseen to demand a special attention of thought, of the mind. Without this attention the process will not be able to continue. Thus the thought must be maintained with a certain quality, a certain intensity. But it is the body that performs the movement. To execute it and express its life fully, the body needs a great freedom. It needs to adapt itself entirely. The least resistance of the body will prevent the thought from following the order of the movement. If this quality in the thought and body cannot be maintained, the movement will not follow the necessary direction. It will be broken, purposeless. In front of the demand, the feeling awakens. The appearance of the feeling brings a new intensity, a unification that creates in us a particular current, a new octave.

These Movements have a double aim. By requiring a quality of attention maintained on several parts at the same time, they help us to get out of the narrow circle of our automatism. And through a strict succession of attitudes, they lead us to a new possibility of thinking, feeling and action. If we could truly perceive their meaning and speak their language, the Movements would reveal to us another level of understanding.

58. Why Movements?

We do not ask ourselves why Gurdjieff introduced the Movements as one of the most important practices for living his teaching. Why Movements? Some embodied a very high knowledge, representing laws. Others were given simply because his pupils needed to work in a certain way. For some periods Gurdjieff devoted several hours each day to Movements, adapting them to correspond to the phase of the work. For example, at times it was the sensation of the body that was not developed, and the attention could not remain on the body. At other times, it was the thought that was not free and could not be open to a subtle energy. The exercises required the attention to be turned in a certain way and to follow a certain path. This brought an experience of a different quality, which allowed the pupil to understand better and see how to find this quality in life. At the same time, work on Movements allowed a direct experience of the laws governing the transformation of energy. This included the symbol of the Enneagram, which Gurdjieff said was almost impossible to understand without the feeling brought by participating in the Movements that are based on it.

The universe consists of energies that pass through us. Each movement inside and outside us is a passage of energy. The energy goes where it is called. We cannot prevent it. We are subject to the forces that surround us. Either we are related to an energy that is a little higher, or we are taken by an energy that is lower. We are not a unity, we are not one. Our energy needs to be contained in a closed circuit, in which it could be transformed. This would allow it to enter into contact with energies of the same quality to form a new circuit, a new current. So long as a current of higher energy is not established in me, I have no freedom.

There is an energy that comes from a higher part of the mind. But we are not open to it. It is a conscious force. The attention is a part of this force that must be developed. Without this force I am taken, and my movements are automatic. The head may understand but not the body. Yet it is the body that must feel this force. Then it will obey, tensions will fall away, and the movements can be free. I will not be taken and the movements will not be merely automatic.

Consciousness of movement requires total attention. The quality of this attention calls us to experience a whole Presence. This perfect attention is a possibility given by Nature. At the moment of a particular movement we no longer think of the movement past or the movement to come. We are not trying to express the form of a movement, an attitude that we make ourselves assume. We are entirely attentive to an energy that needs to be free to remain contained in the body in a certain way. One can know it only in subjecting oneself to it.

The Movements can show us how to be in life, how to experience Presence and at the same time have a freer movement in manifestation. Instead of endless reactions—the conditioned responses of our automatism—there is the possibility of action coming from vision, from a conscious force that is higher. The Movements are a way of living the idea of Presence. The idea alone is not enough. There needs to be an action that brings the energy we are talking about. Through the Movements, when all the energies within us are related, a new energy is produced. We can feel it. It has another quality, another force, and a consciousness that ordinarily we do not have. This energy comes from my mind, from a higher part of my mind where there is an intelligence, a capacity of seeing. I need to be in relation with this part of my mind. Then I will have a vision that is absolutely clear. I see myself. I see other people. I see *what is,* very clearly, without reaction. I see myself as *I am.*

59. *Part of the teaching*

The Movements are part, only a part, of the teaching about the possible transformation of energies in us and the sense of human life. They express the teaching in a language where each gesture, each attitude, each sequence has a specific role and meaning. We cannot understand the Movements apart from the teaching, and we cannot rightly practice them with our automatic thinking and feeling. They call for the participation of my whole Presence. I must open to an energy that could have its own life in me. Then it is the body of energy, the Presence, that is in movement. Unless this Presence is here, the Movements are done automatically. Even if we think they are done well, they express nothing and are meaningless. This kind of practice is a total distortion and has nothing to do with the Movements as they were created.

Those who accept the responsibility to bring the Movements to others are in a difficult position. We repeat certain Movements and try to maintain an interest. But we do not really know what we are doing. We cling to a form that is empty of meaning. We need an experience that we have not lived, an experience of Presence, and of Presence in movement. In fact, we have a very limited understanding of both the teaching and the language of the Movements. It will require years in order to develop the necessary attention. Then, what would be a right attitude today if we wish to serve the Work?

What is required to bring a Movement to others? First, we ourselves need to have done the Movement and we need to know both its structure—the succession of attitudes—and its rhythm, its life. Then we demand, of ourselves and others, correct attitudes and a clear vision of their succession. The positions must be exact. Without precision our work is superficial. Finally, we have to see in ourselves what the attitudes correspond to and find the right tempo to make the Movement alive. Of course, there are always questions. Is it necessary to simplify this Movement and learn one limb after the other? Do we need to begin with an exercise that introduces aspects of the Movement? What will have the most effect on the attention? What sort of demand must be brought, and how? Should something extra be said, remembering always that words provoke thinking and encourage the head to "do" the Movement? And always, what is this Movement, to what does it call? Each time, before beginning a class, we must take a moment for ourselves to remember what we wish to serve, in what we place our trust. The most important thing is my state. I need a conscious attention that is stronger than the automatism. Without vision, without seeing, it is just the ego that brings or does the Movement.

In each Movement there is a succession of attitudes composing a whole, which has to be carried out without mistake. The whole Movement needs to be foreseen simultaneously by our functions during a definite time when everything in us is still. The succession of attitudes reflects the line of developing forces and the state of relation between the centers of energy. Simply repeating a Movement reinforces the automatism and our tendency to rely on the body without the engagement of the thought. So, exercises and concentrating on parts of a Movement are important not only to introduce the Movement but to work on aspects of the attention that need to be developed. At the same time, because each Movement expresses a whole—has its meaning as a whole—we need also to allow the class to experience the Movement in its entirety.

We need to see that different positions and tempos represent different states of energy. For example, when the right arm makes a circle, the continuity expresses a quality of thought that is quiet and does not move; if the left arm maintains a rhythm with a series of positions, it has a different tempo and represents a different energy in the body. We also have to learn how different attitudes affect the disposition of energy in us. When I have taken a certain attitude to allow the energy to circulate freely the length of the spine, a change in the attitude alters the disposition because the direction of the energy changes. If I lower my head, for example, the current no longer passes in the same way; it goes back down. If I put my hand on the chest, I keep the current in this area. If I raise the head, I receive the energy from above. If I put my arm forward, I stop the flow. If I then raise the forearm, keeping the elbow in the same position, I am ready to receive the influx of energy. And if I put the arm down, the energy is received and stored in the body. We have to be very careful in changing the Movements, particularly the order of attitudes that expresses a law. Each attitude, each gesture, has its place, its length, its proper weight. If there is a mistake or if something new is introduced, the whole meaning can be distorted.

We have a tendency to imagine, to let senseless ideas, images and emotions come into our attitudes. But what may take place is more serious, that is, the experience of the flow of energy producing the state intended by the one who created the Movement. It is a science, a knowledge—the most fundamental of all—which can only be obtained by stages, beginning with the relation between centers in action. It has to be decoded and studied in place, in giving oneself to the practice.

60. *Only with a stable Presence*

We are not going to "do" Movements. We are going to try to understand movement. What is movement? How do we put ourselves in movement? From where do our movements come?

We understand movement in a static way, one attitude followed by another, seeing only the outcome without being able to follow the movement itself. We never feel the movement. We see the image of a position and begin to move in this direction. But the movement is mechanical. The position is taken without our knowing how, totally directed by our automatism. And we take each position separately instead of passing from one to another as with notes in a line of music. Nevertheless, what we are is energy in movement, a continuous movement that never stops. We need to feel the energy and follow the movement, letting it flow without the thought intervening in any way. We have to feel this energy as a Presence that must not go away. Then the movement is being done under a vision. It is still automatic, but the vision has an action. The movement is freer.

Before beginning any Movement, I must find this energy, this state in which there is a relation between the mind and the body. The feeling comes by itself. The movement is an expression of this state. Without this state, from where will my movement come? At first, I try to open to an energy that comes from a little higher than my head, and that passes in me. This allows a consciousness that I otherwise do not know. I need to keep it within me, while at the same time my body is in movement. The two need to be absolutely together. This energy is more important than anything else. I am in movement, but the energy remains the same and is stronger than the movement. In order to stay related to this energy, I need to be in a rhythm of a certain intensity and strength. I am "in a rhythm"—what does it mean? Not that one part is in one rhythm and another in another, nor that I do one position in the rhythm but not the next. The energy is everywhere the same.

We do not accept that there is no relation between the thought and the body. The thought turns around and goes its own way. The body does not care and waits for something to be asked of it. For a relation to appear, there needs to be a movement from one toward the other. The relation creates a new energy, which needs to become a Presence that is stable, like a second body. The work has different stages. But for now the whole work is in this, although there will be another stage after the second body has been formed. In order to have this relation, I need to develop an attention that I do not now have, a voluntary attention. If I *will*, I can—if I truly *will*. When this attention, this vision, is developed, my body will obey because it feels a force that is greater, and that will bring it something greater. The effort of relation between the centers, which the Movement requires, brings the energy necessary for the formation of higher bodies. The Movements thus bring the element of shock in a right way. It is this that may allow us to pass the interval between *si* and *do,* which otherwise may never be passed. Only if we have a Presence that is stable, a second body, will we be able really to do the Movements as they were intended.

VI

TO BE CENTERED

We have to find a way toward unity.

Our aim is to be centered in the sense of a concentration of our energies and of finding the center of our being.

In order to become whole, a unity, I must be centered.

For my being to emerge, there must be a quality in my sensation that is equal everywhere, a unity of vibrations, so that a state without waves appears.

The center of gravity is the seat of unity.

I participate in life through breathing.

The perceptible breath is not the true breath, that is, the current which animates inhalation and exhalation.

A SENSE OF THE WHOLE

⬿ *61. The aim of my effort*

We are divided between a movement inward of coming back to ourselves, to our essential nature, and a movement toward the outside. We are engaged sometimes with one, sometimes with the other, and do not succeed in living the two simultaneously. This becomes a kind of opposition, a contradiction, and we spend our lives seeking a way of living in which this tension could be resolved. We need a new approach to this problem, one that does not risk the totality of our being. We have to find a way toward unity. This would include all the centers and functions at the service of the one life force. It would mean that on both sides something is undertaken, something is recognized. These two movements are indispensable to each other. The life force cannot act without me, but I have to give up all pretense of being anything whatsoever by myself, of being able to act independently without it.

Our lives always revolve around a force that strives to be actualized. Yet the force and what is actualized have a different meaning depending on the "I" that is involved. In facing life, I am driven by the force of my ego. I take my life as a web of relations viewed from a center. I feel this center—it is me. I call this center "I," and it is from here that I think and feel. The notion of "I" takes up all the room, and comes back even in my better moments of work. In this it is always a single

131

part of me that takes over—sometimes my thought, sometimes my emotion, perhaps my body. They never act together. There is no sense of the whole.

To be centered means to abdicate, for each part has to renounce the pretense that it is the whole, that it sees and directs the whole. It is as though I submit to an order that is greater, an order on a cosmic scale, and all my parts accept to serve it, to remain voluntarily passive in front of it. My body, my feeling and my head let go. I feel a finer energy in me that moves downward toward its source, as if needing to concentrate again before going back up to nourish the other centers. It is a movement of circulation, of constant balance and relation. For this I need my functions, but a functioning that has no roadblocks. I need my thinking—but not just thoughts, words and images that capture the pure energy of the thinking and make it passive. I need my feeling—but not a feeling taken by images to which it is passively attached. And I need my body, free of any tension that holds back the energy. I see that I need the help of my functions, which otherwise will become an insurmountable obstacle. Without their help, I cannot open to the Presence in myself.

In my usual state, my attention is not voluntary. It is of low quality, without power, and flows passively toward the outside. But this attention has the possibility of being transformed, of achieving a purer quality by maintaining a direction recognized as necessary. By the force of my attention actively turned inward, the movement of energy changes. Instead of going outside, it concentrates within until it forms the center of gravity of my Presence. My whole effort, my whole work, is to maintain this direction—to maintain a body so relaxed that the energy does not leave, a thinking turned toward myself so vigilant that its very presence sustains the stillness of my body, and a feeling of what wants to be recognized, of what is here, a feeling of "I." It is an effort of attention coming from all the parts of myself—to purify the attention in order to concentrate on "I." In this effort I discover a way of functioning that is no longer passive, a work in which the functions are called to obey the movement of attention.

My whole struggle, the aim of my effort, is to come to a certain unity. I can have a more conscious state only at the moment when my centers are balanced and the links between them are maintained by the attention. The different parts of my Presence must learn to work together in the same direction, engaged toward the same aim, to receive the same impression. I see that my vision and understanding, my intelligence, depend on this state of Presence. When I am attentive to this Presence, I feel its life, a mysterious life that relates me with every living thing in the world. My vision of myself is related to the whole.

62. *The first feeling of unity*

Gurdjieff taught that within the physical body there are finer substances that interpenetrate one another and, under certain conditions, can form an independent second or even third body. The physical body works with these substances, but they do not belong to it and do not crystallize in it. Its functions are analogous to those of the higher bodies but are significantly different, specifically in the separation between the emotional and intellectual functions. As we are, everything is governed by the first body, which itself is governed by external influences. In it the feelings, though dependent on accidental shocks, occupy the place of the second body, and the thought corresponds to the functions of the third body. When there are other bodies, the control emanates from the higher body, from the consciousness of the higher body. There is an indivisible and permanent "I," an individuality that dominates the physical body and triumphs over its resistances. And there is consciousness instead of mechanical thinking, with will as a power issuing from consciousness.

As I am, I am defenseless against influences acting on the ordinary level because I am not centered in myself. Being passive, my different centers are necessarily at the mercy of whatever ordinary shock makes them vibrate. But when there is a center of gravity for my functions, an axis, I can receive shocks from another level. So long as my attention remains consciously fixed on this center of gravity, I am invulnerable to the pull of the ordinary level. The shocks from outside do not affect me because their vibration is slower than that of my concentration. At the same time, a vivifying shock from another level communicates to my centers a quicker vibration, which has the effect of cohesion and unification.

When I am quiet, I feel strongly that I am one, that I am whole. I begin to feel that behind all the movements of my ordinary "I" there is something in me that remains stable, like an axis maintaining a certain balance. I have an intuition of a vibration that is totally different in its intensity. It is difficult to attune myself to its resonance, to attune the slow and incoherent vibrations that are moving me. But I listen, and am sensitive to these different qualities. And the more I listen and am sensitive, the more the resonance appears like an underlying sound, a fundamental sound as if in the background, which becomes irresistible. The other vibrations undergo a change, as though the discordant notes attune themselves and the movement quickens by itself. Here, nothing will take place unconsciously. I can only consent and wish consciously—*will* consciously—to be the site of this metamorphosis. This is what I serve, the purpose of my life. To understand this brings the act of letting go, a quieting of all my tensions to correspond to the essential vibration. I need to understand what I wish. I need an awakened sincerity for this blending to take place. Something has to make room.

This opening to Presence requires an attention that is voluntary and sustained by my whole being. I must find in myself a wish and a power of attention, a will, that goes beyond my usual capacity. It is a "super-effort," a conscious effort. I have to remain conscious of being a unity while I manifest, remaining related inside and at the same time relating myself outside. The effort is to realize the relation between the functions and the higher parts of the centers, which brings me the first feeling of unity, of being a whole. It requires a voluntary attention concentrated at the point of division of the forces, and held there. This depends on my feeling of "I," my feeling of Presence. I need to know myself as a whole and to express myself as a whole, that is, to *be a whole*.

But this need for unity can only come if I have sufficiently understood that I live partially, that I am taken all the time in one or another part of myself. When all the ordinary functions participate in self-remembering, there can be an opening toward the higher centers, an opening that comes from the refinement of the attention.

63. *Centered through consciousness*

No conscious movement is possible unless we are centered in an inner form that corresponds to our double nature. Our centers have to be related and permeable to an essential energy that is beyond their understanding. But though we wish it, we do not have this relation or this permeability, so our actions are never conscious. We view the world outside in terms of our self-love, our ego, which is the center of gravity of our state. As such, it distorts the meaning of our perceptions and enslaves us. We do not behave like a living being, a being alive in itself. There is only self-love. We do not know what it is to love.

We recognize that our functions can exist without consciousness, and we begin also to realize that consciousness can exist without functions. We need always to return to our aim: to be centered in ourselves through consciousness. This is both our possibility as human beings and our risk. We may find our true selves, as well as fail.

I begin to see that I live torn between two realities. On the one hand, there is the reality of my existence on the earth, which limits me in time and space, with all its threats and opportunities for satisfaction. On the other hand, there is a reality of being that is beyond this existence, a reality for which I have a nostalgia. It calls to our consciousness, across all the disappointments and misfortunes, to lead us to serve Being, to serve the "divine" in ourselves. If my life is lived only to subsist, the essential being is veiled, obscured. Even if I subsist in an intelligent, reasonable way, I do not see the true sense of my life—I have no direction. I am entirely drawn toward outer existence and thus prevented from becoming conscious of my authentic being. On the other hand, if I feel another reality, under the force of this impression

I forget my life and withdraw into isolation. Thus the world claims me without caring about inner life, and my being calls me without caring about the demands of worldly existence. These are two poles of one larger Self, one same Being. I need to find a state in which I am more and more open and obedient to an essential force in me, and at the same time able to express this force and let it do its work in the world.

If I consider my state right now, I see that I have no real center of gravity, no real "I." I have a habit of calling my body and my other functions "I" or "me." But I do not have an "I" that is true and always the same, that does not change, an "I" that could *will*—not desire, not hope, but *will*. The different parts of me are not related to each other. My feeling does not experience what my head thinks, and my head does not think what my body senses. Their intensity is different, and they do not have a common aim. They are occupied personally, each for itself with its own desire.

My thoughts, emotions and sensations never stop. Considering them as real, I give my attention to them. I am taken and cut off. At times I touch another reality, a reality felt as a void, empty of my ordinary "I." Then I feel a wish *to know*, to be free to enter into contact with this reality. I feel the need for coming together. And as soon as I feel this, letting go takes place in me, a liberation. It is as though a space opens, and in this space the energy comes together to form a whole. Suddenly I feel myself as another being. This moment of unity is a complete change in my consciousness of myself. Nothing remains of my usual way of thinking and feeling.

The possibility of inner growth is of opening to a new functioning that can connect the different centers. The thought needs to become independent in order to keep the idea of self-remembering, a remembering that passes to the moving center, then to the emotional center, and from there connects with the higher centers. For this there must be an inner center of gravity. I need to see what this requires.

AN INNER CENTER OF GRAVITY

❧ *64. Our vital center*

To awake to myself, to what I am, would mean to find the center of gravity and source of my energies, the root of my being. I always forget my origin. And because of this, all my notions of what I am are distorted. The first necessity is to see that I am always losing contact with this source. So long as my essential need is other than to know and to love this source more than anything else, it is my ego that is directing my life and my force. It does this without my even noticing, and all my endeavors, whatever they may be, are conditioned by its appetites, even what I call my "work."

Right work on oneself, according to Gurdjieff, begins with the creation of a permanent center of gravity. This distinguishes the stage of being that he called man number four. This is someone who awakes to himself and asks, "Who am I?" He sees that he does not know he exists, nor how he exists. He sees he is living in a dream and feels a need to know his own reality. He begins to separate things in himself, the real from the imaginary, the conscious from the automatic. Unlike man number one, two or three, he sees with a certain clarity, he knows his situation. The forces in him begin to take a direction, the direction of a center of gravity of attention. To know himself has become the most important aim, the center of gravity of his thought and interest. He wishes to see himself as he is. His center of gravity is a question, a question that does not let him sleep. And in order to know himself, he struggles to bring his attention to the point where he can divide it between a Presence that he tries to sustain and a manifestation in which he is lost. This requires a vigilance that can be maintained only if all the centers work with the same intensity. He must sense, think and feel at the same time, with no one center having dominance. If the balance is broken, the effort toward consciousness stops. Man number four is one who struggles to be able to establish a link between his essence and his functions.

Our aim is to be centered, centered both in the sense of concentrating our energies and in the sense of finding the center of our being, the vital center of our force. We first concentrate the energy, and then see why this center is necessary. From here I can maintain a right relation with all the parts of myself and follow their movements without being lost in them. When I am centered, it is possible to have a contact with the source of my life that is constantly renewed. I do not have to *make* this contact. I have to allow it to be revealed to me, with an attitude that is never sure of itself and that always makes room for the inner being. I make room in experiencing a sense of emptiness, of occupying another space.

In order to be "individual," one must be present at the source itself, at the center where the force has not yet taken a direction, where it has no form. If I could come to this point where my attention is awake before the mobilization of my energy, a new understanding and a new power would perhaps appear. Today I cannot. My ordinary, passive attention only perceives my energy when it is disintegrated, engaged in some reaction or other. The energy is far from its source, and there is no use struggling not to lose it. Nevertheless, I can understand this situation and accept it as my present reality.

65. *Situating the center of gravity*

We need to find a balance between tension and letting go. I do not succeed in knowing myself because I try to know myself as immobile, static. But I am energy that is constantly moving, either toward the inside or toward the outside. The movements come from my different centers. When the movements go toward the outside, the relation with the inside is broken and there is no inner support, no center of gravity. There is tension that seems like a wall. When the movements go toward the inside, the tension disappears but makes room for a slackness that very often ends up in passivity.

I do not know how to engage outside, and I do not know how to — me live inside. I do not know the laws of life. The engagement and return of my energy—the tensing and letting go—take place without sense, order or verification. There is no balance between them and no aim. Inside, my attention, my will, is always passive. At the same time, my body and my functions are active. So long as this relation remains as it is—inwardly passive, outwardly active—no new possibility will appear. I have to feel the necessity to change this relation so that my body and my functions accept a state of voluntary passivity. This can take place only if I actively situate the center of gravity of my attention, the voluntary attention of my whole Presence, the echo of "I."

A certain sensation appears and, with the need to let it spread, there is a letting go that takes place by itself. The sensation becomes definite. It is as if I make room for something essential, or rather an essential Presence makes itself felt in my whole body. I see that I have a constant tendency to interfere, to fix and hold on to this sensation, which hardens it and takes away its life. So I must return to a level, a depth in myself where, without interfering, the balance between the sensation and the letting go is really possible. There is a special tempo. Then a unity appears, not by constraint but through understanding the forces at play. A conscious attention, coming in part from a new feeling, relates the sensation and the letting go.

At the beginning I have a tendency to experience this sensation predominantly in the solar plexus or in the head. But with the letting go, the sensation expands and takes the form of a whole Presence that is rooted in the abdomen. Gurdjieff always pointed to this place as the center of gravity of the being, the point where the second body is attached to the first. I let my energy flow toward this center of gravity, which is a support for the entire upper part of the body. It is also the support for my thought and feeling. As soon as I am centered, I feel my thought is free, my feeling is free. From this center, in a wholly natural way, I can stay in contact with all the parts of myself. I am in an attitude of balance. This is maintained by the sensation, which is renewed as an act of obedience to the Presence whose law I wish to feel. My body is entirely inhabited. It is animated by the Presence, which at this moment is stronger than the body, stronger than the thoughts or desires.

My Presence is as total as it can be. The usual "I" no longer judges and evaluates. I am no longer directed by it. Another "I" appears that is capable of opening progressively to a sense of the higher centers. I feel more stable. In order to experience truly this Presence, I need to adopt a precise inner and outer posture, an attitude that allows a contact with the very source of life from which I come.

66. Becoming second nature

When there is disharmony between inner force and outer form, the true relation in oneself is missing. Either there is an excess of life force that drives everything outward, or an exaggerated accumulation, with a defense of self that is overly rigid. If too much force goes to manifestation, we feel that our inner form is lost and that we are without inner order or direction. Our movements are unchecked, without coordination. If protection of the self is too strong, the movements are inhibited. The force held in check seems too powerful for what contains it. In either case, we feel the lack of an active center, a third element that could resolve the disharmony between outer form and inner life, and make a whole being of me. If there were a center of gravity, the outer manifestation would express a life that would again and again reanimate the whole.

In order to experience a center of gravity, I have to feel a demand at every instant and to receive the impression of the life in me. For this there must be submission, an acceptance of its action. I must constantly make room for it. This is a struggle to free a space so that the impression of this force can remain and allow me not to be subject to forces from outside. In practicing, I develop a faculty to recognize wrong attitudes and to correct them. This must become an ever-present part of my daily life. It is my submission to life. The most difficult thing to attain is submission of the mind. Voluntary passivity always brings suffering for the ego, which can accept it only for very short moments. As soon as I approach the void, a thought or emotion comes from my self-centered "I" and cuts the state. The waves break and invade everything.

I wish to experience this center of gravity, but I never let myself entirely feel its weight, its density. There is always a certain tension, a tendency to displace upward. From being relaxed and soft, I become tense and hard. My will *to do,* my ego, has again taken over. I no longer trust the living force I experience in this center of gravity. I again trust only "me." Even if I begin to feel the reality of this life emerging, I have no control over either my tension or my letting go. And I cannot consider them simultaneously. Either I tense or I relax. Yet there is one complete movement. These two are the movement of life in me. Tension is not opposed to relaxation, and relaxation is not opposed to tension. They follow a rhythm whose purpose is to preserve the living form I seek. What is difficult to understand is the attitude I need in order to let go, the respect that alone will allow an opening that is unconditional. I always want to take or receive *what is owed me,* instead of letting go in order to feel the Presence of being, a divine Presence. I do not let this Presence act on me.

Only if I have struggled for unity over a long time can I understand how difficult it is to redress the adverse effects of these tensions. This is because they involve the whole of myself. In each tension, however small, the whole is engaged. And if the tension has become fixed, access to my being is blocked. Nevertheless, true letting go will appear when I am able to feel the secret source of energy in myself, the source from which my "I" will grow without my intervention. It will hold me

in a new form, very different from that of my habitual tensions, an inner form in which all the parts of myself are integrated. It will give me
a sense of myself, of my true individuality.

My aim is to become whole, a unity. Only then can I know what is
necessary for the whole. For this I must be centered. Tirelessly I turn
again and again toward my center of gravity. What is only occasional
today must become second nature. Without tension, the energy is liberated in a downward movement of letting go. The totality is no longer
threatened. I discover a law under whose influence I wish to remain.
This is the Law of Three, which can make a new being of me.

67. My true form

We have to find an inner order, an inner form. For this the attitude of
the body must be controlled. In a body whose form is controlled, the
inner form can be established. When I work in the quiet, I do not let
myself begin without an order being established around my center of
gravity. I hold myself straight and in balance, supple and without tension. It is not physical relaxation I seek, but to abandon my persistent
ego, which is always eager for authority and has not yet recognized its
master. I must be seated not only in a different posture, I must be
seated as a different person. When I am situated in my center of gravity, there is no ego that imprisons me. What is necessary to understand, above all, is a movement downward to become immersed again
in the source, the wellspring of my life. I need constantly to return and
submit to the force of life, the one true life, of which I am a part. I need
to let the reality of Being emerge, to let the unity of what I am be created in me.

I repeat the letting go of my tensions, of my ordinary "I," which is
in constant motion and does not like to be part of a whole. The chest,
the shoulders . . . everything is relaxed. The concentration of force in
the abdomen sustains the whole torso. Everything is subject to the law
of this inner order. I come to silence and unity in myself. I see that for
my being to emerge, there must be a quality in my sensation that is

equal everywhere, a unity of vibrations so that a state without waves can appear. Then I feel raised up, liberated from the form of my habitual tensions, which express the "I." I am beyond it, aware of my inner and outer attitude as my true form, my personal form through which circulates my essence. I feel the force of life, free of all fear. I am no longer afraid of losing myself. *I am.* This force is irresistible. It is not my force, but I am in it. The force and I are one, provided I obey its law. This means a transformation in all my inner and outer attitudes. If I cannot practice and then transform my attitudes, nothing will remain of the impression touching my being once the experience is over, and I will again fall under the power of my ego, my tyrant. Each tension represents a movement away from unity and brings with it a need for letting go, and each relaxation contains a risk of deviation and brings a need for tension. Behind this law, the whole of me is in play, the balance in question at every moment.

What I exercise is not my body, not my functions. It is the whole being. I do not look at my body from outside with my intellect. The body is the seat, the base of my life, inseparable from the whole. It must be perceived from within. I wish to trust life, trust this irresistible power centered in my abdomen. I seek an attitude, a way of being, in which my center of gravity is imperturbable. For this, the abdomen must be filled with the force of the whole body. If it is not full of energy, the body has no center of gravity and is overwhelmed from the outside. It loses its meaning as a bearer of life. The muscles below the navel are lightly tensed. This brings a certain concentration of force at this place, which needs to be activated by energy coming from all the parts. If my posture is right, the base of the trunk becomes solid like a rock and the abdomen supports the whole upper body, which remains free. There must be no contradiction between the two. One does not deny the other. They are indispensable to each other. The force from above descends toward the center of gravity that supports it. It is necessary to relax the chest and not let it become tense. There must be no duality in the body. The neck is important. If one holds the head badly, the head and the trunk will be separate and will not have the same center of gravity.

I do not try anxiously to do these things one after the other. I try to feel the unity in this attitude, and to appreciate this sensation of unity. Then all distinctions between subjective and objective, inner and outer, are left behind. So long as I obey this new order and place myself under its influence, I have a new form. I see that the center of gravity is the seat of unity. When all my energy is concentrated here, I open to a new sphere of consciousness.

BREATHING

୬ଽ *68. An imperceptible current*

I learn to distinguish two currents of vibration. One comes from thoughts and emotions, and holds me on a lower level. The other is a more subtle current which can awaken and animate other zones of thinking and feeling. I cannot come to a new understanding so long as I have not experienced over a long time the difference between these two currents and their influence on my being. Their action on me depends on the passive acquiescence I give to the first current, or, on the contrary, the conscious vigilance I bring to the second. Through the breathing, by opening voluntarily to a mysterious life-giving force, I can become conscious of this finer current, which opens me to possibilities latent in myself.

I participate in life through breathing. I feel I am in my breathing. It is the way I exist. But I do not trust it. I do not let myself breathe naturally. I inhale but I never exhale fully. I want to intervene, unable to accept this movement of life as it is.

I need to observe whether I breathe from the chest or from lower down, from the diaphragm, and see what is not right with my breathing. I do not let the breathing take place freely: either I resist or I force it to be more complete. In both cases it is an intervention. And even if I know what is needed and try, I never succeed completely in letting it

be. Even when I believe I am simply watching the breathing, I intervene. It is my way of watching that is not right. I cannot prevent my "I"
from believing that it is more intelligent than the life force contained
in my breathing.

I do not know what I am when I breathe. I do not see that the act
of breathing is always modified by images, ideas and emotions that
come from the ego. I must learn to let my respiration take place so that
its rhythm is not modified. I have to come to a state in which my habitual "I" does not intervene. I will never succeed in this without feeling the center of gravity in my abdomen. It is a real event to let the
breathing take place by itself, on its own. I participate in something
larger. I am part of this experience, which transforms me.

The perceptible breath is not the true breath, that is, the current
which animates inhalation and exhalation. We are aware of the air but
not the current, which is imperceptible. It is a kind of magnetism that
produces the action and touches the essential parts of our being. Inhaling and exhaling do not proceed in a straight line. It is like a circle, a
wheel with radiations that touch all the parts of the body. We do not
see the action of the breath on the body, the radiation. In reality, this
current puts the body in contact with all the levels of being. As I come
to feel unity, I will experience a need to breathe more consciously.

69. Stages of breathing

In becoming conscious of the act of breathing, we will understand better the laws governing life and how serving them brings meaning to
our existence. Real understanding of respiration comes through the
experience of different stages.

The first stage is to become conscious of the physical breathing
and to let it be. The respiration goes on by itself. If it is tight and origi-
nates in the chest rather than the diaphragm, this shows that I am
tense and confined in my ordinary "I." I do not allow the breathing to
come and go freely. I take in the air but do not allow complete exhalation, as though I were afraid of not receiving enough air. The first

thing to learn is to let the breathing be without the intervention of my ordinary "I." I have to let the breathing move lower in the body, and let the air go out entirely.

The second stage in breathing is to exercise not only the body but oneself. I no longer place emphasis on exhaling completely, but instead let myself go with the exhalation. I relax not only my shoulders and chest, I relax the whole of myself. I see that my usual respiration reflects a false attitude of my "I." It is not my body but "I" who is not breathing in a right way. In working, I discover that all my manifestations and mental attitudes block the flow of the breath. It is like a resistance to the fundamental rhythm of life, a fear of losing myself, a lack of trust in life.

The third stage will be to experience that it is not I but "It," the universal Being, which is breathing, and to see that breathing is a fundamental movement of a living whole. We learn to become conscious of life and of the Being incarnate in us, conscious of a rhythmic order in which we are included. This is not to observe from outside, holding ourselves apart, but to be one with the experience and be transformed by it. Usually it cannot transform us because we cut ourselves off from reality, lost in our ordinary "I." True consciousness is buried and plays only a secondary role. We must let all our images and preconceived ideas dissolve in order to become aware of its source. We have to let consciousness emerge and play the principal role. Then one can live according to one's Being. This active recognition of the life within brings a sense of obligation to listen to "consciousness," to change and live according to what we understand.

Finally, a man comes to submission and trust in life and the Self. He gives himself up to the cosmic movement of ebb and flow, understanding with his whole being that all forms are created in the void, in silence, and are reabsorbed once they have fulfilled their role. He understands that he finds himself in losing himself. He becomes free from certain subjective limits, but realizes that his Self is a responsible participant in the great life of the universe. He participates in the Whole.

70. *I live in my breathing*

When I am very much on the surface of myself, I have no freedom of action over letting go. When I am much deeper in myself, a moment comes when I have no freedom of action over tensing. Yet there is a level in me at which I can see tensions form and respond to each other without being completely taken by them. I remain aware of something that cannot be taken. This is directly dependent on experiencing my center of gravity, to which I must always return. These movements of tension and letting go are my response to life, and they affect my breathing. When I see that my breathing is never free, the question arises as to its significance and its relation to my thinking, feeling and organic life.

When I am seated in the quiet, I feel constrained by countless tensions, small tensions that hold me as though in a net. At the very moment I sense this, the net loosens. As the tensions give way, my inner life appears as though emerging from a cloud, and I become freer. I see clearly that the posture of my body allows or prevents this freedom. First, the position of the pelvis and legs allows the spine to be straight. The knees must not be higher than the hips. This maintains everything—the trunk, the abdomen, the head. I see that the inner feeling of Presence depends on my tensions. If the solar plexus is too open or too restricted, this life will not appear. The energy needs to pass freely, and the slightest hindrance can prevent the current from being established. As soon as the energy appears, I feel free. I feel myself existing, a new existence I did not know before. And suddenly I am aware of the breathing. I know that I breathe. It is the movement of life that I feel in myself.

I do not concentrate on the respiration, I do not try to relate the thought with the breathing. I have to become one with the feeling of breathing, sensing the inhalation and exhalation as natural and spontaneous, accepting everything so that there is no striving. I hold back nothing, letting myself exhale to the end. When I succeed in letting the breathing take place more freely and completely, I feel that the energy

Cont,

fills my abdomen and that it no longer has the tendency constantly to rise. In breathing, I see thoughts appear and disperse, and I see that behind them there is an energy, the energy of the thinking. The thoughts are not the thinking.

In letting go more deeply, I feel that the breathing is the life of this energy in me. Its elements could nourish this inner Presence. I feel that the routes, the pathways it travels, are important, that they could relate the life of one center to another. I need first to establish a contact through sensation, to become used to feeling the pathways, without expecting anything.

In the moment I become conscious of it, I feel that my breathing has great importance, as if it were the very act of living. I feel it as a living movement, the movement of the one life in which I am included. I exist in this movement. I cannot hold myself apart, observing from the outside, nor fix or stop the movement, appropriating it for myself. I can only feel that I am part of it. I am nothing without it, and it can do nothing without me. I let go, and in losing myself I find myself. I submit to this movement, in which form is created and immediately swept away as soon as it appears. I live in my breathing.

71. *Without fear of losing myself*

my favorite cont thru 151

There is an impression that holds me to the truth of the moment and awakens my attention—the fact that I am breathing. My whole attention is engaged in this act of breathing. I know nothing else. I need to give it all my care. I am one with this feeling of breathing. But I do not try to make a particular effort in breathing. I simply feel the breath— inhale, exhale, inhale, exhale. . . . Thoughts will appear. I observe them as thoughts, simply passing thoughts. I do not try to get rid of them, nor do I lose myself in them. I see them as without reality. And I come back to the breathing. In this state I do not seek and have no desire. I expect nothing.

I breathe, I am this breathing. In order for me to know it, my look must remain on the breathing. When the one is without the other, there is no order, no knowing. Together, they have a sense. Then the breathing takes place without any effort or constraint, and I feel the movement of the breath. This depends on the intelligence of my thought, on its quality, which can bring a look held consciously without words, a seeing. It requires a more complete letting go, a state freer from my ordinary "I," which is always ready to intervene. I try not to direct my breathing. I let it be what it is.

I begin with letting go tensions in the different parts of myself. First, the head. I feel the difference between an energy that is more still and the disordered waves of my thoughts. As I let go, the waves subside. After a certain time, when I feel the energy is freer in the head, I pass to the face and neck, and then to the spine. I hold myself in balance, feeling a depth of sensation that I do not ordinarily experience. My sensation is an obedience, obedience to the free vibration, the free action of the life force in me. Then I pass to the solar plexus. Here also the tensions let go. I obey. I do not direct the energy. It does not belong to me, it is free. But I really know the energy only when I let it go naturally into the abdomen. If there is absolutely no tension in me, if nothing retains the energy anywhere, it goes freely toward its source and is felt as a force of another dimension. I am not afraid to make room for it and do not feel myself threatened.

Now that I feel freer, I turn to my breathing. I breathe gently, without holding back, without fear of losing myself. It is as though it is my self that I am exercising, engaging in a movement that is more than an act of my body. I trust this movement and allow all ideas, all notions, to dissolve. I am not afraid to exhale completely. And I discover a new meaning, a sense of the sacred in my human self.

I see again that I trust only myself. And yet it is the active force of the air that I should trust. When I feel more balanced, I breathe as though through the centers and silently say "I Am." When I say "I," I feel the three centers as though something stands up; and when I say "Am," I also feel them, but as though something sits down. When I breathe in, I say "I" and represent to myself that the active elements of the air are entering. When I breathe out, I say "Am" and feel them flow into and fill my body. I do not try to make anything more of this *"I"* and *"Am,"* simply say the words to myself. With each breath, I follow this order for filling: right arm, right leg, left leg, left arm, abdomen, chest, head and then the whole body.

VII

WHO AM I?

I always believe that I exist and that my imagination of myself, what we call personality, does not.

This ferocious egotism is me, and I have to become conscious of its action.

What I must explore is not beyond the self, but the very basis from which I think and feel.

I do not know who I am. I do not know whence I came. I do not know where I will go.

The wish to be conscious is the wish to be. It can only be understood in silence.

The self belongs to the Absolute. I cannot exist outside the Absolute, outside the Self of the Absolute. The true self is like space—unattached, pure, infinite.

My true nature is consciousness. To know the Self is to be the Self.

EGO AND ILLUSION

≈ *72. The imagination of myself*

In order to know who I am, I need to see what is real in me. The biggest obstacle is illusion. I accept imagination in the place of consciousness, an idea of myself instead of a feeling of "I."

In coming to work together, each of us brings something very important—his ego. I try to understand why I came. I see that it is my ego, my person, who is here, to which I cling, and I see, if I am sincere, that it is mixed up in large measure with what led me here. But it will not be able to help me. To see this, and to see that I still believe myself to be this person, makes me put the question with more feeling— "Then, who am I?"

We are all, such as we are, under the influence of our imagination of ourselves. This influence is all-powerful and conditions every aspect of our lives. On the one hand, there is this imagination, this false notion of myself. On the other, there is a real "I" that I do not know. I do not see the difference. It is as though this "I" were buried under a mass of beliefs, interests, tastes and pretensions. Everything I affirm is the imagination of myself. What I cannot affirm—because I do not know it—is the real "I." It calls to be known and has a nostalgia for knowing, longing to be active . . . to know. But today it is weak. Nevertheless, it

is like a seed, and if my interest is sufficient, the search for this knowing can be the ground in which my "I" can grow.

I need to learn to recognize and separate the real "I" from the
imagination of myself. This is an arduous task because my imagined
"I" defends itself. It is opposed to the real "I," and is exactly what "I" am
not. In thinking of myself, I always believe that I exist and that my
imagination of myself, what we call personality, does not. I have no
idea of this imagination. So long as I do not know it, I cannot know
what I am.

This imagination of "I . . . me" lies at the heart of my usual sense
of self, the ego, and all the movements of my inner life go to protect it.
And this tendency exists as much in the unconscious as in the conscious layers of myself. It is because we want at all costs to protect this
imagination that our experience and our knowledge have such importance for us. The things that we do are not chosen because we like to
do them but because we thereby affirm and assure our imagined "I."

There is no thought or feeling that is not motivated by this. It is, however, so subtle that we do not see it. We are so preoccupied with what
we would ideally like to be that we do not see what we actually are
now, right now in the present moment. Perhaps behind the formation
of this idea of "I" there is the echo of a very deep wish, the wish *to be*,
the wish to be entirely what I am. But today the controlling influence
is the idea of myself, and this imagined "I" desires, fights, compares
and judges all the time. It wants to be the first, it wants to be recognized, admired and respected, and make its force and power felt. This
complex entity has been formed over centuries by the psychological
structure of society.

Do I know this? Not just in passing, or in having noticed it one day
or another . . . but do I really see it at the moment in each action, when
I work, when I eat, when I speak with another person? Can I be aware
of my wish to be "someone" and my way of always comparing myself
to another? If I see it, I can experience the wish to liberate myself from
it, and also see why I wish to liberate myself. So long as I have not understood that this is the essence of my search, that here is the first step

toward knowledge of myself, I will continue to be fooled and all my efforts, all the ways I try to change, will lead only to disappointment. The imagined "I," my imagination of "I," will continue to be reinforced even in the most unconscious layers of myself.

I must honestly accept that I really do not know this. Only in accepting this as a fact will I become interested and truly wish to know it. Then my thoughts, feelings and actions will no longer be objects for me to look at with indifference. They are *me*, expressions of my *self*, which I alone am here to understand. If I wish to understand them, I must live with them, not as a spectator but with affection, and without judging or excusing them. It is necessary to live with my thoughts, feelings and actions, to suffer them, from moment to moment.

73. *Ferocious egotism*

We are not what we believe ourselves to be. Blinded by our imagination, we overestimate ourselves and lie to ourselves. We always lie to ourselves, at every moment, all day, all our lives. If we could stop inwardly and observe without preconception, accepting for a time this idea of lying, then perhaps we would see that we are not what we think we are.

I can have moments of real tranquillity, of silence, in which I open to another dimension, another world. What I do not see is that apart from these moments I am prey to conflict and contradiction, that is, to the violence of my egotistical action, which never ceases to isolate and divide me. Everything I do arises from this action. As I discover new possibilities, I need to know what is at the root of this other part of my nature. I have to see that it is not something foreign that I can put aside when and as I wish. It is what I am, and I cannot be otherwise. This ferocious egotism is me, and I have to become conscious of its action. To see this violence, I have to enter into an intimate and real contact with myself, to observe myself without any image.

Why do we have a compelling need to prove ourselves, to actualize ourselves? A profound impulse is at play: the deep fear of being nothing, the fear of total isolation, of emptiness, of solitude. We have created this solitude with our minds, with self-protecting and egocentric thoughts like "me" and "mine," *my* name, *my* family, *my* position, *my* qualities. Deep down, we feel empty and alone, living lives that are narrow and superficial, emotionally starved and intellectually repetitious. Because our petty "I" is a source of suffering, we wish—consciously or unconsciously—to lose ourselves in individual or collective stimulation or in some form of sensation. Everything in our lives—entertainment, games, books, food, drink, sex—encourages stimulation on different levels. We revel in this and seek to find a state of "happiness," to maintain a pleasure in which we can forget the "I." All the time our minds are busy in evasion, constantly seeking, in one way or another, to be entirely absorbed in something outside ourselves, to be captivated by some belief, love or work. The evasion has become more important than the truth we cannot face.

Revolving around self-interest, our narrow mind diminishes the challenges of life by interpreting them with its limited understanding. As a result, our lives suffer from a lack of intense, strong feeling, a lack of passion. It is an essential problem. When we have real passion in the depths of ourselves, we feel strongly and are extremely sensitive to life—to suffering, to beauty, to nature . . . to everything. We care about life, its possibilities in work together and in relation. But without passion, life is empty, meaningless. If we do not feel deeply the beauty of life and its challenge, then life has no sense at all. We function mechanically. Yet this passion is not devotion or sentimentality. As soon as passion has a motive or preference, it becomes pleasure or pain. The passion we need is the passion *to be.*

Centered in our ordinary "I," most of us do not love and are not loved. We have very little love in our hearts, which is why we beg for it and seek it in substitutes. Our usual emotional state is negative, all our feelings are reactions. In fact, we do not know what it would be to have a positive feeling, what it would be to love. My ordinary "I," my ego, is always preoccupied with what pleases or displeases me, what "*I* like" or "*I* dislike." It always wants to receive, to be loved, and impels me to seek love. I give in order to receive. Perhaps this is generosity of the mind, my "I," but it is not generosity of the heart. I love with my "I," my ego, but not with my heart. Deep down, this "I" is always in conflict with the other person and refuses to share. To live without love is to live in perpetual contradiction, a refusal of the real, of *what is*. Without love, one can never find what is true, and all human relations are painful.

If I do not know myself totally, my mind and my heart, my pain and my avidity, I cannot live in the present. What I must explore is not beyond the self, but the very basis from which I think and feel. My thought craves continuity, permanence, and its wish gives rise to my ordinary "I." This thinking is the source of fear, fear of loss, of suffering. If I do not know my total consciousness—unconscious as well as conscious—I will not understand fear and my entire search will go astray and be deformed. There will be no love, and my only interest will be in ensuring the continuity of this "I," even after death.

74. *Free of fear and illusion*

Is it possible to have a mind with a quality that is always fresh, always new, with a thinking that creates no habits and clings to no belief? For this we must understand the total consciousness with which we live. It functions within a limited frame that must be broken in order for it to be free. What we seek is the state of mind that says, "I don't know." Instead of trying to know what is unconscious, we have to see the false as false. It is the negation of the false that empties the mind of the known. Only a mind that is empty can come to a state of not knowing and discover what is true.

What is important is to see that words and ideas enslave us in formulas and concepts. As long as we are trapped in a net of consoling belief, we lack the intensity and subtlety required for real exploration. Unless I understand this, my observation will remain based on forms, on what I know, and will not be enlivened by the spirit of discovery, as if for the first time. And it will be egocentric, with my ordinary "I" interpreting everything that is presented from its self-centered perspective.

We have to understand fear in our lives, a fundamental fact. Indeed, so long as our total consciousness has not been liberated from fear, we will not be able to go very far, to penetrate deeply in ourselves. By its very nature fear is inevitably opposed to our entire search. But what is the basis for fear in us? Does fear as such really exist? Have we ever experienced it as a reality in itself and not simply the feeling that precedes or follows an event? When we are truly face-to-face with the event—for example, with danger—are we afraid? In fact, fear only arises at the moment the thinking fixes on the past or the future. If our attention is in the active present, to think of yesterday or of tomorrow is simply inattention, an inattention that engenders fear. When we give our total attention to the present, when we are wholly present, fear does not exist. We see that we do not know, that we cannot respond. In this state of complete uncertainty, we can discover that which is true. If we wish to penetrate deeply in ourselves and see what is here and even beyond, we must have no fear of any kind, not of failure or of suffering, and above all not fear of death.

We have never, with our whole being, inquired what death is. It is always considered in terms of survival, as life continuing like a chain or an endless movement. But this survival is only the survival of what is known. In fact, our lives are a continuity of the known. We act from the known to the known. We wish for continuity and cling to survival without ever questioning the origin of this wish. We do not see that it is merely a hollow projection of the thought, that it comes from the imagined "I" created by our identifications—my family, my home, my work achievements. When we realize this clearly, we can approach the question of continuity without sentimentality and without our usual ambition to affirm ourselves.

We need to see that there is no "thinker," that this imagined "I" which thinks "me" and "mine" is simply an illusion. In order for us to receive truth, this must be dispelled, as well as all the other illusions of the thinking, including those behind our desires for pleasure or satisfaction. Only then can we see the real nature of our ambitions, struggles and sufferings. Only then can we see through them and come to a state free of contradiction, a state of emptiness, in which we can experience love. What is important is to live with this void in which the self is abandoned. With this abandonment arises the passion *to be,* a wish beyond thought and feeling, a flame which destroys all that is false. This energy allows the mind to penetrate the unknown.

No movement from the periphery toward the center will ever reach the center. A surface movement trying to become deeper will never be more than of the surface. In order to understand itself, the mind has to be completely still, without illusion. Then with lucidity we can see the insignificance of "me" dissolve in an immensity beyond all measure. There is no time, only the present moment. Yet to live in the present is wholly sufficient unto itself. At each moment one dies, one lives, one loves, one *is.* Free of fear and illusion, moment after moment we die to the known in order to enter the unknown.

TOWARD THE UNKNOWN

✍️ *75. I do not know*

In my search to see reality in myself, I may come to the door of perception. But it will not open, truth will not be revealed, so long as I cling to what I know. I need to have empty hands to approach the unknown.

At the outset I cannot affirm who I am. All I can do is begin to distinguish myself from my ordinary "I," to see that I am not my associations, I am not my feelings, I am not my sensations. But the question then arises: Who am I? I need to listen, I become quiet to mobilize all my attention and come to a more balanced state. Am I this? No, but the direction is good. From dispersion, I go toward unity. My search can continue. Yet I see that the energy of my thinking, moved by all the thoughts that seize it, has neither force nor direction. In order to go toward the source of "I," it must be gathered and concentrated on one question: "Who am I?" I learn not to turn away.

I do not know who I am, and all that I know cannot be an answer. The unknown, the mysterious, cannot be discerned by the known. On the contrary, what I know, what I have learned, prevents me from discovering *what is*. The whole process of my thinking, the conditioning of the known, encloses me in the field of my thought and prevents me from going further. I find pleasure in this conditioning and security, and unconsciously cling to it.

I am unable to face the unknown. I feel it empty, like a void that must be filled. I have a constant tendency to fill it with answers, projecting a false image on the screen of my mind. I am afraid I will not find myself. And in order to resolve this uncertainty, to avoid dissatisfaction, I constantly allow something false to be affirmed. Yet I need this uncertainty, this dissatisfaction, as an indication from my feeling that shows the way back toward myself. It shows the necessity of being more sensitive to the one thing I turn away from, to accept emptiness, the void.

To approach the unknown would mean to come to the door of perception and be able to open it, and to see. But I can see nothing as long as I am taken by words, always putting a name on something and recognizing the object by its name. Words create a limit, a barrier. To enter the unknown, my mind must see this limit as a fact, without judging it good or bad, or submitting to its influence. Can I see myself without putting a word on what I see? I am at the door of perception with an attention that does not turn away.

I learn to listen to the unknown in myself. I do not know, and I listen, constantly refusing each known response. From moment to moment, I recognize that I do not know, and I listen. The very act of listening is a liberation. It is an action that does not flee the present, and when I know the present as it is, there is transformation. I go toward the unknown until I come to a moment when no thought moves my mind, when there is nothing outside myself. I do not know who I am. I do not know whence I came. I do not know where I will go. I doubt all that I know, and have nothing to rely on. All I wish is to understand what I am. Without words, without form, the body and its density seem to disappear. I become as if transparent to myself. Now there is only room for purity, a quality as light as air. I feel that in the search for myself, and only in this search, lies my liberation.

76. *The resonance of "I am"*

In order to know a living energy in myself, the *memory* of it is insufficient. There must be a direct perception of the unknown. But we live in memories, rememberings. Memory substitutes a dead image for a living thing and prevents me from perceiving it. We impose something unreal, something that is not, in the place of *what is*.

I wish to be conscious of this unknown energy that is in me. For this I need to get rid of the idea that I know my body. I must see that the memory of my body, of the known sensation of my body, imposes itself as an answer at the moment of questioning who I am, the moment of incomprehension. And because this answer appears spontaneously, I remain passive and do not wake up and look. I must see this constant tendency to let the memory of sensation preempt the direct perception. I need to see that my body is also unknown.

I feel my essential "I" like an echo of a distant vibration of which I am barely aware. It is as though submerged in my body, and because it is submerged, it cannot differentiate itself. I need to dissociate myself from my thoughts, ordinary emotions and movements, my sensations. Their vibrations of inertia, which condition me, are an obstacle to the consciousness of "I." Yet I have the power to ignore them and not let them invade my consciousness if I concentrate on "I," this echo of a powerful vibration that could transform me.

When I feel deep anxiety and dissatisfaction, as we all do at different times, it is because I am not listening to the finer, more subtle vibrations of my Presence. I do not let them animate me. I am not available. I am always, again and again, moved entirely by the vibrations of inertia of my functions. But anxiety and dissatisfaction are not enough. I need a more conscious feeling and a more conscious thought directed on this underlying current. I must come to understand that behind my thought there is something, behind my emotion there is something, behind my movement there is something . . . and I must actively go in the direction of this "something." As I am, my energy is too fragmented, too passive. It is not magnetized in a direction.

I become aware that in order to go beyond my present state, a greater concentration is necessary. When I understand this need, a movement takes place of concentration toward what is seeking to come into being in me. In this voluntary movement, my attention becomes active and refined, and the movement passes a threshold where words are no longer necessary, where my ego is pacified and my body is still. *Who am I?* In a state of questioning without words, I approach a void. I accept putting nothing there, knowing nothing, and am wholly attentive to the silence. I am entirely present to the question *"Who . . . ?"* as if it were a magnet attracting all the force of perception. Behind all our life, all our activity, the resonance of this question must be stronger than the insistent call of the movement toward life. *"Who . . . ?"* I wish to penetrate the state before thinking arises. So I observe from where this thought comes. Gently, very quietly, I penetrate the state. Absolute tranquillity is necessary.

Who am I? I listen to the resonance of the question. And I begin to hear the resonance of the response, which I perceive through a sensation of life, of a current of life. It shows me that at this moment my essence is touched. My work is not imaginary, not only on the surface. It has penetrated more deeply.

I belong to this life whose echo I feel, and wish only to attune myself to it. I listen in myself to the resonance of "I am." It must become more important than everything else. This is my soul itself that is here.

77. *Silence*

I have a preconceived idea that a state of silence, of peace, is deprived of energy and of life, a state where there is a stop, the suspension of everything that generally moves me. In fact, silence is a moment of the greatest energy, a state so intense that everything else seems quiet.

More and more I feel an attraction for the consciousness of *what is*, of what I am. But I am not really open. The ego takes a long time to give way, and there is a limit I do not pass. I feel that to receive the real, a transformation is necessary, a break from my conditioning. To know who I am, I need a perception of myself beyond the capacity of my senses and functions. For this I need silence and tranquillity. The perception of "I" that is revealed in the stillness must be as strongly established as the notion of myself rooted in the body.

To have an experience of reality, there must be a sense of space. But the space created by our thought is restricted and narrow. We isolate ourselves, we measure and judge, and from this limited space we think and act, even believing we bring something to others. Because it is all our thought knows, we believe this space to be very important. Our ordinary "I" clings to it out of fear of being nothing. Yet in this small space the only feeling that appears arises from the opposition between this "I," this "me," and what is not "I." The thought cannot open to another dimension, the vast space in which there is silence. And a feeling without limit cannot appear.

Escape from this narrow space will not come from thinking. By itself the thought cannot be silent. It is only when I die to all I know and all I have learned that I can open to something new. Only then can I really know myself—that is, know how I live from moment to moment. This action alone will take away my fear of being nothing and bring my mind the energy required to be completely silent. Sometimes there is a stop between two thoughts, and for a moment I sense the space expand beyond all limits. It is only within this space, a vast space which the ordinary "I" cannot reach, that the thinking becomes silent. Then I no longer seek an answer and, in giving my entire attention, I enter the unknown. I do not seek, I perceive. I do not have to seek the good; the attention is the only good. This attention is the process of meditation.

It is the quiet itself that is important, silence as the fact itself, not what one obtains through it. We need to discover the nature of silence, when thought, feeling and body are all silent. What takes place when thought is really quiet, and also feeling? The silence . . . does it become awake to itself? In being attentive to the nature of silence, I feel an intelligence awaken. What is important is its appearance, not what it illuminates. This intelligence is sacred and cannot be at the service of my ego, my ambition. The silence that appears when I see myself taken by illusion is revealing, but only if I do not wish for it. I feel the action of reality on me, but I do not give myself up to it. I learn to let my thought flower and thus come to an end. The field is free; I offer no opposition. Thinking becomes a light for itself and no longer seeks experience. It is necessary to pass through the world of the known to enter the unknown, the void, the real.

I begin to understand that silence does not come because I seek to become silent. It comes when the mind sees the process of thought and its conditioning by the known. For this it must observe as one watches a beloved child, without comparing or condemning. One observes in order to understand. It is only when I know this conditioning that silence and tranquillity are sought not for security but for the freedom to receive the unknown, the truth. Then the mind becomes very quiet. This opens the door to a state that is reality, with immense possibilities. The mind is no longer an observer of the unknown. It is the unknown itself.

The wish to be conscious is the wish *to be*. It can only be understood in silence.

78. Inner solitude

Our ordinary "I" thirsts for continuity. Our mind is never still. We dare not remain without thinking, without doing something, face-to-face with emptiness—a terrifying solitude. We are afraid to be alone because we are afraid not *to be*, not to experience. Our lives are a continuity of the known, always acting from something known to something known, not daring to approach the unknown. But the known cannot enter into contact with the unknown, and a thinking based on what we know cannot commune with the unknown. We must die to the known in order for the unknown to be revealed.

How then to confront the real in myself? I will truly meet the real only when I understand the functioning of my ordinary "I" and its incessant desire to perpetuate itself. What can this "I" experience? In order to know myself, I need to see with clarity, tirelessly, the movements of my ordinary "I." The way to this knowledge is arduous, but it brings incomparable joy and silence. The "I" rises ceaselessly and always falls, constantly pursuing something, winning and losing. But it is always frustrated. It always wants "more," and its desires are contradictory. In order for me to understand this, the thought must not intervene. There must be no judge who, in taking sides, would keep the conflicts alive. There must be neither a subject nor an object of experience. Then there is a direct relation. And it is this direct relation that gives rise to understanding. There is a silence that emerges not from reaction but when the process of thinking is understood.

A moment comes when I experience a feeling of total solitude, when I no longer know how to relate to what surrounds me. Everywhere, always, I feel alone. Even when I am with close friends or my family, I am alone. I do not know my relation with them, what actually connects us. This feeling of solitude and isolation is created by my self-centered thought—*my* name, *my* family, *my* position. I need to live with this solitude and, passing through it like a door, come to something much greater: a deeper state of total "abandonment," a state of "individuation." This is no longer a state of isolation, because the isolation is included, as well as the entire process of thinking and experiencing, with all the provocations and responses involved. When we understand this process on all levels of consciousness, we are free from influences in that our thinking and feeling are no longer fashioned by outer events or inner experience. When the mind is without provocation or response, there is "abandonment." Only in this state can we find the real.

To live silence, to know *what is,* I need to come to the sensation of a void, empty of all my imaginary projections. I try to emerge from this world of illusion that hides my reality, to not let myself be influenced by it. I concentrate on *"here . . . now."* I do not seek—as I always do—to fill the void. I feel I am this void. Accepting that there is nothing, I seek neither shelter nor guarantee. Feeling myself as an observation post that sees only emptiness, I seek silence. This inner silence means abandon and submission. My ordinary "I" submits, and my mind is freer in an attitude that transcends thoughts and words. This is like meditation without mental activity.

I need to understand the feeling of real solitude, even if I feel not seen by those around me, not understood, and experience this as sadness. Solitude from what is ordinary, imaginary and false is something very great. It means that for the first time I know that "I am." It is a solitude from all the known and from all that is not right *now,* in the present moment outside of time. This solitude appears as a void. But it is not a void of despair. It is a complete transformation of the quality of my thinking. When the mind is free of all talking, fears, desires and pettiness, it is silent. Then comes a sense of complete nothingness, the very essence of humility. At the same time, there is a feeling of truly entering another world, a world that seems more real. I am a particle of a greater reality. I experience solitude not because something is missing but because there is everything—everything is here.

MY TRUE NATURE

✎ *79. The veil over my reality*

The belief that I am my body casts a veil over my reality. I cling to the form and always take the object as real, hypnotized by the attraction toward matter. In my effort to be present, I always want to have a sensation of a form, a new form, but nonetheless a form. My ordinary functioning and the way I sense my body prevent me from becoming conscious of what I am in my true nature. A knowledge beyond my usual imagination, a new knowledge, will be revealed only when the notion I have of myself is no longer rooted in my body.

I need sincerely to accept that I am not my body, my mind or my emotions. My real "I" is not temporary. My thoughts, my sensations, my states are continually changing, but the "I" is always here. Something does not change. All these states are like phenomena appearing on the surface of my being. They are in perpetual movement. Yet something remains immobile, unaffected by the movement. My real "I" remains silent, as though submerged in my body. Nevertheless, it seeks to know itself. And the more the "I" seeks to know itself, the less it participates in the body in which it is submerged and the more it participates in consciousness. The question "Who am I?" then sounds like an echo, coming from another world through my higher centers in order to resonate in the lower centers. This echo is what I can know today of another nature in myself.

I ask this question and concentrate, but not in order to obtain consciousness, the real "I." I concentrate in order to lift the veil of thoughts that stands in its way. We are under the domination of our thinking mind. This is our slavery. So long as this mind dominates me, I believe that I am my thought, that I am my body, and I cannot know consciousness, my true nature. So long as there is not consciousness, I am obliged to ask who I am. In the moment of consciousness the question does not appear.

More and more, I feel the need for stillness and silence. Behind the forms of my continual thoughts and emotions, there exists a very fine energy that is not to be projected outside. It allows me to know what I am in my essence. But to come to the emptiness in which this living energy can be felt is difficult. This is because even the wish *to be*, which appears in me as a wish *to know* and is pure in its origin, is betrayed by the form it takes. Can I trust, entirely, what is in this emptiness? Or do I reserve the right to judge, to calculate, to remain a cold observer in front of an energy in which I do not recognize myself? How to go toward awareness of this subtle energy, at each step seeing the trap of making it conform to some design or of limiting it by ascribing a known meaning?

I am seated here. Who am I? I want to answer. And I see that I cannot answer, that nothing in me can answer. I can only listen, in order to hear better. Silence emerges . . . silence, stillness. And as I sense this, it is as though my entire being wished to enter this silence, to allow it to be established. At the same time, it is not I who can impose the silence. It is here. This silence is in me, it is me. It is as though a door were opening, allowing me to feel a vibration that the usual noises prevent. This is no longer "I" as I know myself. I feel something to which I did not know I was called. I discover in myself another dimension that requires a new way of being.

80. *What I really am*

To know oneself means to know one's true nature. In asking who I am,
I want to know my true nature. I am in front of a mystery. Something
more myself than all I know is calling to be recognized. It is as though
I were going to be born to myself. I want to be able to see what I really
am. This depends on me, depends on the truth of my wish. I need to
hold myself under a look that calls me to be what I am. None of my
usual perceptions will help me to approach this experience. I must go
beyond them all in order to come to a perception impossible to foresee
in advance. There can be no words, words imprison me; no memories,
memories imprison me; no formulated wish, formulations imprison
me. I recognize all this is useless and let it go. One thing alone brings
me closer to what I really am—the concern, above all, to be true.

I have accepted the idea that I do not know what I am. But it is just
an idea, a theory, and I do not understand what it means. In my usual
state of consciousness, what I can perceive is limited by the functions
that govern these perceptions. I perceive things with my thought, feeling and sensation, and with these try to become conscious. But the
functions work on a level that is very ordinary, automatic. They are
functions of the lower centers in me. What I wish to know is much
higher, more pure, endowed with qualities that these functions cannot
perceive. I want to know what I really am in my true nature, my very
essence, in which all my possibilities are contained. I wish to return to
the source of *what is*, of the only reality, of the "self." The self belongs
to the Absolute. I cannot exist outside the Absolute, outside the Self of
the Absolute. And yet I consider myself as outside the Absolute, and I
address it as outside me. I confuse the true self with the body and its
functions. But the true self is like space—unattached, pure, infinite.

I feel a greater and greater need to come to a state of quiet and
peace. Yet this state has nothing passive in it. I am actively conscious of
this peace, a state in which my centers are in balance. This is how I experience it. And I understand what Gurdjieff meant in *Beelzebub's Tales
to His Grandson* when he wrote that, before beginning to meditate,

Ashiata Shiemash brought himself (by all sorts of methods) to the state of "all-brained-balanced-being-perceptiveness." I perceive a state of *life*, of a kind of vibration that nothing else can equal, the vibrations of my Being. From this source, this living material, come waves of vibrations of another kind—my thoughts, my desires. . . . But this is like the ocean and the waves that rise and fall. They are one and the same. What is essential is the life that animates it, a life that is permanent.

81. Who am I?

Who am I? The question sounds in me. It is a call from Above, from higher than what is moving in me. I hear it poorly and wish to listen, to hear it not only with what is more or less available at this moment . . . my thought, my ordinary sensing. I wish to hear it with my whole be-ing. I *wish*, I *will*, because my wish, my will, alone can bring this. It becomes serious for me. I wish to open in order to make room and recognize the Presence of a life, of a force before which I must bow. I have to feel animated by this life until the sensation of my body, of the form of my body, is less strong than the awareness of the force vibrat-ing in my whole being.

Usually I limit my sense of "I" to my body. There are inside and outside, subject and object. I see my body and the things around me separately. But I do not see this force in my body, this force that creates both my body and the things around me. Yet I am at the same time this force, this form and this consciousness. The consciousness unites the whole in a single Being, the consciousness "I Am." This is the only Be-ing, the eternal Being. The one who sees is not outside consciousness; he does not see himself. He Is. To Be is to realize "I Am."

I offer myself to this realization. Nothing else exists besides this opening. I give myself to it—now, and all the time, "I Am." There is not one moment when I am not. But I must submit to this reality and, whether it appears or disappears, always be ready to open to it. This prepares me to penetrate my true nature. There must be an uncondi-tional submission to something whose grandeur I recognize. It is not enough to want the true "I," the Self, to be revealed because I desire it. This means that I command the Self, that I feel in a sense more important than it. Rather, I must await its will. I must have faith in it, not a blind belief but a faith that is conscious. My sole reason to Be is to recognize the Self.

Who am I? This question resonates in my Presence as if, from a central source, an extraordinary power were making its existence felt. It is as if an underlying current were created that brings me the experience of a new life. I feel I need to become conscious of this power, to attune myself with this source in order to be connected to it and obey it. This wish for consciousness is like a demand for constant purification, the center of attraction toward which the rays of my attention converge. From all the parts of myself, my attention is activated to concentrate on this central vibration. When my thought and feeling are attuned to it, another knowledge of myself is revealed, and I feel my question differently. In the experience of knowing, what takes place is a direct movement, like an electric current. The knowing is an experience of being because at this moment I know my state of being.

82. *My true nature is consciousness*

There is in me a suffering in being limited. I do not accept forms limited by time or change, space or multiplicity. There is a sole, a unique energy within which change takes place but which itself is always the same. It takes different forms but tends to reintegrate into what in essence it is—infinite, one. I have an irresistible wish to be myself, free of all that weighs me down, all that makes me dependent. I wish the happiness of being entirely myself, without any reservation. I feel it is not to be sought outside myself, in someone or in something else. The only source of happiness is the fact of *being,* without expecting any profit or reward, just the revelation of *what is.* I love *what is.*

I hold myself here trying to see my barriers—my tensions, my thoughts—so that, in this seeing, they can fall by themselves. I do not judge them or wish to substitute something better. I become sensitive to something they hide toward which I am drawn, as by a magnet. It is as though I pass beyond. And I have another impression of myself, an impression of matter that is alive, of a life in which the density of my body disappears. Then I come to a second threshold, where I feel that I am no longer a compact mass but an infinity of living particles in movement, in vibration. I feel myself as participating in a Being whose force gives me life, which I then radiate around me. It is like a kind of cosmic breathing in which I take part.

I must never forget what gives life to the form. The form alone does not exist. That which "*is*" in the form, that which has taken form, is the essence of what is questioning in me. I seek therefore to return to the source. The more the "I" seeks to know itself, the more it participates in consciousness and the less in the body in which it is submerged. All thinking comes from the thought "I." But from where does the thought "I" come? When we look within and return to the source, the thought "I" disappears. And when it disappears, the feeling "I am" appears by itself. Then we attain consciousness, our true nature. When we know our true "I," something emerges from the depths of being and takes over. It is behind the mind. It is infinite, divine, eternal. We call it the soul.

There is no death. Life cannot die. The coating is used up, the form disintegrates. Death is an end—the end of everything known. It is a fearful thing because we cling to the known. But life *is*. It is always here, even if for us it is the unknown. We can know life only after we know death. We must die to the known and enter the unknown. We need to die voluntarily. We have to free ourselves from the known. Once free, we can enter the unknown, the void, the complete stillness, where there is no deterioration—the only state in which we can find out what life is and what love is.

Which is real: what I am conscious of, or consciousness itself? Deep down in my being *I am* already what I seek. This is the impetus of my whole search. When consciousness is here, I realize that consciousness is me. I and all that surrounds me are the same consciousness. My true nature is consciousness.

The search for my self becomes the quest for the Self, more and more profound. The Creator appears as the "I," the "Self." Whether it is manifest or nonmanifest is immaterial when one remains turned toward it. There is no object to know. The Self is always the Self, and *to know* the Self is *to be* the Self. When the true nature is known, there is Being without beginning or end—immortal consciousness.

VIII

TOWARD A
NEW BEING

The Fourth Way is a way of understanding that requires the awakening of another intelligence.

The level of being is determined by what enters into one's Presence at a given moment, that is, the number of centers which participate and the conscious relation between them.

The first conscious shock—to awake to oneself—is for coming to a more collected state that allows us to open to our being.

It is necessary to die to oneself in order to be born again— that is, to die to one level of being in order to rise to another.

The waves, the movement and the energy are one and the same. What is important is to understand the energy itself, the pure energy.

My wish to be is a cosmic wish, and my being needs to situate itself in a world of forces. There is a cosmic need for the new being that I could become.

The Fourth Way has always existed, but only within a limited circle. Today it can renew the weakening link between the two levels of the cosmos.

MY BEING IS WHAT I AM

🪶 *83. Can being change?*

Ordinary life is under the law of the circle of mechanical influences. The way of development of being is opposed to everyday life. It is based on other principles, subject to other laws. This is the secret of its power and its meaning. Without the help of a way, of an influence of another order, no change of being is possible.

The Fourth Way is a way of understanding. The magnetic center which leads one to a group following the Fourth Way is different from that which leads toward a monastery, a school of yoga or an ashram. This way demands another kind of initiative. It demands a broad mind and discernment, that is, the ability to distinguish the mechanical from the conscious in oneself. It requires the awakening of another intelligence. What can be attained does not depend on obedience. The knowledge that results is proportional to the state of awakening, of understanding.

The Fourth Way begins from the idea of different levels of being. But what is being? The level of being is determined by what enters into one's Presence at a given moment, that is, the number of centers which participate and the conscious relation between them. The level of being determines everything in our lives, including our understanding. My being today is not unified. It is dispersed, and therefore without consciousness. Can being change? Can my being become different from what it is today? This is where the idea of evolution, of work, begins. The first step is to recognize that through a certain effort I can live a moment of more complete Presence. Then I will see that the slightest difference in the level of being opens new possibilities to know and to act.

My being is what I am. Since I do not know myself as I am, I do not know my being. I do not even believe I need this knowledge. But unless I acquire all that is possible on the level at which I am, I cannot receive more, I cannot understand more. At the same time, I must recognize that understanding can only change little by little. A moment of new understanding brings a certain knowledge, but this is insufficient to transform my being. Nevertheless, it can show me that in my present state of being I am unable to receive more, and can only consider the next step. If, for example, I see that I am dispersed, and not collected, I can work on this step. Only when I have truly understood this one will I be able, in a collected state, to see the next step toward feeling my Presence as a whole.

Change in being comes about through transformation. In the analogy Gurdjieff used, it is like a mixture of metallic powders transformed into a chemical compound through a process of fusion. This requires a special kind of fire, a heat produced by "friction" in the inner struggle between *yes* and *no*. The resulting compound corresponds to the second body, the formation of a single "I," whole and indivisible, which is "individual" in that it can resist influences from outside and live its own life. This chemical compound can then, by a certain work, undergo further change.

The Fourth Way is to be lived, experienced, not simply thought or believed. The ideas brought by Gurdjieff contain knowledge from a higher level that we must live in order to understand. But this knowledge is in code. This means that any person speaking about work, or otherwise attempting to pass on this knowledge, may not know what he is talking about. Unless we are able to live the ideas and decipher the code, this knowledge will always be deformed, be used for other ends, and produce results contrary to its original meaning.

The demand to live the teaching implies respect for forms that have been given, but without being afraid to modify them when that the need is indicated by sound understanding. It also calls for a certain attitude toward traditional teachings. We should not allow false complacency to close our minds to other ways. Indeed, we can find many principles and practices in common. But comparisons can be useful only after we have understood the way that has been transmitted to us. We have to guard against judging with our mind before we have allowed our intuition, which is at the heart of the experience, to bring us knowledge. Studying general themes is one thing, but following steps on another way is very different, especially experimenting with practices of other teachings. If we truly enter this way, the experience engages the energy in certain channels to produce results that depend on understanding. In this case, to approach another teaching is a serious matter, especially if one submits to a practice or discipline that produces a shock on the mind. If the result does not come from understanding, it can bring an attitude, even a crystallization, that leaves no freedom to go further.

84. *The intensity must increase*

Everything in the universe declines or evolves in an endless movement of energy. According to Gurdjieff, the laws underlying this universal process were known to ancient science, which assigned man his proper place in the cosmic order.

In our lives we never fully accomplish what we intend to do. All our movements and actions are subject to the Law of Seven. They begin in one direction but cannot pass the interval in the octave. We go up to the note *mi* and return to *do*. To go further, there must be an additional force from within and from without. Today it is mainly our head, our thought, that is touched by the work. The body and the feeling are indifferent and recognize no demand so long as they are content. They live in the moment itself and their memory is short. Yet the wish must come from the feeling, and the power to do, the "capacity," must come from the body. These separate parts each have a different attention, whose force and duration depend on the material they have received. The part that has received more material has more attention.

We believe we can work without intensity, but this will not lead to real change. To allow a contact with the higher centers, the intensity of the lower centers must increase. These centers, each of which vibrates at a different frequency, must come to the same speed. We have to proceed, as in an octave, from level to level, learning to see the distance between energies and recognizing that they can come together only through intensification. What is necessary in us as well as around us is to create a more active energy that is able to resist surrounding influences and find a stable place between two currents of different levels.

Even without conscious effort, the body produces a very fine energy or material, the final product of the transformation of food, which Gurdjieff called *si* 12. This is the material used by the sex center which, when united with its male or female counterpart, can develop independently as a new organism. But it can also participate in a new octave within the body. When all the cells are permeated with this matter, there can be a crystallization, a formation of a second body. The way of the shrewd, the astute man—the accelerated way that Gurdjieff called "haida yoga"—includes the transmutation of the energy *si* 12 for the development of the higher bodies. Gurdjieff never spoke of this delicate work, or even gave explicit indications about it, but there is a key to be found. For example, the friction within us that is necessary to produce the substance for our "I" is identical with what takes place externally between the masculine force and the feminine force in action. The power of *si* 12 is evident in the experience of sexual union, which is for most people the only experience that allows an opening to a state of unity without conscious effort. The rhythms of all the functions submit to this experience, and there is a fleeting moment of happiness when one feels the absence of the ordinary "I." All too often we seek to forget the self in this intense passion, an identification in which we can lose ourselves completely. But immediately afterward the "I" reclaims its rights and we return to the narrow circle of our ordinary thoughts and feelings. Without an understanding of the forces at play, the experience serves no purpose in the search for consciousness.

✎✎ 85. *Degrees of the octave*

In Gurdjieff's teaching, work passes through the degrees of the octave, degrees of intensity. He described the process as follows.

First, there is a note, a vibration that comes from a higher octave and sounds as *do*. It is like an opening to a new vision of a quality that was not here before, to an idea from a higher source. Then, because of a relation between the energies, a stronger intensity begins to appear, a vibration given by a higher octave. We have feelings, sensations, belonging to layers that are deeper, and pass to the level *re*. A new seeing appears that brings a new understanding, a conviction. Here, there is a certain light, but it is still insufficient. It has the power to illuminate what surrounds it, but one feels a necessity not to project outside. The attention must stay free. What sees appears more essential than what is seen. We come to an intensity of perception of the idea that cannot be more intense. We are at the note *mi*.

The proximity of another degree appears, a sensation of another possible level. Nevertheless, it seems inaccessible by the same means, without the intervention of new help. One feels that to pass to this new degree, the vivifying power of the idea must increase. This does not depend on the idea alone. It needs a support that will allow it to last, a force by which it can be nourished. This is an important moment. The thinking is no longer enough. A second center must come into play. The whole body must voluntarily offer its participation. It must allow this force to intensify through it, to manifest. It feels the quality of this force and refuses its automatism in order to receive the action. The body submits consciously in order to allow the conscious manifestation of this force from another level. This is decisive. The struggle is between two octaves—one must take authority and the other accept it. If this is resolved in favor of an inner sensation, the interval is passed—the octave is saved. This is the note *fa* that sounds.

The sensation must be definite; *fa* needs to become established. It must exist in my Presence as a complete sensation—stable, with all the new ideas and feelings that accompany it—in order to pass to the degree *sol*. Then, exactly what took place with the original idea begins again. But this time there is no longer a force from outside. It takes place with a force of my own. The thinking and the body are no longer enough. A new feeling must appear—the feeling of being. I feel myself subject to a force that is beyond me, a will that is beyond me, and I see the process of inner transformation intensify in the fire of the wish *to be*. The concentration then reaches its peak. And from the union of these three forces appears the independence of the sensation of self, the consciousness of self with its own individual life—a new octave.

The octaves are superposed and must not mix. Descent is obligatory if one mixes with vibrations of lower notes.

✍ 86. First and second conscious shocks

In the ascending octave toward consciousness, remembering oneself is the shock that is necessary to pass the interval between *mi* and *fa*— the first conscious shock. It brings a force that can only come from the wish, the will. We must make the will grow degree by degree, step by step.

The current in which we live keeps us at a level on the earth on which the energy is taken continually in reactions. This is because our centers are not related. Without a relation, there are only reactions, and the energy is not transformed. Transformation is possible only through relation with a higher energy. A relation is indispensable, a conscious and sustained relation. But the state in which we live, the level of energy of our thought and of our body, does not allow us to receive the action of this higher energy. It is as though it did not exist.

It is my ordinary "I" that does not allow this relation. The material of my thought keeps its authority, and prevents the automatic movement from stopping. My body is not sufficiently touched. In order to provoke a stop, suffering is necessary so that a third force can appear. Then the attention becomes voluntary—I wish not to be taken, I wish to remain free. At this very moment I feel I must have the freedom *to be*. I experience a will for freedom. The degree of this will of the attention produces an opening of my body to a finer energy. Everything depends on this opening. I need to feel the energy in my mind and in my body simultaneously with the same force. My attention needs to last and not diminish.

All the centers are involved. If one reaches *fa,* it can draw the others toward *fa*. All the centers must be in front of the interval for the intensity of vibration to increase. The relation between the centers is the shock necessary to pass the interval, which will never be passed without it. In our working on this relation, a force appears, and we then feel a vibration that opens the door to a different level.

In proceeding further with the octave, the question of the second conscious shock can appear only when I have been consciously present for a sufficiently long time. In this effort of Presence, my feeling warms up and is transformed. It purifies itself, and my emotions become positive. But this does not last; my emotions fall back and again become as usual. This shows that what in me observes, what watches, has no will. The interval between *si* and *do* is very difficult to pass.

I seek to be present to what I am, but I do not feel it. It does not touch me. I feel my incapacity: I have no feeling, no substance, that would allow me to become conscious of myself. In this conflict a feeling appears that is different from my habitual emotions. The question of myself has a new urgency. I must be here for my functions to obey, and for this there is a need for will. I feel that I do not have it but that I can call it. I must *will*, because *I am*. This second shock—an emotional shock—changes the whole character of a person.

When we can remember ourselves, be open to ourselves, for long enough, we are put to the test by the intervention of the subjective "I" in the face of other people's manifestations toward us. At the moment the impression is received by the mind, I react. It is with this reaction that the notion of "I" bursts forth. I identify with the form projected by my thought. So, if I wish to go further, I need to be shocked, shaken, by seeing the selfish reaction of my ego, defending itself out of fear of being denied. In order to be free from this fear, I have to experience it, to wholly live with everything it entails.

With a second conscious shock, it is possible that consciousness opens and we see reality. This is an emotional understanding of truth. At this moment I realize that my emotion is no longer the same. There is no closing, no negation. I do not refuse. I do not accept. With this vigilance, which does not choose, a new feeling appears and a new understanding, not born from opposites. This is a feeling that embraces everything, a feeling of unity, of being. I am transformed, and in this new state I feel a new order appear.

A COLLECTED STATE

87. *Repeat, repeat*

The first conscious shock—to awake to oneself—is for coming to a more collected state, a state that allows us to open to our being. When my energy is contained, it does not serve the same aims as when it is being eaten by all the outside influences. Because it has another quality, the energy can serve other aims, enter into other combinations.

We are in front of the absolute necessity for a change in our inner state. As it is, our state does not allow us to remain free. There is no unity in us, so the energy is taken. As we come to understand this, we try to maintain a state that is more related, more collected. But we are still not transformed, and we easily lose this state. What makes us lose it?

The relation between my mind and my body is not strong enough. The ego is always here. I am not animated by an energy of such intensity that it could completely transform me. Today, this is not possible. I need to pass through different stages in which the relation between the mind and the body becomes stronger and stronger until I no longer feel them as separate but as a single Presence. For this I need to keep a certain intensity in myself that nothing can make me lose.

When I see myself dispersed, not collected, I do not try to bring myself back. This would be forcing. I remain in front of this dispersion.

Then there is a spontaneous movement of letting go. I become conscious of what it means *to be*. Here is the secret—to see and to suffer. There is reality and, at the same time, there is "me"—my ordinary "I"—which pursues an attitude that will let it preserve its continuity. It may be afraid for moments, but it is cunning and never truly shaken. So long as I have not seen this and suffered with it, nothing new will appear. I must accept this.

A collected state is a state of collected attention, in which the attention is as whole as possible. This state does not come about by my thought resolving to be collected in order to obtain something better. It comes by seeing—through the vision of my dispersion, of the lack. In order to see better, I collect myself. The attention which was taken is freed to engage in a movement that is more active, more charged with intention. In this it responds to the deepest wish in me, the wish to be what I am. A double movement takes place: a movement of awakening, of sensitivity, of vision and a movement of letting go, of receptivity, which needs to become deeper. The two movements complement each other. Yet, because this has to be perceived at the very moment, and everything is continually uncertain, it requires an attention that is always finer, more and more alert, acute. Then there is a moment when it seems a blending takes place. A great tranquillity appears, like a silence.

In order for me to come to a collected state, the sensation, the thinking and the feeling have to turn inward, trying to find a common tempo, an accord in which they do not diverge and disconnect so easily. Without this prior accord nothing can be done and no conscious attention can appear. The better the accord, the more right the action. There is a seeing of oneself and of the response to be expressed, which takes the whole into account.

We must accept that the state of dispersion is normal so long as we have a limited capacity to concentrate. We have to repeat and repeat coming to a collected state. Only repetition will lead to shortening the time required for preparation and increase the time available for practice.

There is an exercise that was specially created for coming to a collected state. I begin by representing with all my attention that I am surrounded by an atmosphere extending a yard, more or less. This atmosphere is displaced according to the movements of the thinking. I concentrate all my attention to prevent the atmosphere from escaping beyond its limits. Then I draw it in consciously, as though sucking it in. I feel, throughout the body, the echo of "I," and silently say "am." I experience the total sensation of being.

88. *My thought does not wander*

All the time I need to return and deepen what Gurdjieff called the "collected state" so that it becomes indispensable to me. This is a state in which my centers try to be attuned in order to know this being, the being that I am. When all the centers are engaged in the same question, they awaken and come closer. When they are truly together, I can *be,* and I can *do* something consciously. But only when they are together.

When I am in my usual state, I am taken by the particular associations that last touched my self-love, such as vanity or envy. This is my unconscious thinking. When I am collected, I have another quality of thought. What determines a collected state is that my thought does not wander. It does not leave me. With associations my thought wanders, but when I am collected it remains in me. My feeling also does not project itself. I am occupied with feeling "I am." When I am collected, my thought is conscious. But only when I am collected.

I want to learn to be in a more collected state but cannot because my thought, my sensation and my feeling are not in accord in taking an action. I have a sensation of my body, but my feeling is indifferent. I think of being, but my body is occupied with something else. And yet what I am, in fact, is a body, thought and feeling. Even though I know this, I cannot experience them at the same time. They do not all have the same intensity or even look in the same direction. I feel myself divided, uncertain.

Seeing my state makes certain tensions fall. I am less on the surface. My attention is more penetrating and reaches deeper in me. I let go, not in order to relax but because the more I let go, the stronger the movement of collecting becomes, the movement of coming together. I let go in order to feel contained in myself. I concentrate on the point where my thoughts arrive and disappear, and I go beyond. My effort is not to suppress the thoughts. I see that they are shadows, phantoms. I let them float. Thoughts have no substance. The substance is in the source.

The mind is then capable of true silence, of a tranquillity that comes when it has seen its own activity form a center separate from the rest, which limits it. Without this tranquillity, my mind will never be capable of knowing its own movement. And its movement is immense, immeasurable. Our mind is our instrument for search—so long as it is not influenced by ready-made answers. Can the mind be in a state of not knowing? Can it be so in a way that is true, simply a fact, not an affirmation? If the mind can remain in front of this, accept it as true, feel poor in knowledge, the mind can really be in a state that is the highest form of thinking. Then the mind is acute, profound, clear, without limits, and can receive something new.

I am here, very still, without knowing what I am, without making efforts to know. I see that knowledge cannot be grasped. My mind has become quiet, without movement, related to the sensation of this stillness and to a feeling of this state of being. There is stillness, but it is not empty. In this collected state, a reality begins to work in me. It is not I who apprehends, who knows this reality. It makes itself known. I have to let its action work. I feel the need for a letting go, and I relax naturally. All my centers are more sensitive, more acute, more perceptive. There are layers of myself that I have never penetrated. To see this frees me.

89. *I feel, I sense, I watch*

Our work is to understand better the collected state, a state in which I engage in a new order. Each part of me has its place in maintaining a unity without which no real knowledge and no conscious action are possible.

In order to experience this collected state, I try to understand my presence in this body, what I am in this body. I open to a sensation, an impression carried by the nerves to the brain. Usually when this takes place it immediately arouses suggestions or associations with past experience, and sets in motion all that is in my memory. These get mixed up with the impression, obscuring it so that I cannot know what is real. All our sensations are distorted by this. So I see that a sensation of the real in myself will depend on being less invaded by suggestions and associations, on being freer from them. For this, their movement must subside, slow down. It depends very much on the state of my muscles and on my breathing. Above all, there must be a real relation between my mind and my body.

First, I need to find a position of my body in which there is no pressure or tension to hinder a pure sensation. I try to find a right posture. Everything is still, relaxed, and yet alive. The joints, the muscles, even the skin, need to be relaxed. I pay great attention to the skin. The sensation of the body changes. I am here, I am still, with a sensation of reality. But in order for it to be true, something more is needed. I feel my own existence, but I also sense it. The awakening of my feeling immediately calls the participation of my thought. *I feel . . . I sense . . . I watch.* And I see that, in this state, this relation must be closely followed by the attention or it will immediately be lost. We are too ready to lose it. Here we need to have a will that does not come from an affirmation, a hardening, of one of our functions—only the will *to be. I feel . . . I sense . . . I watch.* If I am sufficiently awake, with my energy entirely collected, I have the impression of a living Presence. I know this Presence by the sensation I have of it. But I know its nature, its quality, by the feeling which is also here. Without it this quality will not be revealed. And because there is a ray of thought which lights up the whole, I awake to the fact that "I am."

But I am disconcerted by this impression. I do not remain collected. My attention fluctuates. Sometimes it is my sensation that takes me, sometimes the feeling, sometimes the thought. And in this activation they leave the general rhythm, the general tempo of my being. In order to find it again, I need to quiet the instability, and I let go naturally and deeply. I learn the true meaning of relaxing. I let go, I give up, for the sake of collectedness. When the relaxation is deep enough and I am more collected, I see that the state of my body has great importance for the capacity of my attention.

Regulating the global "tonus"—the overall degree of tautness of the thinking, sensation and feeling—changes the sense of inner space in which movements of energy take place. Once a certain stability is established, it becomes possible to capture the energy spent in automatic functioning and maintain the thought on a chosen support. By influencing the rhythm of ideas that arise, this provides a kind of mastery over the associations, making it possible to become aware of the flow of thoughts without interference or censure. There can then be a current of unified thought.

90. How do I listen?

We are trying to understand a state of quietness in which we could become conscious of the reality of life. This would be without expecting something, without wishing for something, and without belief or fear. For this I need to be seated in a right posture, neither too high nor too low, feeling that this place is my own, in this spot and in this body. I am quiet in front of quietness itself.

I consider myself, I look at my state and what it allows, and at the same time I look at the different parts of myself. I see they are each occupied differently. The body is passive, heavy, asleep. I sense its weight. The head is restless, dreaming, suggesting ideas and images. I sense its tension. I even sense in which part of the head I am tense. My feeling is indifferent. But in my way of looking, something is in question—my self, what I am. And I see that I cannot answer. In the state I am in, I cannot know. I am not free. I am in question, so I listen. How do I listen?

My thought stops for a moment to see better, and the attention that is freed turns to my body. Under this look, my body awakens and becomes sensitive, very sensitive. A contact is established between the body and this thought. And if the thought keeps the fullness of its vision and the body the warmth of its sensitivity, this awakens another part of myself that was beginning to be felt as missing. Their intensity wakes up the feeling. I am touched, and I feel a current is established in me which is like a closed circuit. I feel that I am here, that there is a Presence with an energy which fills this body. And it is the feeling I have for this existence, this Presence, that allows the awareness to last. This feeling is fragile, unstable, but I am helped by the deep need I have for it. I learn what it would be to have a sensitivity that touches everything in me. It is never enough. I do not feel; I am not touched deeply enough.

When my thought, my sensation and my feeling are turned in the same direction with the same intensity, there is a change in the state of consciousness that transforms me. This state cannot be easily undone from the outside, but can be demolished in a flash simply by my inner weakness, my passivity. I need a thousand times to experience both this possibility and this fragility together, in order for a new wish, a new will, to appear. I have to know what I wish, what I profoundly wish. I have to know the need of my being.

FROM ANOTHER LEVEL

✐ *91. A more intense energy appears*

The energy coming from the higher centers is always here, and I am less or more open to it. My body and my functions are also here and constantly expend the energy. These are two different worlds, two levels of life, but between the two there is nothing. On one level the head says "yes" and the body says "no." Yet two opposing forces do not bring a conscious state, a state in which there is no contradiction. A third factor is necessary, a factor capable of situating what says "yes" and what says "no" in a whole, a unity, which is beyond their individual existences.

There is a movement of Presence, a passage, which I need to value. I see that when the attention of the head turns toward the body, the body also becomes attentive. The movement of my thinking changes a little, and that of the body also. At the same time, there is an interest, a feeling, that awakens in me. But I see that it is weak, that each part has a tendency toward separation, to return to its habitual movement. I feel these two forces in me: the "yes" and the "no." This duality is always here, but I do not understand it because I do not stay in front and I accept being divided. Although a certain movement of relation, of unification, occurs, I am unable to resist my automatic movements. My attention is passive and is taken. I suffer, but if it serves nothing, this suffering does not help.

In order to have a relation between my thought and my sensation, the body needs to be touched by a thinking that comes from another level, from a part of the mind that brings a more subtle, purer energy. The body feels this movement of energy. It understands that it cannot receive it in its passive state, and feels the necessity to open, to let go all its tensions. And as soon as the thought and the body are turned toward each other, the speed of vibration changes. The body frees itself in order to let the energy of the thought pass. The two must have the same force. This is the most important thing. I look . . . I stay in front. I stay very still to allow the energy to pass. If my vision remains clear, and if the force is the same in the thought and in the body, under this look an exchange takes place. A more intense energy, with a speed I did not know, appears and becomes established in me. It has a new quality, a new intensity. I need to respect this movement, to submit to it. My body opens to it, my thinking opens—the same force, the same respect.

The relation of thought and body demands a very strong attention to bring about a transformation of the energy. When the force coming from a little above the head appears, I need to give myself to it. The whole difficulty is here. I do not give myself. I need to see my resistance and suffer from it, to see that it is the ego which resists and that the ego needs to give up its place. This is what is called dying to oneself. Then there is a gift, a complete relation that allows this force to act.

92. *Exercise of divided attention*

We could say that the attitude we take, our inner and outer posture, is at the same time our aim and our way. I begin by considering my physical attitude. I see that in my habitual posture, my attention is a prisoner of my body's attitude—I am not free. I adjust my posture. I ask of my body that it free itself of tensions, that it enter into a new attitude where there is no tension—my back very straight, the arms, the head, all without the least tension. The breathing then has more force. It is free. Yet I feel as though the act of breathing, though essential, in itself is insufficient. I feel a need to open more deeply.

When I turn the attention of my thought to enter into contact with my body, my mind opens. The cells that vibrate are not the same as those engaged in my usual thinking. It is a part of the mind that can have a relation with a more subtle, pure energy. This is the energy of a higher level, which, Gurdjieff explained, is constituted by the real thought, the prayer, of certain beings. In order to have a connection with this level, I need a conduit, like a wire that reaches as high as my thinking allows. I can then take in, or rather suck in, the energy and let it pass through the connection.

As an exercise, given by Gurdjieff, I divide my attention into two equal parts. The first half I direct to sensing the process of my breathing. I feel that when I inhale the air, the greater portion, after passing through my lungs, returns outside, while a small portion remains and settles in me. I feel that this penetrates inside, as though spreading through the whole organism. As only one part of my attention is occupied in observing the breathing, all the associations continue to be noticed by the free part of my attention.

I then direct this second part to my brain, trying to observe clearly the entire process that takes place, and I begin to feel something very fine, almost imperceptible, freeing itself from the associations. I do not know what this "something" is, but I see it appear—small, light, so delicate that it can be felt only after practice brings the sensation of it. Half of my attention remains occupied with the breathing, and I feel the two at the same time.

Now I direct this second part of my attention to assist this fine "something" in my brain to flow, or rather fly, directly toward the solar plexus. What takes place in the brain is not important. What is important is that what appears must flow directly to the solar plexus. Consciously, I concentrate on this, and at the same time I feel that I am breathing. I have no more associations. And I feel more fully that "I am," "I can," and "I can will." From the air and from the mind, I receive food for different bodies, and I see then with certainty the two real sources from which the "I" can be born.

The practice of this exercise brings the possibility of an active thought, and with active thought the "I" becomes stronger.

93. *My body needs to open*

In the movement of opening there is a limit beyond which we do not pass. To go further it is necessary to die to oneself in order to be born again—that is, to die to one level of being in order to rise to another. What needs to be accomplished—and always remains half done—is the complete relation between the centers. It requires opening to a higher force, an energy coming from a higher part of the mind. This is the most difficult thing. I do not wish to open.

In order for the higher force to unite with the body, the body needs to open entirely to it. I feel a movement from the brain that descends toward the body, an energy coming from above. In order to know it, my attention has to be very active, wholly turned toward this movement, and must not lose its intensity. What is important is to have the right attitude in front of this energy. I must feel the necessity to give myself to it consciously so that it can act. Then a feeling appears, a new energy is produced that penetrates my whole body. I am touched by the quality of this energy. It has an intensity and intelligence, a vision which I do not know in my usual state. I feel that I am free, that I am not taken.

This demands something completely new from me. What I am—this active attention—needs to find its place between two levels so that this energy can last. I am open to this force, and at the same time I need to act on the level of life through my automatism. Without me—without "I" being here—this will not be done. The attention has to remain continually conscious both of this higher energy and of the body, of the force that makes it live. I am inhabited by these two movements of energy at the same time. If I lose one, I am no longer able to act in the world. If I lose the other, I am taken by my reactions, my automatism. I must learn to act and at the same time receive impressions without losing the opening to this energy from above.

I begin to see what I habitually call "I" and to recognize that by myself I am nothing. At the heart of this humility there is a feeling that comes from the higher parts of myself and appears like a light, an intelligence, and with it confidence. Then I see I wanted to change something that was not mine to change. Now I can serve. I no longer intervene, and a silence comes by itself. In this silence an unknown energy is revealed and acts on me. Consciousness is here. It does not need to have an object. Although it makes me aware of my body, in these impressions it is not my body but the light of consciousness that is perceived. It reveals what I am and what the things around me are.

When I feel a pure energy, without limit, I see that it is sufficient unto itself. But this energy is in movement. It has waves and is always in movement. The waves, the movement and the energy are one and the same. And yet the wave is the movement, not the energy itself. What is important is to understand the energy itself, the pure energy.

94. A cosmic scale

Each person has an ideal, an aspiration for something higher. It takes one form or another, but what matters is the call to this ideal, the call of his being. Listening to the call is the state of prayer. While in this state, a man produces an energy, a special emanation, which religious feeling alone can bring. These emanations concentrate in the atmosphere just above the place where they are produced. The air everywhere contains them. The question is how to enter into contact with these emanations. By our call we can create a connection, like a telegraph wire, which links us, and take in this material in order to let it accumulate and crystallize in us. We then have the possibility to manifest its quality and help others understand—that is, to give it back. True prayer is establishing this contact and being nourished by it, nourished by this special material, which is called Grace. As an exer-

cise for this, we breathe in air, thinking of Christ or Buddha or Mo-
hammed, and keep the active elements that have been accumulated.

We need to understand the idea of a cosmic scale, that there is a
link connecting humanity with a higher influence. Our lives, the purpose of being alive, can only be understood in relation to forces whose
scale and grandeur go beyond ourselves. I am here to obey, to obey an
authority that I recognize as greater because I am a particle of it. It calls
to be recognized, to be served and to shine through me. There is a
need to put myself under this higher influence and a need to relate to it
in submitting to its service. I do not realize at the outset that my wish
to be is a cosmic wish and that my being needs to situate itself and find
its place in a world of forces. I consider it my subjective property, something I can make use of for personal profit. My search is organized on
the scale of this subjectivity in which everything is measured from a
subjective point of view—me and God. Yet at a certain point I must
realize that the origin of the need I feel is not in me alone. There is a
cosmic need for the new being that I could become. Humanity—a certain portion of humanity—needs it. And I also have a need, with their
help, to capture the influence that is just above me.

We feel that without this relation with a higher energy, life has not
much meaning. But by ourselves alone, we will not have the force to
achieve it. A certain current, a certain magnetism, needs to be created
in which each person finds his place, that is, the place which will permit the current to be better established. Our whole responsibility is
here. The traditional ways all recognized and served this aim in a manner that corresponded to the development of people in a given place
and period. Today we need to find again the contact with this energy.

This is why Gurdjieff brought the help of a Fourth Way, which
excludes nothing and takes account of the development of the different
functions in contemporary people. This way is not new. It has always
existed, but only within a limited circle. Today it can renew the weakening link between the two levels of the cosmos. This calls for a great
work. The first step is to establish centers where we seek to live this

way with others. The experience proceeds with ups and downs, with responsibility more or less assumed, in a play of forces through which a certain liberation can emerge. But it still involves only a limited number of people, and this force needs to be felt on a much larger scale of humanity.

IX

IN A STATE
OF UNITY

There is only one great life. I can enter into the experience only if I have first come to unity in myself, only if I have come to be a whole.

I am able to see a form, but I cannot know through my senses the true nature of what it is. My thinking knows forms but cannot grasp the reality behind them.

Seeing does not come from thinking.

Attention is the conscious force, the force of consciousness. It is a divine force.

The wall of tensions is the wall of my ego.

Sensation is the essential experience on the road to consciousness.

I have to maintain a continual sensation in all the activities of my daily life.

THE ACT OF SEEING

🪶   *95. Another vision*

I seek what I am, to be what I am. I have a habit of thinking of "body," on the one hand, and of "spirit or energy" on the other. But nothing exists separately. There is a unity of life. I wish to live it, and I seek it through a movement of return toward myself. I say there is an outer life and an inner life. I say this because I feel myself as distinct, as existing apart from life. There is, however, only one great life. I cannot feel separate from it, outside it, and at the same time know it. I must feel myself a part of this life. But it is not enough to desire this or to seek an intense sensation of it. I can enter into the experience only if I have first come to unity in myself, only if I have come to be a whole.

There are two movements in me: a movement of energy from above which, if I am free enough to listen to it, penetrates and acts through me; and another movement, dispersed and without order, which animates my body, my thought and my feeling. The two are very different, and I cannot bring them into accord. Something is missing. My attention is unable to follow them at the same time. Sometimes it settles on the void, the infinite, on emptiness; sometimes on the form. When the attention settles on emptiness, it is the form that dissolves. When the attention is on the form, the sense of the void disappears. It is necessary to pay the price.

Can I be free enough to receive what is unknown, behind all my avid movements toward the outside? This unknown, which is behind and beyond, cannot be perceived by my senses. I am able to see a form, but I cannot know through my senses the true nature of what it is. My thinking knows forms but cannot grasp the reality behind them, the reality of what I am, which appears just before and after each thought or feeling. What we experience—sounds, forms, colors, thoughts—cannot exist without a background. But this background cannot be perceived by my senses. It remains unseen, not experienced. The forms and the reality are parts of a single whole, but they exist in different dimensions. The real is not affected by the material of my thinking and cannot absorb it. Reality is on another level. Yet the material of my thought absorbs the real and constructs illusions based on forms. The form acts as a veil hiding the reality. When the reality of myself is not felt, I cannot help but believe in this illusion and call it "I." Nevertheless, the illusion is only a mirage which dissolves the moment silence is established.

I have to see that there is a space between thoughts, a void that is reality, and I need to remain as long as possible in this space. Then another kind of thinking appears, clear and intelligent, a thought of another level, another dimension. I see that the usual thought, which is limited and measurable, can never understand that which is beyond measure. With my usual vision I see the physical aspect of the world. With this other vision I see another dimension in which the immeasurable has its own movement. If my centers are absolutely still, without any movement, the energy can pass through them. I see what I did not see before. I see *what is*. In this seeing there is light, a light that is not ordinary. Things appear and disappear in the void but are illuminated, and I am no longer so taken by them. In this seeing I can understand my true nature and the true nature of things around me.

It is not a matter of fighting indifference or lethargy or anger. The real problem is vision—*to see*. But this seeing is only possible if we return to the source, to the reality in us. We need another quality of seeing, a look that penetrates and goes immediately to the root of myself.

If we look at ourselves from outside, we cannot penetrate and go deeper because we see only the body, the form of the seed, its materiality. Reality is here, only I have never put my attention on it. I live with my back turned to myself.

96. *Seeing is an act*

The question is not what to do but how *to see*. Seeing is the most important thing—the act of seeing. I need to realize that it is truly an act, an action that brings something entirely new, a new possibility of vision, certainty and knowledge. This possibility appears during the act itself and disappears as soon as the seeing stops. It is only in this act of seeing that I will find a certain freedom.

So long as I have not seen the nature and movement of the mind, there is little sense in believing that I could be free of it. I am a slave to my mechanical thoughts. This is a fact. It is not the thoughts themselves that enslave me but my attachment to them. In order to understand this, I must not seek to free myself before having known what the slavery is. I need to see the illusion of words and ideas, and the fear of my thinking mind to be alone and empty without the support of anything known. It is necessary to live this slavery as a fact, moment after moment, without escaping from it. Then I will begin to perceive a new way of seeing. Can I accept not knowing who I am, being hidden behind an impostor? Can I accept not knowing my name?

Seeing does not come from thinking. It comes from the shock at the moment when, feeling an urgency to know what is true, I suddenly realize that my thinking mind cannot perceive reality. To understand what I really am at this moment, I need sincerity and humility, and an unmasked exposure that I do not know. This would mean to refuse nothing, exclude nothing, and enter into the experience of discovering what I think, what I sense, what I wish, all at this very moment.

Our conditioned thought always wants an answer. What is important is to develop another thinking, a vision. For this we have to liberate a certain energy that is beyond our usual thought. I need to experience

"I do not know" without seeking an answer, to abandon everything to enter the unknown. Then it is no longer the same mind. My mind engages in a new way. I see without any preconceived idea, without choice. In relaxing, for example, I no longer choose to relax before knowing why. I learn to purify my power of vision, not by turning away from the undesirable or toward what is agreeable. I learn to stay in front and see clearly. All things have the same importance, and I become fixed on nothing. Everything depends on this vision, on a look that comes not from any command of my thought but from a feeling of urgency to know.

Perception, real vision, comes in the interval between the old response and the new response to the reception of an impression. The old response is based on material inscribed in our memory. With the new response, free from the past, the brain remains open, receptive, in an attitude of respect. It is a new brain which functions, that is, different cells and a new intelligence. When I see that my thought is incapable of understanding, that its movement brings nothing, I am open to the sense of the cosmic, beyond the realm of human perception.

97. Beyond my usual perception

I believe I understand unity. But if I really knew what unity was, there would be an irresistible wish to live my life in this state. I could no longer accept feeling dismembered and seeing these parts, whose material encumbers my Presence, remain isolated, taking me away from the consciousness of my reality. Nevertheless, I begin to be drawn to the difference between what I am in a state of unity and what I am in a state of dispersion. I become especially interested in the energy that constitutes the vibrating link between the centers. When it is here, this energy brings a strong acceleration of my functions, together with something like an empty space in which a new force can appear.

There is an energy in me, a life that is always in movement but does not project outside. To feel this requires a certain tranquillity, a certain silence. It is only in the void that another reality can appear. At the same time, there is also in me an energy that is projected outward by my functions, taken by their inexhaustible reactions to impressions coming from both outside and inside. I do not have the attention necessary to confront all these impressions and reactions. But I am shocked when I see the speed with which I unknowingly react. Is it possible to receive impressions without reacting so quickly, to let the impression penetrate and act on me? For this I would need a pure perception of what is here, a perception not mixed with a reaction. In my ordinary state, my attention goes no further than noticing what is present. The moment is very short, too short for me to grasp the nature of the thing as it is. Yet this is the moment of knowing. We are generally not interested by an impartial perception of things "as they are." We always judge them or treat them from the point of view of our personal interest. With every perception we instantly attach a label that distorts the vision. Afterward these labels determine our actions and reactions.

I feel the need to go beyond the limits of my usual perception. I need a new perception, an attention that like a sixth sense could receive impressions apart from the thinking mind. This kind of attention would be fluid, all-inclusive. It is very difficult to find in myself, first of all because I do not feel the necessity. I always seek in the same way. I believe that I can touch something real in affirming it—for example, that I can deepen sensation by trying to know it better and better. But if I wish to have a new perception, I cannot look for something positive. There is only my ignorance. If I feel this complete ignorance, there will be a break, a rupture that undoes the bonds that imprison me. It will bring something like an inner expansion, and my attention will pass beyond the limit of known impressions. There is no stairway to climb. I have to leap. To become conscious I must let go of all that is known. Really knowing is a state in which everything is observed, experienced, understood and—because it is unable to serve in the following moment—abandoned as useless.

98. *The most important thing*

What we have learned—all our words and memories—gives the impression of continuity, the illusion of my ordinary "I." But, on the scale of energies in us, this material is not very high. What allows the passage to a higher level at every degree is the intensity and quality of the attention. It is attention that gives the capacity to see. Attention is the conscious force, the force of consciousness. It is a divine force.

Vision, inner vision, is the liberation of an energy that is beyond thinking. It is a total awareness of life because to see is to embrace totality at the very moment. We cannot see part by part, little by little, over time. We have to see the whole. It is an act of perception of what is true without interpreting what is seen. If I am distracted by anything whatsoever, my conditioning is such that I cannot see freely. My thoughts are mechanical. They are a mechanical response to a question or an impression. The response may take time and come after an interval that is more or less long, but it is still mechanical. Vision, on the other hand, is observation without thought, without the security of words or names. In a state of pure perception, there is no more aim and no attempt to respond. One simply lives the fact.

The act of seeing is an act of deliverance. When I see what is real, the real fact, the very perception, is deliverance from it. I need to disengage from the all-powerful value I give to knowledge, to my opinions and theories. The very act of seeing something as a fact has an extraordinary effect by itself without the participation of the thinking. If I can remain in front of the reality without reacting, a source of energy appears that is not the thought. The attention becomes charged with a special energy that is liberated in the act of perception. But this state of observation can come only when there is an urgency to understand and to see, and my mind gives up everything in order to observe. Then there is a new kind of observation, without any knowledge, without belief or fear, with an attention that remains firm and stays in front in order to know. It is an attention that neither denies the fact nor accepts it. The attention simply sees—going from fact to fact with the same pure energy. This act of pure seeing is an act of transformation.

We need to understand the role of conscious attention. In the play of forces, either energies are taken or they serve to create a relation that produces a higher vision, a freer energy. Conscious attention requires a relation between the centers. But it is difficult to come to this relation because their vibrations are not of the same frequency. How could the centers be related? What would "reconciling" mean? This would require an energy that would contain everything and be conscious of it. This energy must do nothing other than contain. As soon as it takes sides, it ceases containing and is degraded.

I listen, sensing vibrations of another intensity, wishing to be attuned in order to know them. To be attuned requires the appearance of attention as a third force—a vigilance, a look without expectation, a capacity of seeing that is much stronger than before. It cannot appear unless the thought and the body have the same intensity. This seeing is the most important thing. It maintains the relation between two centers and allows a new energy to be formed.

CONSCIOUS SENSATION

🖋 *99. Life is in me*

We begin to realize that in fact we hold nothing under our look, under our attention. I am here, attentive to myself. Yet I do not perceive myself entirely, as a whole. I am drawn to feeling one part more than another, and I do not have a complete sensation of the whole of myself, a sensation that is everywhere the same. The essential characteristic of voluntary thought is to fix on something in order to know it. But I am still unable to hold any object under my look, unable really to see. This act of seeing is difficult to understand.

Through sensation I could be aware of being here, through the organic experience of sensing. But my sensations are generally mechanical. I receive them and respond without knowing how. The awareness I have of sensations is poor and fleeting. The knowledge they bring does not go far. I do not know what value to give them. Because I do not hold them under my look, I can be completely misled about their meaning.

In the beginning, sensation is almost the only instrument for self-knowledge. It can give a power to watch over many things and to repeat experiences that we can then identify. This creates an inner world. Later, consciousness will have to become deeper, more interior. Yet the impulse to look into the depth of oneself is an indispensable step in the evolution of consciousness. Nothing is either certain or pure without this.

I need to attune my centers in order to hear the vibration of an energy that is not yet degraded. I listen to its resonance in myself. This is what takes place in praying, in meditating, in reading sacred texts, in repeating sacred words. But I need to understand the step I am taking, and not go beyond what I understand. My contact, my communion, with the difficulty will liberate me through knowing. So I listen with my own substance to the vibrations of an unknown energy in me.

I see that I never allow an experience to take place in myself. I always resist the full experience. This is because I want to lead it. I do not trust the experience, I trust only me. Because of this, it does not transform me. When I begin to perceive a subtle Presence in myself, I feel it as something alive that calls for its action to be felt. But I cannot feel its action deeply because I am separated from it by a wall of tensions, that is, of my mental reactions. The unknown in this Presence provokes suggestions and impressions that give a shock to my mind. The mind reacts by presenting a form, and with this reaction the notion of "I," egoism, springs forth. This is not the real "I," which is behind it and which alone has intelligence. This is the ordinary "I," my ego, which believes it is affirming itself in the reaction. The wall of tensions is the wall of my ego.

More and more I feel the need to experience certain impressions. This need is very strong, as though I could not live without these impressions . . . and, in fact, I cannot participate in a certain life without them. Indeed, the need is so strong that, for lack of impressions, I seek outside myself the shock that has to come from within. Life is in me, but I cannot feel its vibrations. They are too fine, too subtle for what I am now. Even my desire to be penetrated by these vibrations, to absorb them, brings duality and a tension that holds back the energy. With this tension I cannot become conscious of the nature of this energy. Its vibrations do not reach me. I feel this, I feel my incapacity. I am unable to be transformed. In my tension I feel my refusal. Life is here, very near, but my "I" is still closed, turned in on itself.

100. An inner stillness

Until now I have not understood my relation with my body. For me to become conscious, my body has to accept and understand its role, not because it is forced but through real interest. In order for unity to appear, my body has to participate consciously, voluntarily. For this it must find the attitude in which it is free, without tension.

In the opening to Presence, there are two steps to be understood: first, the seeing, that is, the moment when I hold myself entirely under my look; and second, the letting go toward which the look has led me, the release that follows the shock when I see. In order for me to have a real perception, an act of knowing, I need an attention that is as total and as even as possible, an impartial all-embracing look that does not take one side or the other. The most important thing is to discover whether I am capable of such a look. When my attention becomes truly active and my mind acquires the clarity of this look, there is a letting go both in the head and in the rest of the body, which becomes still. At this moment I can experience a Presence that has no need to project outwardly and is maintained under this look. I have the impression that this letting go takes place from top to bottom, and that my inner volume changes, as though no longer confined to my body. Here I approach the meaning of relaxation, not an artificial letting go but one that appears as I understand the act of seeing.

At the moment I see, there is a shock, a stop in which the finer energy in me becomes free to follow its proper direction. I do not force it to change course; it changes by itself. Then I know an inner stillness, a state without waves, without ripples. There is no movement. Yet I recognize this letting go as an action, an act that does not depend on me but that transforms me. At this moment I know what this energy is, an energy that does not take me. It is what "I am." If my attention remains whole, if the look on myself lights everything, an opening appears that I experience as something given—a filling out, an opening in the abdomen. With this perception, I have a moment of knowing. I discover something real and see a direction for study in which I can only proceed step by step.

Knowledge of opening to Presence requires the passage in me from one density of vibrations to another, a movement inward through sensation. For this there must be an empty place free of tensions, felt as a void, void of my ordinary "I" which no longer affirms itself. Then I can penetrate the world of finer vibrations. Sensation is the perception of these vibrations. The more I feel the life in my body, the more I recognize that the sense of Being would not touch me without its participation. I feel it through my body. But it is not I who grasps this, it is the life force making itself known. This is a very different inner movement that brings a deep letting go, which I can sometimes also experience alone in nature.

 101. A conscious posture

Sensation is the essential experience on the road to consciousness. I need to understand what it would be to have a conscious sensation.

We wish to know who we are. Each of us knows the difficulty. I come to a quiet state with a little more stillness and silence, but as soon as I emerge to respond to life, I am the same as before. Nothing has changed. What responds is not really "I." Something in me has not been shaken. I never have the feeling of being at the root of myself, of reaching my essence. And I am never entirely touched. There are always hidden parts that refuse.

My body is the first to refuse. It knows nothing of my wish and lives a life of its own. Nevertheless, it could participate in the process of knowing. It is the receptacle, the vehicle for the energy in us. If we look within ourselves, we see that the energy is concentrated either in the head or in the solar plexus. Perhaps there is a little in the spine, but nothing in comparison with the other centers. And there is nothing in the lower part of the body. It is as though the body had no real importance. Yet it is only in and through the body that the energy can act.

I feel this energy beginning to appear. In order for it to act through me, I need to see my automatism and to recognize that if it becomes stronger than the conscious movement, the energy falls back to its lower level and once again I am taken. The position of the body is very important. My automatic posture holds back the energy and conditions my thinking and feeling. I need to see this, to live it, so that a conscious suffering appears which calls for a new posture, a conscious posture that, like an electromagnetic field, allows the action of this energy on the body. Its position must therefore be precise, and be maintained by a close and continual cooperation between my thinking, my feeling and my body. I need to feel at ease, with a sense of well-being and stability. Then the position itself can allow the mind to come to a state of total availability, naturally becoming empty of agitated thoughts. In the right posture, all my centers come together and are related. I find a balance, an order in which my ordinary "I" is no longer the master but finds its place. The thought is freer and also my feeling, which now is purer, less avid. It respects something.

As I let myself open to this energy, there is absorption without judgment, without conclusion, and my attention maintains itself patiently without effort and silently penetrates beyond what I know. This is like an inner expansion. I feel a greater unity between my body and what animates it. A center of gravity, my vital center of energy, has formed by itself. There is no more contradiction in me, no more refusal. I have found in myself this primordial center of energy, and have passed beyond the struggle, the duality between my body and my psyche. The more I experience this state, the more my essence is touched. But as soon as I lose contact with this center of gravity, the energy surges back toward the head or the solar plexus, and the false notion of "I" returns. I believe this contact is easy to maintain. Yet even the idea of maintaining it is false. This center of gravity must become second nature to me, my measure and my guide. I must feel its weight in everything I do. Otherwise an opening to the higher centers cannot take place.

When I experience being this living Presence, conscious of itself, I feel that it is the Presence that is breathing. The freedom of my center of gravity depends on the freedom of the breathing. When I let the breathing take place without interfering, another reality appears, a reality I did not know. I need to see that this experience is my essential food and must return to this state as often as possible.

102. *In a quiet body I breathe in*

I have a new impression of myself but it is fragile. I am not sufficiently steeped in the sensation of being a living Presence, and the feeling revealed here is still too weak. Tensions reappear. I feel them. But I know what they separate me from, and because I know it, they fall away. This is a movement of ebb and flow in which my feeling becomes stronger. It loses its negative and aggressive elements, and opens more and more to a sense of the subtle, the higher, a sense of life itself. My intelligence has to understand the meaning of my tensions, and something in me needs to leave more and more space—not out of obligation but from necessity, a necessity of my being. I seek to understand this state-without-tension which brings me closer to the void, to my essence.

I become aware of a world of finer vibrations. I feel them, I have the sensation of them, as if certain parts of me were irrigated, vivified, spiritualized by them. Yet I am still not entirely under the influence of these vibrations. I realize this. But I feel an ever greater need not to resist them. My usual "I" has lost its authority and, as another authority makes itself felt, I see that my life has meaning only if I am attuned to it. In working for this accord, I feel as though situated in a closed circuit and that, if I could remain here long enough, the miracle of my transformation would take place.

In order to feel these fine vibrations, I must come to a real stillness of the body, a state without any tension where the thought is simply a witness which without comment sees all that happens. I will then understand what it means to have a pure sensation—a sensation with no intervening image. My body is under this vision with no tension. Relaxation appears by itself as my seeing becomes clear, and with it I feel that separate islands of energy in me need to be more deeply related.

This fine sensation is a sign of incarnation, the moment of penetration when the spirit materializes and takes on a definite density.

In a more objective state, where an order is established, my breathing can take on new meaning. Only in this state am I capable of receiving the finer elements of the air and of absorbing them. I feel the energy circulate freely in my body, with nothing stopping or deflecting it, nothing projecting it outside or fixing it inside. It flows in a kind of circular movement, which takes place without my intervening. I feel it as a movement in which I exist. I discover my breathing—the absorption and discharge of energy.

I breathe in. . . . I breathe out.
I know that I breathe in. . . . I know that I breathe out.
In a quiet body I breathe in. . . . In a quiet body I breathe out.
Slowly I breathe in. . . . Slowly I breathe out.

I am awake to this breathing that is taking place in me. I am awake to my body. I do not separate them from each other.

In a light body, I breathe in. . . . In a light body, I breathe out.

The body feels lighter. I let myself exhale completely, all the way to the end.

Without avidity, I breathe in. . . . Without avidity, I breathe out.

I feel the impermanence of the movement. I do not seek to hold back anything whatsoever.

Feeling free, I breathe in. . . . Feeling free, I breathe out.

Words and forms lose their power of attraction. A kind of clarity lights the state I am in. I become deeply quiet in order to awaken to what I am.

VOLUNTARY ATTENTION

✍ *103. The feeling of lack*

In us there is a force that descends from above and a force that ascends from below. These energies are not related. This relation is something that Nature did not provide for in human beings, even though we are here to play a cosmic role. Man has to relate himself to the higher force that is in him. For this, he must see his incapacity and his refusal, and at the same time feel the wish to be related in the depths of himself.

When the energy of attention has a different movement in each of the centers, there is no force capable of its own will. So I need another attention, a purer attention less burdened with the material of my thoughts and capable of having an action on the centers. This kind of attention does not come because it is made captive, nor by forcing—I cannot make it appear, just as I cannot force love to appear. Attention comes when it is needed, when it is called by a feeling of necessity. If I really see that I do not understand, that I have lost the direction and the meaning of my life, then at that very moment my attention is called to be here. Without it, I will never be able to be what I am. I do not have the necessary energy. But when I feel this absolute necessity, the attention appears. So I have to come to the feeling of lack, of not understanding, not knowing, a feeling of being insufficient.

I can daydream as I walk along a road. But when I have to walk on ice, on a slippery frozen path, I cannot dream. I need all my attention not to fall down. It is the same inside myself. If I have no real interest in myself—if I keep thinking I can answer everything, and pretend that I am able—I will continue dreaming and the attention will never appear.

I have to experience my nothingness in this moment and my incapacity to be present. I have also to feel my lack of interest, my lack of wish. It is an important moment, an interval where the intensity weakens and there is insufficient force to go further. I see my slavery to my functions. Perhaps I also see that a force from another level is here. But if this force is not engaged, if I am not related to it, my functions will take the energy, and I will be even more enslaved than before. There must be voluntary submission, a voluntary obedience. I wish to stay in front of this insufficiency. I do not see it enough, I do not feel it enough, I do not suffer from it enough. To feel this lack calls a more active attention. It is as if a door opens to a much finer energy. This energy passes through the head and descends in me, provided the space is free. My whole work consists in allowing this passage so that the energy can circulate. Everything depends on my attention. If it weakens, the functions reassert their power and reclaim the energy.

This circulation requires a voluntary attention, which I never needed before. I see that a certain will is necessary. I say, "I wish to be." With "I," I open to this force that passes through my head, through my thought; with "wish," I experience a strong feeling that allows the energy to pass in the body; with "to be," I sense myself as a whole. And I feel that there is a Presence in me.

More and more I realize I need will, a wish to be that comes from deeper in myself, a force that gives me a sense of existing. This shows me my true place and awakens me to an order, to a relation, that will otherwise not appear.

104. *Obedience and will*

Two opposite poles act on my Presence and communicate entirely different vibrations. I know their action by my sensation of them. I am sensitive to the attraction of the earth; I obey it. And I am sensitive to the attraction coming from higher spheres, and I also obey it. But I do not realize this; I am too passive. Here are two forces, two currents, two densities without a relation with each other. In order for the higher force to be absorbed and influence the heavier matter, there must be a current of intermediate intensity, another voltage that could galvanize the whole. This would be a purer emotional current in which the material of my usual subjective emotions does not enter. This current appears when I awaken to the vision of these two forces acting at the same time. As soon as I awaken to this vision, I am seized by a will, a wish that is the essence of the feeling of "I" in all its purity. It is the will to be what I am, awakening to my true nature—"I Am."

Today something is open that calls me toward a relation with the higher, but this does not come about by itself. I feel I have to obey a higher energy, an authority, which I recognize as the sole authority because I am a particle of it. And I need to serve it in order not to lose my relation with it. There are two kinds of obedience. If I try to obey in my passive state, unconsciously, I lose myself and cannot serve. But if I come to a more active state, I can voluntarily obey in submitting. This requires a state of conscious passivity in which only the attention is active and the functions are intentionally maintained in a passive state. I have to silence all my usual activity, disengaging and quieting my thought, emotion and sensation. My attention, now voluntary, can then be turned toward knowing "what is" and what "I am," knowing how much I am true. Only a voluntary force can liberate me from the power of an involuntary force. All the parts of myself are related in a total attention that leaves nothing outside its look. In the act of being present, I voluntarily obey and submit, renouncing my own will and at the same time asserting a different will over the functions.

The first sign of obedience to something greater is conscious sensation. And I can have a conscious sensation only if I am voluntarily passive. When I feel my insufficiency, when I feel the lack, I see the need for change and suffer a hunger, a need to be nourished. My thought is called toward a deep sensation, which awakens a feeling. But this feeling is weak, and I am afraid. I do not yet believe it, and the feeling disappears. The ego reasserts itself and everything disperses. I need to see that to begin again requires humility, sincerity. I must look again for a deep sensation. I obey either the current that brings me force or the one that takes it away. If the attention is not placed consciously on something, it must be taken. This is a law from which I cannot escape. It is no longer enough that two energies are turned toward each other. There must be a movement toward one another that is active enough to provoke a new inner movement that calls the feeling.

I begin to see that my whole struggle, my possibility or impossibility, is a question of attention. One force calls my attention in order to act on me, and another force takes it and disperses it through my functions. But there is no one present in the middle to know what I want, nobody who feels responsible. The sensation of lack, of what is truly missing, is the most important thing. I alone can resolve the question . . . if I *will*.

105. *Developing conscious force*

Real observation of oneself is the function of the master. As we are, we have a limited capacity of attention, only that of the body, the head or the feeling. With the will of man number one, two or three, using all our concentration, we can control only one center. We cannot obey voluntarily, consciously. Nevertheless, we can make an effort of self-observation, a practice that strengthens the attention and shows us how better to concentrate. We can begin to remember ourselves and, if we work conscientiously, see what is needed.

For us, there is the possibility of two kinds of actions: those that are automatic and those taken voluntarily, according to "wish." To wish, to will, is the most important and powerful thing in the world because it allows us to take an action that is not automatic. We can, for example, choose something we wish to do, something we are not ordinarily capable of, and make it our aim, letting nothing interfere. It is our sole aim. If we *wish*, if we *will*, we can do it. Without will, we cannot. With conscious will, everything can be obtained.

I need to develop a voluntary attention—that is, a conscious attention—which is stronger than my automatism. I must feel the lack of relation between my mind and my body, and see that this relation requires a voluntary attention maintained on both parts. It calls for a will that is not my usual will, one that comes from a new and unknown feeling. Only a conscious attention, which is the opening to a higher force, has the power to prevail over the automatism. But for this the attention must always be occupied voluntarily. A conscious force cannot be automatic. The attention can be stronger or diminish, but the moment it ceases to be voluntary, it is taken. The moment it is no longer voluntarily turned toward this relation, the energies separate. I become fragmented and the automatism again takes over. The opening to a higher force must become constant.

In order for the conscious force to develop, I have to maintain a continual sensation in all activities of my daily life—in walking, in speaking, in every kind of work. It is an attitude in which the attention is active and the body consciously passive. My attention needs to be wholly occupied with two things: feeling and following the sensation of Presence, and, at the same time, dismissing the associations, that is, not allowing them to take me. I have the sensation and feeling of my Presence. My attention is on this sensation. And the thought is wholly engaged in watching what I am experiencing, with no possibility of representing anything by words or images. The seeing is the most important thing, a higher force maintaining the relation and allowing the energy to concentrate. The body feels the quality of this force, its master, and refuses its automatic manifestation. It submits in order to receive the action of this force and let it intensify. There is a struggle: one energy must take authority, the other accept it. Everything that is usually dispersed concentrates. An atmosphere collects by itself. There is a definite sensation and at a certain moment I feel animated by a new energy, a feeling of being.

X

A PRESENCE WITH ITS OWN LIFE

We can know God only through sensation. Pure sensation is the name of God—pure, burning sensation.

A relation between the three lower centers is absolutely necessary for opening to a new energy.

I begin to feel this Presence almost like another body.

To stay in front is voluntary suffering.

I awake in order to be whole, to become conscious with a will to be.

I create a struggle between the "yes" and the "no" for my being. Only at this moment does the work begin.

A conscious man no longer suffers—in consciousness one is happy. But suffering thus prepared is indispensable for transformation.

A PURE ENERGY

 106. A particle of the highest

We live in two worlds. The reaction of our functions to impressions is our contact with the world below. Our perception of the fine energy in us represents the contact with the world above. We are also inhabited by two simultaneous but opposite movements—one toward the outside, the other toward the inside. In our organism, certain cells multiply in order to create and maintain the body. Others, germinating, contract and concentrate, saving energy for later creation. In manifesting in life we believe that we are creating, but real creation takes place through drawing in, through absorption. The role of our Presence is in connecting the two worlds.

There is a life force in me that I do not feel, do not hear, do not serve. All my energy is constantly called outside by thoughts and desires, aimed only at satisfying my avidity. When I see this useless expenditure, I feel the need for greater tranquillity, for a state of stillness in which I awaken to a pure, free energy in me. I need to come to a different inner density, a different quality of vibrations. This is, in fact, a spiritualization in which the spirit penetrates matter and transforms it. I must have a strong and deep experience of passing from one materiality to another. My sensation becomes more and more subtle as the attention purifies and concentrates, penetrating the body and permeating everything that surrounds me. There is no other way. For this I learn to come to solitude in which this internalizing, this concentration, is possible.

In order to know this subtle sensation, I assume a right posture and find an attitude in which the body and mind become one. My mind is lucid, clear at each moment, entirely attentive. A movement of deep abandon, a letting go, takes place, a door opening toward inner freedom. I learn what tranquillity is, and that it can only be attained through sensation, which becomes finer as tensions are reabsorbed. The sensation is subtle and penetrating only where there is no tension. This is a layer in me, beyond mental forms, that is never reached by my usual consciousness. I feel it as a void, an unknown essence, empty of my ego. The fineness of vibrations in what I perceive as emptiness is beyond what I know of my usual density, the usual form of my being.

In this state my thought and feeling include the forms. My thought, immobile and without words, is capable of containing words and images. My feeling, the feeling of my essence and not of my form, is able to contain the form. Knowledge of what is true appears by inclusion. My thinking remains free in order to penetrate, not reacting or choosing, without clinging to security. In front of the necessity to see, my ego ceases to affirm at all costs its identity, its form. It gives way to the feeling of essence, to the will to be *what I am,* which depends on neither form nor time. I have an impression of an expansion taking place well beyond the limits of my body. I do not lose the sense of my body, and even have the impression of containing it. There is a sensation of a very special energy, which I feel is life itself. My mind is still, embracing the whole. I can experience this so long as this seeing is the need of my whole being. If I give myself to it, this energy could be the beginning of a new order in me.

I am a particle of the highest. Through sensation I can know this. We can know God only through sensation. Pure sensation is the name of God—pure, burning sensation. The body is the instrument for experiencing this.

107. *Feeling this Presence as alive*

Our separate centers of energy receive impressions and respond from material previously recorded. Each center responds from its own point of view. Each has energy of a certain quality and can only know what corresponds to it. But there is in us an energy of a much higher quality than that of these centers. This reality cannot be perceived by them separately. They are too passive. In order to open and be permeable to this higher quality, they have to unite and become more active so that their vibrations intensify. The work is to increase the intensity of the lower centers in order to allow a contact with the higher centers.

When I come to a quiet state, free of all tension, I discover a very fine vibration, a reality I could not perceive before. It comes from another level to which I am usually closed, from a higher center that cannot come into play unless the other centers let go, become quiet. I can be related to the highest energy if I accept voluntarily opening to it. But this opening is difficult. The state, the level of energy of my thought and my body, does not allow it. The thinking remains captive to its own material, and its automatic movement cannot stop. The body is not touched enough. The ordinary "I," keeping its force, does not permit the relation with the higher energy. It is as though the energy were not here. For the relation to appear, suffering is necessary. Through suffering the attention becomes voluntary, and the intensity of its will can produce an opening of the body to the finer energy. Everything depends on this opening. Then a force from above, from another part of the mind, can act. . . . My state is transformed.

I need to understand that a relation between the three lower centers is absolutely necessary for opening to a new energy. The opening can be sustained only if the relation is stable. This energy needs to become a Presence. I have to feel it as alive, with its own density, its own rhythm, a Presence that has a separate life that I need to preserve. The sensation of it cannot be held too tight or it will lose its sense, and it cannot be too subtle because then, as I am today, I will be unable to attune myself to it. This energy has to fill the whole of my body. And I must have the impression that it is from this energy that I move. Everything has to be subordinated to it. I must let it take over.

In opening to this new energy, I experience an inner order in which this Presence, experienced as a whole, can see all the parts. It can act through them, provided my attention remains active with the same intensity everywhere. This inner order requires a total attention. The new current of energy, which all the rest must obey, needs to take on force and become permanent. The connection between my inner Presence and my body is the connection between this Presence and life.

108. *From a higher part of the mind*

There is an energy that comes from a higher part of the mind, but we are not open to it. It is a conscious force. It needs to appear, to pass in our body, to act on us. It cannot pass in us or act on us today because there is no relation between the mind and the body. When I am subject to the automatism, there is too great a difference in vibrations between higher and lower. The attention, which is part of this force, needs to be developed.

I am sitting here, now. From where could I try to have a relation with my body? From where could I see the way I am? . . . It is from a part of my mind to which I am not open. To relate to my body, I have to open my mind, quiet my mind. It must not think about all sorts of things. It has to remain motionless in the stop between two thoughts until it becomes more sensitive and perceptive, more alive than what is seen, what is under its look. When my attention is more active, my thinking is freer and I begin *to see*. This seeing is a direct contact with the higher energy in me. Another intelligence appears, and a relation with my body becomes possible.

This force coming from a higher part of the mind needs to pass in the body and find a place that is free in order to act on the other centers. There must be room so that a vibration can be produced. The slightest tension makes it impossible. In order to receive this life in me, I must have a state with no tension . . . nowhere. I become still. And when real stillness is possible, I can be open to an energy that fills the body. All trace of limitation disappears. I feel light, as though transparent. My Presence seems more alive than my body, more intense in vibrations. One force needs to take authority, the other to accept it.

Even when a relation appears between the mind and the body, it is not enough. It does not last. For a moment the relation is here and then . . . an instant later, the two parts are not together. So, there is something more that is necessary. A force needs to be developed, a conscious attention that can last. This depends on me. Either I can abandon the effort or, if I wish, if I will, I can be more attentive. I am responsible. My responsibility is precisely in the act of seeing.

109. *To become a vessel*

My attention is not free. It has no conscious direction. When I am in front of this, I feel it and I feel the need to open. Because I see it, I let go deeply and my body opens. My mind also. There is a movement of coming together. My attention increases. I allow the movement to take on force. Suddenly I feel a new energy appear, which comes from a much higher level and passes through me. I feel that I am the instrument through which it can act. Yet I do not let it act on me. I am too tense and I still want to act myself. At the same time, there is a wish to pass beyond the limits of my ordinary "I," to know myself animated by the life force in me. For this all my centers of energy must have no other aim than to become a single whole, united with this current coming from the higher centers. All the energy in me is then contained as in a closed circuit, not by an effort of constraint but through the relation of my different parts. I need first to become a vessel and later to know the channels by which this life passes in me.

In order for a force from above to be absorbed and influence the heavier matter in me, there must be a new circuit, one with a higher intensity capable of electrifying the whole. This requires a current of purer feeling, free from my usual subjective emotions, an intense state of attention that can appear only when I sincerely see that I do not know, that I really know *nothing*. When I recognize this and this state appears, my automatism slows down. For a second I see what it is hiding, and I see the automatism itself. I see the subjective circle within which my thoughts and feelings turn, and I see beyond it. I feel myself the center of a double movement: one movement of coming together which allows access to a purer force, and another of letting go in which this force can be absorbed. These two movements complement each other in the fluidity of life. There is a moment of greater stillness in which life makes me feel its action on me. Then, through my sensation, I perceive vibrations of another quality and penetrate a world of fine matter. This produces something like a magnetic field that reflects the energy needed for higher consciousness, bringing energy of a different emotional order.

The sense of my life today is to be entirely available to the immaterial Presence in me through a state in which I will be completely passive and yet very awake. This requires a balance between the intensity of presence and a greater and greater relaxation. It is as though I felt another body living in me. To come to this state, I need a right posture, an attitude in which I am grounded, maintaining an inner center of gravity. I have to open to this vital center where contact is made with the life force, to feel the wellspring from which this force naturally flows out and returns. The sensation of my Presence opens and expands freely when the energy descends and accumulates in the abdomen, but this sensation weakens when the energy, according to its tendency, disperses and rises again toward the solar plexus and the head. My center of gravity is the central point between a descending and an ascending movement. It is neither my heart nor my head, but it gives them such freedom that it allows a blending with the higher centers.

A right attitude also requires right breathing and a right tone of the muscles, in which the energy can circulate without constraint. When there is a balance between tension and letting go, I have the impression that the energy flows in channels that I did not know. Yet I feel that the movement of coming together is governed by a kind of respiration in which energies blend and are dissolved in the body.

A BODY OF ENERGY

⚜️   *110. This immaterial Presence in me*

What in us corresponds to the role of organic life for the earth? Special organs of perception, the higher parts of the centers, receive a direct impression of a finer energy. This is perception beyond mechanical functioning, a more conscious perception. It requires the formation of a kind of net or filter that maintains within its mesh a substance that could be experienced as a second body. My Presence has to become like a second body in order to receive this finer energy and let it show through. For this I need to accumulate active elements that begin to live their own life, to create their own nature within the physical body, their own world and events.

I am here. I feel a need to see myself. My body needs to open to a force to which it is closed, a force that comes from above, from a little higher than my head. My thought does not allow me to open to it. My body also does not allow me to open. I see that my body needs a conscious state, a state of absolute unity. I take a very straight posture, and am aware of my whole body having the same energy everywhere. It is not the body that is important, it is this energy that fills it. The force has a greater intensity than the body if the body lets it act. The force comes from above my head and passes through my body if there is no tension. It passes down the back, between the legs and ascends again by the abdomen, the chest and the head. This is a force that has its own movement and needs to have its own life in me.

I then feel a movement of relation taking place. It is not I who does this, but I need to make room in order for the movement to proceed. It becomes stronger, quicker and I feel a transformation in me, the presence of an energy with its own life. My body becomes quiet in order to let the energy from above pass in and unite with it. This union creates a new force, more intense, a more intelligent energy. It forms something like an inner body, which is undone as soon as the relation is undone. Our work is to bring about this relation, and to stay vigilant in order to sustain it. To recognize the truth of this immaterial Presence in me, I need to be entirely, totally available to it.

I begin to feel this Presence almost like another body. I do not try to imagine it, but I do not reject this impression when it comes to me. This Presence may seem at first to be contained in my body and then, through an opening or expansion, as though it contains my body. In any case, I feel that it exists with its own functions. This other body has its own thought, not an associative thinking, but seeing. It has vision, a capacity to see, as one of its properties. Words, images and ideas appear, but are as though contained in the vision. Words are not of its nature. The vision is not affected by them; neither does it affect them. There is no tension. This other body has feeling, not emotions but a power of relation, of love. Emotions are nearby, ready to appear, but they are contained in this feeling. Emotions are not of its nature. It is not affected by them; neither does it affect them. I can experience the Presence in this way so long as the axis of my energies is maintained, so long as there is a center of gravity. The right sensation provides the key, a sensation that obeys this Presence whose law I wish to feel. It is the sensation of a quality, a fineness, which is like the birth of being. This second body is "I" in relation to my body.

111. *A mass of energy*

I wish to become conscious of my existence. If my attention is as usual, dispersed, I feel myself as a form, as matter, a person. When my attention becomes finer and my perception keener, I feel myself as a mass of energy in movement, a body of energy. Currents of moving particles pass through me, whose movement does not stop. I sense myself no longer as matter with a solid form, but as energy animated by vibrations that never cease.

I feel this energy as if it were magnetized, drawn toward unknown ends. I try to observe this attraction pulling in different directions. I feel that there is no current that is my thought, nor any current that is my feeling, or my sensation, my movement. There is no such thing as each person's thought, each person's feeling. Rather, there is a current of force maintained in a certain sphere by what attracts it and makes it gravitate there. It is necessary to pass beyond.

According to the sphere in which it is maintained, the thought is more pure or less pure. It is the same for the feeling. What holds my thought and my feeling in a particular sphere is the repeated contact with a certain order of ideas to which the thought submits, the hypnotic effect. My centers react to the least shock from the disordered vibrations invading my Presence. Without a relation with a more conscious force, the centers are prey to all the large and small shocks that shake them. If I am not related to an energy of a higher level, I am bound to be taken.

To know what "I Am," my whole being needs to quieten in an act of total attention. When there is no wave, no ripple on the surface, I can see if there is something real in the depths. Then I will see if there is a Presence like a second body, which I will know by its density, its own movement, which I will feel as distinct. I cannot act on it, but it can act on me. This Presence is as though independent of my body, but for now seems attached to it. Nothing in me—not my body, not my thought or my feeling—as yet recognizes it. The centers do not realize that a relation with it is not only possible but indispensable. In order to maintain a contact with this Presence, I must have a center of gravity that relates my ordinary "I" and my essential being. This sphere of force keeps me in balance and, by excluding conflicting influences, brings tranquillity. It gives power over the sexual energy and, in opening an inner door, allows it a new creative role.

This Presence, this body of another density, needs to have an action on me. I must have a close relation with it. For finer energy to penetrate and be absorbed, a kind of space must appear in which reactions do not arise, a zone of silence that allows this Presence, this second body, to expand with its subtle vibration. I need a circulation of energy that is free, that is stopped nowhere. I do not intervene. The energy is distributed according to an order beyond my understanding. This free circulation takes place through the breathing, which nourishes this Presence by the air, bringing active elements we are not aware of. This breathing is a participation in the forces of the universe. But it is not just any kind of breathing. It is very light and subtle . . . as if this Presence were breathing.

112. *An exercise for opening*

There is an exercise that Gurdjieff considered most important for opening to a different state of being. It is an exercise one cannot undertake without being prepared. And I am prepared only when I truly feel the necessity for it.

I like my body and will do everything to save it, to make it comfortable, to give it food, to anticipate its desires. I have not yet measured the strength of my attachment to it. I also like my thought, my mind, and will do all I can to maintain its continuity. I do not yet see how crucial it is for the thought to preserve this continuity, which is part of my idea of myself. But I can know my real nature only through feeling, through a feeling of participation, a movement of communication, of communion. It is not our body or mind, although each plays its role, but our feeling that is at issue in the immediate possibility of knowing what we are.

My work has brought me to recognize and to feel a Presence in myself. I am afraid of not knowing how to be in front of this. It poses a question to me, a question that I do not face. I do not know what attitude to have, and I cannot know in advance. It is the life of the question that can show me the way.

This exercise begins with the consciousness that I am here. I say to myself, "Lord, have mercy," each time with a sensation in the four limbs, successively—right arm, right leg, left leg, left arm. I do this three times, and rest for one or two breaths. Then I breathe consciously, saying "I Am": with "I," I take in the active elements of the air and mix them with the result obtained in the four limbs, and with "Am," I exhale and distribute this into the sexual region. I repeat this second step three times.

I then recover the result from the sexual region and send it to the spine, exhaling with "Am." I begin again the filling of the four limbs, remix with the active elements of air, recharge the sexual region, recover from the sexual region and send it to fill the solar plexus. And I do the same to fill the head. Then I feel the whole Presence "I Am" throughout the body.

I nourish this Presence by taking the active elements from inhaling and sending them into the legs and the abdomen, then in succession the chest, the right arm, the left arm and the head. I make an inner act of engagement, saying to myself, "I wish to be. I wish and I can be. I will do everything to make this last for a specific time. I will take all necessary measures to crystallize in myself this result for being. I will do everything to be."

113. The substance of "I"

Once again I recognize this substance, this force, crystallized in me by everything I truly live of this work. I feel it. This force is behind all my movements, like a subtle Presence. It could allow me to participate in life in another way and bring a different relation with other beings. But, even in feeling this force present in me, I do not respect it. I give nothing of myself to it. I wish for it, I ask its help, but I do not give what it needs to have its own life in me, its own form. My center of gravity has not changed.

If I wish to find in myself this "will to be," the will to hold this Presence as the very meaning of my life, I need to *see what I serve* . . . not think about it, believe it or desire it, but *see it* from moment to moment. For this I first need to establish a relation between my body and the material that Gurdjieff calls the "substance of 'I.'" This substance is scattered in the body. I practice recapturing it through the mind in order to let it melt and be dissolved in the whole organism, so that it is not fixed anywhere. I say "I" to myself, and it is as though I breathe in this material as I see it melt. Then I say "me," letting this more subtle substance spread evenly in the whole organism, so that a second body can be formed. I repeat this a number of times. In order to see that all the material is distributed evenly, I experience a look from above, a sense of "I" above the head. My body then seems a small thing among everything else, like a drop of water in a glass. I see especially that the "I" is really the intelligence, the master of "me," which is content to be under its look. To have two bodies is the greatest luxury.

When I become aware of the movement of breathing in and redistributing this fine material in me, I realize that I can, by my attitude, allow it to take shape according to pathways and centers of gravity particular to it. I become sensitive to feeling this attitude, and in practicing this I see that a very close relation is created between my body and this fine material. I can feel this substance of "I" in the body. It is of another order. But for now it is without its own force, powerless, without material. I need to have a more lasting awareness of it as a totality. Later, crystallized, it will have power over my manifestations.

The work has different stages. At this point, the formation of this new body, the astral body, is the basis for our work. After it has been formed, there will be another.

VOLUNTARY SUFFERING

🪶   *114. To stay in front*

How do we open to a higher level? When there remains even a residue of conceptual or intellectual meaning, there can be no pure awareness. The finest and highest energy I could know does not animate me. It is not here. I need to feel this, to feel that my force is taken and I cannot be transformed. I am not open to a higher level, a higher thinking. I have to suffer this lack, to stay resolutely in front of it. Little by little this will become more important than anything else. But it requires giving all of myself. And the ego always reasserts its dominance. To stay in front is voluntary suffering.

We need to reconsider the question of an inner attitude that could lead to transformation of our consciousness. What we are today no longer corresponds to what we were some years ago. What has changed? And what has not—what, in fact, has become even more fixed? The more real part of our being is hidden because it is beyond our usual consciousness. Nevertheless, we can see the force with which it insists on appearing in order to give a form to our lives. It is stronger or less strong, more accepted or less accepted, but this reality is a fact. And this fact means that we are no longer the same. Something has changed in us. But what has not changed is that we assume no responsibility in front of this reality. We have no conscious attitude in front of it, no way of being. We do not take our state seriously, and do not see the danger.

We are in front of a real question. There are two possibilities: on the one hand, contact and unity with the essential energy of our Being, and, on the other, the refusal of our ordinary "I," which is afraid of suffering and of being eliminated. In front of this situation we are cowardly. We postpone, we discuss, we complain, and we do not become independent. Nevertheless, we are at least ready to face this. We are at a turning point that offers us an opportunity. But it also presents peril, for nothing is easier, as we are, than to fail. My aspiration is stronger and stronger for this essential force. At the same time, I live with a continual concern for my own well-being, the desire to satisfy all the avidity of my ordinary "I." This contradiction leaves a taste of remorse.

I am not free. I am not available. Questioning this, I become aware of what, in my unconscious, refuses. Yet I must not oblige myself to be available, or discipline myself. It is not a question of failing or succeeding, but of seeing whether I wish to be open to this essential energy. This brings about a deep letting go in a right and natural way, and allows a certain freedom. I pass beyond the recriminations of my ordinary "I." My entire being depends on the feeling I have for this energy and my capacity to communicate it to all my centers. If they become integrated with it, a unity will be created that is maintained by their sharing the same life. This letting go is never assured and needs constantly to be verified. This movement comes not from a right of possession, but reflects an act of love.

My centers feel this energy, feel my attitude. I leave room, I allow a movement toward a unity that has its own balance, its own form. But the centers do not yet understand their purpose, what they must serve. In each part there always appears, underneath, the automatic habitual movement that draws the energy outside. I need to stay in front, to experience a confrontation between these two movements, which depends on the relating force of my attention. I am in front of a law. There is in me the possibility of a new state of being. But I know only its fluctuations because, even when I have an intimation of this reality and am touched by it, I do not truly appreciate it. I do not truly wish for this reality. I do not love it.

✍ 115. I must live the insufficiency

In order to have a contact with the higher centers, it is necessary to increase the intensity of the lower centers. Their vibrations have to intensify through seeing and suffering the lack, a conscious suffering. "Yes," we think to ourselves, "I know. My mind and my body must be together." But what does it mean? Do I feel, do I have a sensation of the energy that is in my mind, the energy that is in my body, the energy that is in my feeling? Can I see their movements? How do I understand the change that needs to take place in the centers?

Energies cannot remain isolated—either they are taken or they act. I cannot help but be taken if I am not related to an energy of a higher level. I need to be in contact with an energy whose quality frees my attention from the action of other energies. But the connection is difficult to establish. I am attached to all my actions. There is a feeling that has not appeared. I need a conscious relation that keeps me from being taken right and left, and a feeling that allows the relation to last. For this I must stay in front, I must live the insufficiency. Above all, I have to see that in this effort the intensity is never the same in the head and in the body. So the relation is never real.

Throughout the course of our work we encounter resistance in ourselves. At each moment there is negation of whatever is affirmed, sometimes with violence. Yet without this negation we might not have the possibility to evolve. Our energy would not be transformed. When, for example, energy is freed for a deeper sensation, there is a refusal that appears—doubt, fear, some negative emotion. And instead of helping to make the sensation stronger or more alive, the energy passes to the emotional and intellectual centers, which then vibrate in a coarse and brutal way. Without being transformed, the energy is projected in outer movements, in talk or actions that leave us weakened. Nevertheless, if at the moment the opposing force appears I see in what the negation consists, I can wish to stay between the two thresholds and, by a special effort, come to separate the elements that feed off this negative emotion. If my effort is sincere and if it is sufficient, a contact may be made with another kind of feeling, with another emotional current. For that I have to be present at the moment of friction. I have to live this without taking sides in order for a finer energy to be produced.

In trying to let this energy circulate freely in me, animate me— that is, be my master—I come to know the limits within which this is possible. I feel places, always the same, which are knots of contraction, where an attitude of my ego persists that I have great difficulty undoing. It is a grimace of my face, a stiffness of my neck, a smug movement in raising my head, or a turning away without accepting. I need to know these points where my refusal hides, where my ego protects itself and is not touched.

I suffer from my lack, my incapacity. I am closed, the passage is not free. I suffer this, that is, I stay in front, accepting the friction between the "yes" and the "no." I see the resistance, the passivity, and I see myself give up, abdicate my wish *to be*, in order to go toward sleep. I struggle to stay in front, not to prevail but to observe the constant changes in myself. With this staying, an energy of a higher quality develops, a more conscious attention. There is a constant demand for a conscious sensation. The thinking and the sensation intensify through the active force of this attention, which maintains a relation between them. A new feeling appears when the conditions of suffering are accepted, even wished for. I accept my powerlessness and I suffer. In this staying in front of my insufficiency, the energy intensifies and becomes an active force that obliges the passive force to obey.

116. Conscious struggle

We wish to be conscious of the inner Presence as a second body in us that must live its own life. It needs to have an action on our physical body and not be demolished as the body also lives its own life. For the moment, what is important is to let this energy grow in us, to take on force. We must feel that it needs a connection with a higher energy. The question is how to allow this new body to develop, how to absorb subtle vibrations until they saturate my Presence.

Our work is to be vigilant, to see what can sustain this body. This requires an attitude, consciously maintained, in which the largest part of my attention is held within, engaged in this desired penetration. This practice, which conserves energy, is an act of creation. The vision of what takes place in us is the most important thing. The result comes from this seeing and from the friction between opening to the unknown and the response of our functions. This is the beginning of a "crystallization," the formation of something indivisible, individual and permanent—will, consciousness, "I." I awake in order to be whole, to become conscious with a will *to be*.

The second body has as its substance a finer intelligence, a sensitivity. Like the physical body it requires food for its development. A struggle, a conscious confrontation, is necessary to call an energy that would not otherwise appear. When our attention is strongly concentrated in front of the various movements of our thinking, feeling and body, this produces a substance similar to electricity. It is necessary to accumulate this material for a second body to be formed. The way is long, but the substance can be created in us by conscious effort and voluntary suffering. The new body will then have a possibility of action on the physical body. What is important is the continual struggle between our head and our "animal," between our individuality and our functions, because we need the substance that this conscious confrontation produces. It requires effort again and again, and we must not be discouraged because the result of our work comes slowly.

There is in us naturally a permanent conflict between the psyche and the organic body. They have different natures—one wishes, the other does not wish. There is a confrontation that we must reinforce voluntarily by our work, by our will, so that a new possibility of being can be born. It is for this that we undertake a task, something precise that reinforces this struggle. For example, my organism has the habit of eating or sitting in a certain way. This is its conditioning, but I refuse to obey it. There is a struggle, a conscious voluntary struggle between a "yes" and a "no" that calls the third force, the "I" that is the master who can reconcile.

The body is an animal, the psyche a child. It is necessary to educate both, to put each in its place. I have to make the body understand that it must obey, not command. For this I must see what takes place in me. I must know myself. Then I can take a task that corresponds to my possibilities and exercise a conscious will. I create a struggle between the "yes" and the "no" for my being. Only at this moment does the work begin.

Our experience of suffering is never voluntary. It is mechanical, a reaction of the machine. What is voluntary is to place oneself in conditions that bring about suffering and to stay in front. A conscious man no longer suffers—in consciousness one is happy. But suffering thus prepared is indispensable for transformation.

XI

THE ESSENTIAL BEING

Our essential nature is immobility, the great force of life in which all movements appear.

I see the world beyond my form and, through this vision, I see the world of form.

The essential effort is always consciousness of "I." Everything is related to this—touching my essence.

Faith is the lived certitude of having gone beyond the limits of my ordinary "I."

In seeing my ego and the real "I," I liberate myself. This is the death of my ordinary "I."

The ordinary "I" is a phantom, a projection of my self. In fact, everything I take as manifestation is not something separate, but a projection of the essential.

Reality has no continuity. It is beyond time, outside duration.

RECOGNIZING A
FALSE ATTITUDE

117. Stages of work

Our essential nature is immobility, the great force of life in which all movements appear. Yet, at the same time, we are energy in movement, a continual movement that never stops. If our functions could be at rest—even for one, two or three seconds—we would come to a new knowledge of our true self.

Change in our being comes about through transformation of energy, a work that takes place in successive stages over time. First, there is a state of observation, of "critical watching," in which I become aware of a false attitude in myself. This is not a mental representation but an inner awareness of the body that reveals all the flaws of imbalance from the functioning of one center alone. Second, as the false is recognized and felt, there is a letting go of what impedes me. This is a state of "trust," the opposite of wanting "to do." It is a dissolving of what has become fixed, abandoning a way of thinking that transforms everything into an object. This means accepting what takes place without relying on any mental representation. The predominance of "I" shows in the body. The accent in my breathing passes from inhalation to exhalation.

The third stage is marked by becoming conscious of the essential Being. The form of "I" becomes permeable. Everything that was hardened is dissolved and reconstituted for the formation of the second body. In the fourth stage there is trust in the essential, admitting the formless without classifying or naming. This requires the courage to endure the state of no longer understanding, that is, to be under the radiance of Being and to stay there, taking the risk again and again of dropping my deeply rooted attitudes and convictions.

In transformation the question is not how to achieve a more open state but how to allow it. The energy is here. Our role is not to make this energy appear in us, to make it pass in us, but to let it pass in us. If I do not submit to its action, the passage will not take place. In fact, the more I "try," the more the way is blocked. Nothing gets through. The active force and the passive force are always present in us. What tries to be active—my thought, which always wants something—needs to remain passive. Then the attention is active. A feeling appears, a feeling that transforms everything because it allows a relation.

In me, in what I am, there is a Presence that is pure, a thought that is pure. It consists of innumerable waves, but in its nature it is pure, vast and without limits. It is wholly sufficient unto itself. The waves are simply waves, not the energy itself. It is I who produces them. If I see the waves and do not try to stop them, they will subside by themselves and not disturb me. They will become quiet, and I will feel the pure nature of my mind, my thought. The waves are one and the same as the energy, but I take them for something else, something they are not. The energy always has waves, always a movement. But both the wave and the energy are in reality the same. What is important is to know the energy itself, the pure energy. If I were truly present, there would be no waves, no movements in me.

118. A flagrant contradiction

We are not what we believe ourselves to be. I always say that I seek, but in reality I am sought. I do not know this enough. Something I could believe in is missing, something absolutely true that would be like new knowledge, a force that would prevail over my inertia.

I need to have a force in me coming from a higher level of the cosmos. It must become part of what I am. It should emanate and radiate in me. But the state of my being, my consciousness, does not allow me to feel it. I am separated from reality by the mirage of my reaction at the moment of receiving an impression. This prevents me from remaining open to the totality of what I am perceiving. There are always words, subjective emotions and tensions, and this movement does not stop. I do not know this movement and cannot rightly evaluate it, and so a new order, a sign of my transformation, does not appear. I have a way of taking myself as an object, always thinking of "me," always with a complaint. This way of being preoccupied with myself is false and can teach me nothing.

I wish to be conscious of what I am, who I am, and I see myself respond: "I am here. It is I." At the same time, I feel this is not true, it is not really "I." Yet this is the way I think. And when I say "I," I feel myself as the center of everything. I affirm myself. Things only exist in relation to me: I like them, I do not like them; this is good for me, that is bad for me. I am separate, distinct from everything. Even my wish to know myself can come from this self-centered attitude, from my ordinary "I." I am always ready to defend and support this "I," this center of gravity which, deep down, is not really what I am. Alongside the affirmation of this "I," there is something that does not affirm, that does not demand—something that *is*. At each moment of affirmation I refuse myself and I refuse others.

We are not what we believe ourselves to be. There is in us an essential impulse toward consciousness that comes from an innate need to realize the totality of our being, a wish leading toward the transformation of ourselves. We know this wish is in us, and at certain moments we are touched by it. But it is still not a fact for us, and our self-centered consciousness is not transformed. In fact, we are exactly like all those around us whom we find petty, stupid, mean, envious and so on. Like them, we are not aware of the impulses that move us and create the current in which we live. We continue to compare ourselves with others and believe in our superiority, hiding behind ideas

and hopes. But we do not want to see this. We believe that we will succeed in knowing what is beyond our habitual state without taking into
account what prevents us, without even understanding the fabric of
our thoughts, feelings and actions. This creates in us a certain hypoc-
risy. We have not yet seen the flagrant contradiction between our
wish for a larger consciousness and the impulses driving our habitual
behavior. We have not accepted that in order to find the truth, we
have to understand the source of our thought and our action—the
ordinary "I."

We always hope that something will come about all by itself, but
transformation takes place only if, little by little, I give myself to it entirely. We have to pay with the effort of self-remembering and the effort of self-observation, giving up the lie of believing in ourselves for a
moment of reality. This will bring a new attitude toward ourselves.
The most difficult thing is to learn how to pay. We receive exactly as
much as we pay. In order to feel the authority of a subtle Presence, we
have to pass beyond the wall of our ego, the wall of our mental reactions from which springs the notion of "I." It is necessary to pay. Without paying, we have nothing.

119. The affirmation of myself

The movement of energy in us is continuous. It never stops. Rather it
passes through phases of intense projection which we call tension, and
phases of returning to oneself which we call letting go, relaxing. There
cannot be continuous tension and there cannot be continuous relaxation. These two aspects are the very life of the movement of energy,
the expression of our life. From its source in us, energy is projected
outward through the channel of our functions toward an aim. In this
movement the functions create a kind of center that we call "I," and we
believe that this projecting outward is the affirmation of our self. This
"I," around which our thoughts and emotions revolve, cannot let go. It
lives in tension, is nourished by tensions.

This ordinary "I," our ego, is always preoccupied with what pleases or displeases it—what *"I"* like or what *"I"* dislike—in a perpetual closing that becomes fixed. It desires, fights, defends itself, compares and judges all the time. It wants to be the first, to be admired and to make its force, its power, felt. This *"I"* is a center of possession in which all the experiences inscribed in our memory are accumulated. And it is from this center that I wish "to do"—to change, to have more, to improve. I want to become this, to acquire that. This *"I"* always wants to possess more. With ambition, avidity, it always has to become something better. Why does the *"I"* have this exaggerated need to be something, to make sure of it, and to express this at every moment? It has a fear of being nothing. Is not identification, at its core, based on fear?

This *"I"* constantly seeks to establish permanence, to find security. So we identify with all kinds of knowledge and belief. The experience of identifying is all that we know, all that we value. But we will not achieve permanence by identification. This process can only lead to conflict because of the limitations of our thinking mind. It deals only with form in time, with something finite. This mind cannot imagine something beyond—in the realm of *what is*—and it cannot bring anything new. Yet real security does not come by escaping from this mind. It is possible only when the thinking is truly quiet, when the accumulating action of ambition and desire comes to an end.

In order to see *what is*, I have to recognize that my state cannot be permanent. It changes from moment to moment. This state of impermanence is my truth. I must not seek to avoid it or place my hope in a rigidity that seems to help. I have to live, to experience this state of impermanence, and proceed from there. For this, I have to listen. Yet if I only listen to what I wish to hear, I will never be free. I have to listen to whatever appears, and in order to really listen, I must not resist. This act of listening, of being present, is a true liberation. I am aware of my reactions to everything that takes place in me. I cannot avoid reacting, but for reactions not to stop me, I must be able to go beyond them. I have to continue until I see that it is everything I know that keeps me from approaching the real, the unknown. I must feel all the conditioning of the known in order to be free from it. Then my search for silence, for tranquillity, will be a quest not for security, but for free-dom to receive the unknown.

When the mind is freer and truly quiet, there is a sense of insecu-rity, but within it there is complete security because the ordinary "I" is absent. My mind is no longer moved by the wish "to do" on the part of my "I," by its demands, by its ambitions, even for my own inner growth. In this tranquillity all the responses, reactions and move-ments of this "I" are left behind. My mind is at rest, stilled by the vision of *what is*. An order is established that I cannot institute myself but to which I need actively to submit. I feel a kind of respect, and suddenly I see that it is trust. I have confidence in this order, in this law, more than in myself. I entrust myself to it with my whole being.

120. My attitude expresses what I am

There are in us two different centers of gravity around which we re-volve. Our ordinary "I" is always responding to defend its existence. The other center is the real substance that we are, the reality that seeks to appear in us and be expressed through us. One cannot exist without the other. They need each other. How can there be a relation between them? What attitude on my part would allow a new unity to appear?

I need to watch in order to see that my attitude is false. My ordi-nary "I" tenses, even if I merely hope for consciousness to appear. So I need to trust this other center of my being, this core that needs me. I believe that I trust it, that I am not relying on my ordinary "I," which can "do" something. Yet even the way in which I trust reflects a "do-ing." It is not that this "I" is in itself bad, but that it turns away from what is beyond it. I need to see this until it brings me a shock.

The way I am in my body can either signify distortion or reflect an inner form that develops in a right way when there is no forcing. The authenticity of what I am is expressed by the combination of the atti-tude of my body, the quality and relation of tension and letting go, and the breathing that takes place in me. It is something I need to experi-ence constantly. For this I need to watch. If I watch, I can glimpse the movement of concentration of my energy in my head or solar plexus, which upsets the balance of unity in me. I feel wrongly situated in myself. This is a moment of becoming conscious of a false attitude. Then I need to feel strongly what a right attitude would be, with a new center of gravity. I need to have a real impression of it, so that afterward I will wish to find it again. If I become sensitive to this center of my essence, I will see that right away a letting go takes place. It takes place at the same time as the right attitude appears. Can I trust it? Can I stay and not intervene?

It is in my attitude that I express what I am, here, at this moment. My ordinary "I' expresses itself through constant tension in the body above the waist. This is a habitual form that I trust but one in which the reality of what I am cannot appear. I can only see this false attitude when the chaotic movements of my thoughts and feelings come to a stop. In this stop a space appears . . . silence. I feel alive . . . more alive. I am conscious of being here, of existing, fully and completely. This awareness goes beyond and contains everything. It includes my body, without which it would not be possible. My body is like a mirror reflecting the light. I see the world beyond my form and, through this vision, I see the world of form. I feel a wish *to be*, a consciousness, which brings me to the heart of these two realities and allows them to play their role. There is a sense of a real "I," of "I Am," and my ordinary "I" no longer turns away, no longer fears being annihilated. It knows why it is here. It has found its place, its purpose.

A REALITY IN ME

121. A wholly different vibration

Forces from all worlds pass through me, from the lowest to the highest, the most pure. And I do not know it. I do not feel them, I do not serve them. For this to be possible, the barriers that separate me from my essential being must fall, and I have to become conscious of myself as a whole.

There is in me a sense of insufficiency, of dissatisfaction that is not understood. It sets in without any real questioning about its source, and without the feeling of self being engaged. Instead of a perception of the real fact, which could call a new attention, there is a reaction. My mind remains passive, judging, demanding what it does not bring itself. I do not understand either the nature of the dissatisfaction or the nature of the reaction. The reaction is not put in doubt, and my feeling does not change. It cannot change because the being, my being, is not concerned as a whole. And this dissatisfaction, which in fact reflects the need of consciousness to grow, is appropriated by the ego.

When I am touched by an event on a larger scale, I realize that there is a reality beyond the reach of my habitual way of being, an elusive energy beyond my known tension and relaxation. I see that I vacillate between tensions of all kinds and the relaxation, voluntary and involuntary, that follows them. Yet I never see the tension—intellectual, emotional or physical—in the moment itself as tension. I see only the result: the word, the image, the form it produces, the emotion in reacting for or against. The tension itself, the movement of energy, I do not see, and so I am subject to it. Since tension and relaxation make up what we call our life, giving us the impression of living, we are avidly attached to them. It seems that everything would collapse without them. But these movements hide something more real, something that I do not see because my attention is caught. How can I know this?

When our attention is placed on ourselves, we become aware of tensions within our whole body, which we feel as a hardening of matter. Yet they could be felt as vibrations of different kinds, each having its own speed, its own density, its own sound. A movement, a tension, could be felt as sound or as light, producing a current that is more magnetic or less magnetic. These vibrations are chaotic and keep our attention dispersed, in the dark. I feel myself taken by them, unable to disengage. Nevertheless, from behind the chaos, I may feel the action of a vibration that is wholly different in its intensity. This vibration is more subtle, and it is difficult to attune the slower vibrations that hold me back, which are too incoherent. But there is something that responds. I feel an influence more luminous, more intelligent than my usual awareness. And I feel a wish to obey this influence, to serve it. In order to attune myself, I become more sensitive. Now my tensions seem useless, even bothersome, and fall away by themselves. I become permeable, as though each and all the parts of me were attuned to the wavelength of this subtle vibration.

The essential effort is always consciousness of "I." Everything is related to this—touching my essence. What contains the energy is temporary. The energy is permanent. I recognize this in stillness when, with a pure attention, a kind of sixth sense, I disengage myself from associations and reactions that distort my vision of the real. I need a conscious attitude, an impulse coming from all three centers, in order to touch my essence, the current of life in me. At this point, I see my reaction in receiving an impression and I am not wholly lost in it. This experience is what could be stable, forming a new center of gravity in me. It is here that I need to hold myself. Here is the only work, an engagement from which can be born the substance that becomes the material of the second body.

122. Sincerity

To know myself is not an idea, not a hope, nor a duty. It is an irresistible feeling, yet I do not know in advance where it is leading. I wish to find something that is truly me. I open to questioning. I see that my thinking is full of itself and knows only its own activity. But seeing this frees me from the thought, frees the energy. I can see, and I feel the wish *to be*.

In order to approach the threshold of reality, the unknown, I need uncompromising sincerity. Everything I know is known through the conditioning of my thinking mind. In order to know my true nature, I have to pass beyond the activity of the mind. This does not mean to deny it, to wish to change it or to oppose it. Rather, I have to understand its functioning and see how it conditions me. Then there is an acceptance, with a certain clarity and peace, and an attitude that allows my first contact with the unknown. My mind itself is seen as part of the unknown, and the knowing that constitutes its functioning, its way of bringing its memory, appears in another light. I see that, in seeking security in the mind, I lose myself in it, I give myself to it. If I wish to know myself, I have to see this conditioning at each moment and not be fooled by it.

A time may come when I see that I do not know, when my mind is emptied of the contents of memory—I do not know what I am beyond my usual consciousness, and I have nothing in me that could know. So long as I have not lived this fact, the experience I have of myself remains superficial. My sensation belongs to the state maintained by the known, which does not allow me to penetrate the deeper layers of myself, unknown to my usual consciousness.

My different centers will be related not by forcing but by understanding in the very moment their lack of relation and the limitation that this implies. It is possible to become more aware of the sensation and, through letting go, to have a deeper impression of the energy in me. But I see that my thought does not really blend with my sensation. On the contrary, the sensation becomes completely disengaged from the thought. A kind of contradiction arises between these two centers, and the more I try, the greater it becomes. I feel the lack of something essential, something intimate, that would reveal a new understanding. How can I evaluate this condition in which I find myself—get to the bottom of it?

The meaning of sincerity appears in the questioning itself, in facing the problem. At the moment the question arises there is a call to feeling, which appears in the form of sincerity. The demand here is for uncompromising sincerity. Without sincerity I will not know. The more I face the real fact, the more I stay in front, the more my emotion is purified. I *am* sincere. My emotion blends with the thought and the sensation, and I feel myself different, unified. This is a transformation of my state beyond the state of my ordinary "I," an abdication of my own will to correspond to the will of the void. In this voluntary passivity I live my transformation, passing from one density to another.

The wish for uncompromising sincerity makes me sensitive to listen to myself, and leads me to the threshold where I could pass from my ordinary awareness to a wider consciousness. When my sincerity is tested, the feeling of myself is put in question. Around what does it revolve? I wish to leave the realm of my thoughts and emotions in order to be attentive to something more true. When I approach the threshold of an unknown reality, I observe the impulses—the thoughts and desires—that drive my actions. There is a new attitude, a new way of being. But this is not something that is assured. I find it only at the precise moment when I have a burning need for sincerity.

123. Faith

Today I ask myself the question: Do I have faith in something? When is it that I feel faith, and when does doubt appear? Between faith and doubt there is a continual movement back and forth, but I am unable to hold this under my look or understand it. What is missing?

My thoughts and my emotions, coming one after another, have a meaning and purpose, but I cannot discover it. They are just a part, a small part of my Presence. Behind them there is a life force that they hide from me. When these thoughts and emotions appear, I submit to them as though they were essential. But they are not the essential. To accept this theoretically is one thing, but to live it, to actually experience it, is something else. Through a single part I can never feel the whole. Yet if I understand the whole, the place and importance of the part become clear. I know why it is here. So my mind, my thinking, needs to see the whole. As long as I am taken by partial movements, stopped by them, my vision will remain false. I need to feel the whole in order to know truth, reality.

It is necessary to experience and recognize in myself a reality that is almost impossible to grasp but which nonetheless I cannot doubt. It must appear more real than everything I think I know of myself as essential. It is at this moment that faith is touched in me. This is not a faith that has been instilled, not a belief in an ideal. It is a moment of actually recognizing that I have lived something beyond the perception of my senses, and that I have known it through a feeling beyond my usual feeling of myself. At the same time, faith is not at my disposal. I feel something in me demanding to be recognized, not because I think it but because, wishing to listen, I feel its action on me. When I simply think of me, I never receive the impression of myself in this way, because to receive it requires more than my thought alone. Yet this impression is exactly what I need most. This is what brings faith— the lived certitude of having gone beyond the limits of my ordinary "I."

Is this possible for me? If I enter into the experience, I see right away that I expect something from it. But there is nothing to expect— everything is here. Nevertheless, I continue to expect. I expect a sensation, that is, something I know through my body. I believe that my thinking and my body must do something. When I realize this, suddenly I see this approach is false and I feel freer. A moment ago it seemed that on one side there was my body and on the other, an energy. Now, because I am no longer thinking with words, my thought does not go to one or the other, and my attention can include the whole. This gives me an impression of extraordinary fullness, an impression of life.

Unfortunately, thoughts and words reappear. I again doubt. I no longer understand, no longer know. Yet I wish to understand.

> *That I am seated, I know.*
> *That I have a body, I know.*
> *That I have a Presence, I know.*
> *That I am a particle of life, I know.*

This faith acts on me. I listen to it.

Faith cannot be transmitted. Not even an atom can be given by one being to another. It comes from understanding.

124. *Remorse of conscience*

On the way toward inner rebirth, it is the true feeling of love that enables one to cross the second threshold. But before pure feeling can appear, one has to pass through faith and, from a force nourished by hope, acquire discernment. For this it is necessary to have a renewal of intelligence and a knowledge that reinstates an order of values in which personality submits to the real "I."

To believe, to hope, to love are all indispensable for evolution of being. But they can be lived only if, at the same time, voluntary suffering allows true, higher feeling to appear. It is necessary to feel remorse of conscience. The voluntary effort is to prepare conditions and stay in front of my inadequacy—to suffer my insufficiency. In this way a will develops that would not otherwise be produced, and a feeling arises that is not a reaction. When one is touched by a higher force, the experience of suffering is not the same.

In moments of inadequacy, unable to approach the reality of myself,

I feel behind all my manifestations a constant suffering, as if something precious were missing. It is a sign. Until now my awareness has not been true consciousness. I have been living only with my ordinary functions. Now I know I can go further, I can reach a deeper level in myself. And at certain moments I succeed in touching my essence, as though feeling a new center of gravity. This essence is like a newborn child that I have to nourish and strengthen. It is here that I need to concentrate, to hold myself in my work.

More and more I feel a need for the spiritual in me, for spirit to penetrate and transform me. Yet the passage is not free. I remain on the surface of myself, conditioned by an inner lack of relation. Even if I have a strong feeling, I am always on the surface. So long as I do not face this, I cannot penetrate deeper in myself. But when I see and feel it, a kind of suffering arises, a feeling of lack, of insufficiency. Do I accept being in front of this insufficiency, or do I in fact refuse? The suffering is not from my attachment to the idea of myself, my self-love, nor from some failure in the past. It is a suffering from my own indifference, my incapacity, from how I am living now. I need to feel remorse of conscience so that I have a vision of this insufficiency, a clear seeing of the lack.

My deep wish is to submit entirely to an inner voice, the feeling of the divine, of the sacred in me. I know that a higher energy—what religions call God or Lord—is within me. It will appear if the mind and the body are truly related. God is here when two forces are opposed and a third unites them. We can ask for help in order to unite these forces in us. We can say, "Lord, have mercy," in order *to Be*.

THE EMERGENCE OF "I"

✎ *125. The extraordinary impression of existing*

I need truly to recognize in myself two states of being. I have to see the difference between a state in which it is my ego that acts and another state where the whole of me acts, in which I feel that I am whole. I see more and more that everything I believe I know comes from my thinking, even what I take as sensations. It is all simply a projection of my thought. But behind this there is another "I" that is beyond the thinking, the feeling and the body. I begin to know that this "I" exists, that there is a separate principle of consciousness—pure thinking—which sees and observes the ordinary "I."

In my search for consciousness, the ego, this ordinary "I," could be the pivot of my efforts if it consented to serve rather than be the master. But this is impossible when my different parts act separately and independently, without taking account of the whole. So, instead of serving and helping my development, my ego swells and bars the way.

Who am I? It is impossible to answer. I see I am not my body. I let it become passive. I am not my ordinary thinking. It, too, becomes passive. In the face of this questioning, I see I am not my egotistic feeling, which also becomes passive. Who am I? There is a letting go, a relaxation, which becomes deeper and deeper. I let go, not in order to obtain something. I let go out of humility because I begin to see that by myself

I am nothing, and at the heart of this humility a trust, a kind of faith, appears. In this moment I am tranquil. I am at peace.

In this deeper letting go, I open to the vital center of my force in the abdomen, and a relation appears between the energies of my different functions. This contact makes me feel that the totality of my being is secure. Everything is integrated, everything in its place. I feel I am part of an order that is right and involves me as a whole. My body is at rest, not straining in any direction. There is a continuous movement of letting go downward toward this center of gravity. From here the energy goes out as I engage in life and returns as I come back to myself. In this movement of deep letting go, I have the impression of an energy that has been freed, liberated without effort, without my doing anything. This happens as a result. Neither my thought nor my emotion can take charge of this energy. It does not belong to them. It is a transcendental force that acts as long as I obey it. If I accept and do not resist the experience by trying to direct it, this energy will transform me. I need to live it and obey it consciously. This movement is the movement of my being.

When my body comes to a state where there is no longer any tension, I feel the fineness of the sensation of stillness. It is like the birth of being. And I feel the fineness of the thought, which reaches a level where it penetrates and registers everything that takes place. I come to the extraordinary impression of existing. And when I am quiet in this way, immobile, totally without tension, I feel that my breathing has an importance that I never give it, a great importance. It is by this act that I participate in life, an act greater than myself. I exist in this movement, a living movement in which I am included. It is not my body that breathes. It is "I" who breathes.

126. The death of my ordinary "I"

I remember myself in the moment when I do not see myself as an object, when consciousness leaves no room for division. It is the moment when, feeling consciousness, I feel I am consciousness. I feel "I." Remembering oneself is the emotional shock that occurs when all the energies in us come into contact. This emits a creative vibration that is immediately subject to the Law of Seven. So, remembering oneself cannot remain static.

In my habitual state my experience is vague and nebulous. Thoughts, waves of emotions and tensions arise. The thoughts do not come all at once; they arrive one after the other. It is the same with the emotions. When one thought has passed, another arises. But between the two there is an interval, a stop, a space that is extremely important. Behind the movement that has begun and finished, there is a reality that is hidden from me. In this interval I can become aware of what is behind the movement. No thought lasts; what appears must disappear. The disappearing is as important as the appearing. It is part of the same fact. And if I can live the two, accept them both, I am beyond the appearance and the disappearance. I contain them. In this moment, my centers enter into relation with each other, a relation that comes by itself.

Opening to our essential being, the higher centers, requires a state of unity. But, in our usual state, our center of gravity is always refused in favor of the ego and displaced toward the upper part of the body. This cuts us off from our true form. The separation from our essential nature brings suffering. When it is strong, this suffering brings an opening that allows a coming together toward unity. There must be a decision, a determination to follow the way through which our essential being is calling us. This requires a perpetual contact with this essential being if we are to become able to serve and express a force that transcends us. We need to die to one level—as ego—in order to be reborn on another.

I wish to open. I feel the need to risk my established position. And I feel the need for silence, a real silence, emptiness. At the same time, I would like to take, to have, in order to subsist in my usual way. I do not submit, do not recognize, do not serve. I want to serve myself. And I need to accept this fact, to live it, to suffer it rather than seek a way out. To resolve it today would be an escape, a way of brushing aside what is inevitable. I feel closed, indifferent. And I feel this reality that calls me but that, at the same time, I do not trust. I do not have faith in it. I want it to yield to me. I am afraid, afraid of disappearing.

In order for me to pass beyond this fragmentation, this separation from my essential being, all the energy in me needs to blend. It needs to be entirely liberated. Do I see the necessity for this? Do I accept it, do I wish it? For this, an absolute tranquillity needs to appear in all the parts of myself. This is not in order to succeed, or to receive and appropriate to myself something marvelous. Rather, it is to see my nothingness, my attachment, my fear of losing the meaning I attribute to myself. Instead of always wanting to be right, I see my contradictions. I see myself hypnotized by my imagination. I see everything together, both my ego and the real "I."

In so seeing, I liberate myself. For a moment I am no longer the same. My freed attention, my consciousness, then knows what I am essentially. This is the death of my ordinary "I." To remember oneself means to die to oneself, to the lie of one's imagination. I have the taste of understanding through awareness of the lack of understanding. In remembering oneself, it is the letting go of the ego that allows a new consciousness to penetrate. Then I see that the ordinary "I" is a phantom, a projection of my self. In fact, everything I take as manifestation is not something separate, but a projection of the essential. Returning to the source, I become conscious of that which arises not to fall back, that which is not born and does not die—the eternal Self.

127. I see reality

In order for me to receive and transmit energy of a higher level, there must be an inner organism, like another body living its own life, in which each element works toward maintaining the whole. As in the physical body, no part can work independently for itself. This is what ought to take place in the inner organization for all our centers. Their functioning should assure the life of a Presence, another organism related to higher centers. A new order needs to be established. For this I have to separate the subtle from the coarse, not to discriminate, to make judgments, but in order to keep them distinct, until one nature lives its life in the other. This creates a new circuit, an emotional current purer than the usual subjective emotions. If there is a deep letting go, a finer energy can circulate freely in me. I then feel the Presence like a magnetic field. And I feel the need to have a conscious sensation and to make room for the inner being.

Knowing cannot take place when there is an image or a judgment. It comes when automatic thought and subjective feeling are suspended, and a tranquillity appears that allows the attention to be free. Because I need to know, to see, my attention enters into contact with *what is*. And in this contact there is an action that takes place, a blending that brings a Presence with its own life, its own rhythm. I see the constant duality, the fragmentation and contradiction preventing this blending, preventing unity. As I see it, the energy is transformed.

When both the mind and the body are entirely still, there is neither thought nor movement . . . only fact, only *what is*, fact without pleasure or pain. This experience of fact can never be mechanical. It cannot be approached with an opinion or a judgment, because this will then become the fact and take the place of what we wish to understand. Fact teaches us. In order to follow its teaching, our listening and our observation must be intense. The intensity of attention disappears if there is a motive for listening or observing. Our usual suffering comes from a thought that feeds on itself, forming the ordinary "I." This "I" is like a machine fed by the thought and the feeling. Seeing fact destroys this machine. Only consciousness of fact will bring understanding, consciousness without choice, consciousness of every thought and feeling, of their motive and operation. No system or method will do this. What is important is to see the constant change of facts in oneself, more important than to seek to go beyond. Consciousness of self as one is, without theories or conclusions, is meditation. When our thoughts and feelings blossom and die, we enter another sphere. A movement outside time appears, which the thinking cannot know. We no longer seek experience and no longer ask anything from it.

The transformation that can take place in me is transformation of my consciousness by another kind of thinking and another kind of feeling. This will come about only through the way of pure vision, which changes me entirely, as though by a miracle. In seeing from moment to moment what I am, I abandon all that I pretend to be. Everything is engaged in this—my emotions, my thought, my body—each intensely active. It is under these conditions that seeing appears. An energy is liberated that alone gives me the force to look deep in myself and not turn away, not stop.

What is most important for me is *to see*, to see without the reaction of my memory and regardless of what I see. Whatever the fact—ambition, jealousy, refusal—the act of seeing it reveals an enormous power. As the fact itself blossoms, there is understanding not only of the fact but of the action that seeing produces—the change in my consciousness. The very act of seeing brings this change, and the truth of what I see transforms my attitude toward life. Consciousness opens—I see. I see reality, and this becomes all-powerful for me. I have an emotional understanding of truth.

Reality has no continuity. It is beyond time, outside duration. Truth must be seen instantaneously and then forgotten, unremembered in the sense of memory of what has been. The perception disappears, but since the mind is unencumbered it may reappear the next day, or even the next moment.

128. *The radiance of Presence*

My being has an origin, a source that is alive, a source of life. I have a way of thinking that distinguishes matter from energy, body from spirit. But nothing exists separately. There is a unity of life. I am at the same time that which creates and that which is created, without any division. With my help, a new body can be created through which the one unique life force in me can make its action felt.

I always make the mistake of trying to force my way toward being, as if I could oblige being to appear. The opposite is true. It is being that constantly strives toward the light of consciousness. It needs a passage that allows it to radiate. But on the way it meets the hard crust of the ego and is blocked by it. In order for being to have an action, a void must appear before it in which a finer vibration can be sensed. Only in emptiness can its vivifying power be felt, only when there are no tensions or any disordered movements of the ego wanting at all costs to prove its identity, to affirm its authority. Each tension is testimony of my ego. In each tension the whole of me is engaged.

I now understand that conscious sensation is the first sign of obedience to something greater, the first step toward a true feeling. Here I glimpse the possibility of a direct perception. My tyrannical "I" submits and no longer dominates, no longer trying to show its strength. I feel another force, not a power that I possess but one in which I am. At this moment there appears an energy coming from a higher emotional current, irresistible so long as it is obeyed. It is this energy, a cosmic force passing in us, that all traditions call "love."

As I become empty of all pretense of knowing, my feeling becomes more stable and purified, able to weigh opposites, that is, able *to know*. When the action of being is felt as a necessity and as something I truly wish, I become capable of communicating this feeling to all my centers so that they are integrated into a single whole. This creates a kind of atmosphere like a thin, sensitive layer, a filter, which is capable of capturing what otherwise would be incommunicable and of letting the most subtle elements show through. This atmosphere is not a wall— the wall of my ego falls. It is like a filtering screen conscious of its mission. Everything depends on the fineness of the filter, whose quality and stability can become the object of my search.

This atmosphere is necessary for the action of my being. It is like a new circuit of another intensity, through which I become conscious of a current of pure feeling for the true, the real. This current is capable of electrifying the whole but can appear only if there is a unity of attention in all my centers. I need this unity in order to know myself.

I have to escape the circle of my habitual "I," letting my crust dissolve, so that life can expand in me and I can absorb the radiations of my being. Then there is not an independent body and a Presence foreign to it. They are one and the same thing—the radiance of a subtle Presence that I experience through the contact, constantly renewed, with the very source of life from which I come. Another "I" appears, shows through my flesh—this Presence made of another substance.

XII

TO LIVE
THE TEACHING

The miraculous is the entry into an action of a conscious force that knows why and how the action is performed.

In order to create, it is necessary to be liberated by voluntary death, the death of the ego. Creative vision only belongs to one who dares to look into the depths of himself as far as the void.

Understanding comes only when the spirit is still.

The highest form of intelligence is meditation, an intense vigilance that liberates the mind from its reactions.

We cannot be without relation; we always obey a relation. Either we are related to something higher or we are taken by the lower. It is a struggle of forces.

In my essence I rejoin the one who sees.

There is no before, no after, only life itself.

CREATIVE ACTION

✥   *129. "I am" in movement*

From where do our actions, our movements, come? When the centers are not related, there can only be reaction. In our usual state the centers do not have the same associations, the same aim, the same vision. Real action belongs to a state beyond our ordinary functioning.

There is in us a perpetual movement of energy that never stops but that gives birth to all kinds of other movements of energy. Every movement is a displacement from one position or attitude to another position, another attitude. We never see both the position and the displacement at the same time. Either we concentrate on the position and ignore the movement, or we focus on the movement but lose sight of the position. So we can foresee a movement and set it in motion, but we cannot follow it.

To follow a movement requires a certain inner vision. Usually the energy of my look is passive, my attention not free. I look through an image, an idea, and consequently do not really see. I may have a sensation of my body, but I do not feel the movement of the energy that is contained in it. In order to feel this movement, the state of the body must change. And the state of the thought and feeling must also change. The body has to acquire great sensitivity and a power of action wholly unknown to it. It must recognize that it is here to serve, that it is the matter, the instrument, through which forces act. The body must see that it needs to obey, and that an understanding between it and the thinking is absolutely necessary. Then a new kind of movement can appear—a free movement. It will not take place without me, without my attention. And the more total my attention, the freer the movement will be.

To maintain a relation between our centers, an action has to be performed at a certain tempo, a certain speed. But we always move at our habitual speed, which is a tempo of inertia, a tempo without vivifying attraction. The action is not lived by all of me. Either the body does not wholly take part and the thought loses its freedom, or the thought is not active enough and the body follows its own habits. So our action creates nothing new, nothing alive, no "sound."

In the Gurdjieff Movements, which can show a new quality of action, the tempo is given and we have to submit to it. In our own work, we ourselves need to find the right tempo and then equally submit to it. Otherwise the work will not transform us. I need to feel that my body and my thought have equal participation, the same force, the same intensity. Then the sensation of the energy contained *in the body* can be stronger than the sensation *of the body* itself. I can follow the movement. "I am" in movement.

130. *The miraculous in action*

In coming together to practice the work to be present in practical activities, we are drawn by an irresistible desire for the miraculous but find ourselves working at mundane tasks like construction, cleaning, cooking, pottery. How do we relate these two, the miraculous and life? Through action. Without action, there is no miraculous and no life.

When we think of an action, we never think that actions can be radically different in themselves, in their quality. We see clearly the difference between wood and metal, and we are not mistaken. But we do not see that, in their quality, actions can be as different from each other as different materials. We are blind to the forces that enter into our actions. Of course, we know that our action is meant to reach an aim, and we expect a result from it. We always think of the aim, of the result, but never of the action itself. Nevertheless, the aim does not determine the action. It is the quality of the force entering an action that conditions it, that makes it automatic or creative. The miraculous is the entry into an action of a conscious force that knows why and how the action is performed.

Each act, everything we do—working with wood or stone, making a meal or a work of art, or thinking—can be either automatic or a creation. In my habitual state I always proceed by repetition. When I have to produce something, the first thing I do is collect my memories on the subject. Then I put together all my experience and all my knowledge, and go forward. My head applies itself, my body follows, and at times I am interested. But all this is merely automatic, and something in me knows it. There is no need for the action to be performed in one particular way or another, and I can do it at a tempo that pleases me. I may succeed in doing something well, but this has no power to change me. It contains no power of action, of creation.

The situation is completely different when my action is not a repetition but something new, an action that can only take place in the present moment to respond to a need I recognize right now. Then there is only one possible speed, and no other tempo can replace it. In a creative action, this comes from a life force that is irresistible, recognized as a truth I obey. And it is this force that sees what has to be done and directs my thought and body. It creates an act and an object, which contains a dynamism and intelligence that are irresistible. The word must be said, the sound emitted.

In order to act in this way, I need to be free, without any image or idea, without thought trapped in memory. Freedom is not freedom from something, but freedom to be in the present, in a moment that never existed before. Action is immediate, without the intervention of thought. I never know; I learn. It is always new. In order to learn, I must have freedom to look. The thinking is silent, entirely silent, free. It sees. In this state, we can understand and carry out an action with all the parts of ourselves. We can even act together with others, provided that, in this moment, all have the same seriousness and intensity.

An action depends on the way my energy is engaged at the very moment I act. I have to be conscious of this at the moment of action and feel the movement of the energy going toward its goal. Once the movement has begun, it is too late to intervene. What has been launched no longer belongs to me. Nothing can stop it from giving the results that will follow—whether good or bad, strong or weak, pure or distorted. Everything is thus determined by the disposition of my different centers at the moment of the action. Each act requires a certain freedom of my body, a one-pointedness of my thought, and an interest, a warmth for what is being done. This will bring me a new way of living.

131. Effective through being

Let us try to understand a state of creation. This is a state in which we know *what is*—not what could be or what should be, not something on which we put a name . . . but simply *what is.*

Can we know a state that does not reinforce our ego? Because everything that reinforces the ego brings division, isolation. This includes all the experiences we have, all the experiences we go through, on which we put a name. We register impressions and react to what we see and feel. And it is this process of reacting that is the experience through which we go. We put a name on the reaction. Indeed, if we do not name it, for us it is not an experience. But is it possible to receive the impression and not have the experience, to be in a state of "nonexperience"? For it is only then, when we are completely immobile and the ego is absent, that creation can take place.

In trying to perform any action effectively, I distinguish two kinds of sensation—one with tension in which the energy is stopped, and another without tension in which the energy is liberated. In working, I can try, as I usually do, to succeed by achieving more and doing better, or I can try in another way, becoming effective through my being. When I undertake something unfamiliar, an object or aim to be achieved, there is tension. My ordinary "I" both wishes to succeed and feels incapable. I am separate, and I want at all costs for my identity to be recognized. My ego is in the way. The tension prevents me from rightly carrying out what I have to do. I need to see this. The level of tension determines whether I can be conscious of my being and of the object of the action.

In engaging in an action, what I am seeking is not to perfect my performance but to become effective through my being. The true relation between my being and the aim depends on carrying out the action without the participation of the ego. To discover this has great importance. Then I need to find a feeling of unity that is not destroyed by the agitation of my ego. I have to come to the point where there is no more tension, no separation between me and the aim, where my ego no longer wants to be recognized.

I cannot come to total immobility, a state without ego, a state of "nonexperience," by forcing . . . nor by fear, nor in order to obtain a reward. I need to know the functioning of the "I" on every level, from its automatic movement to its deepest intelligence. I have to see that whether the thinking turns around in the cage it has constructed or becomes completely still, in either case, the mind has no power to create. And when the mind is not trying to create, there can be creation. But this is not something we can know in advance. No belief, no knowledge, no experience can help. All of that has to disappear, to be abandoned. It is important to be poor—poor in knowledge, poor in beliefs . . . poor in everything that is in the realm of the ego. But I will let this all go only if I know it, if I see the process of this functioning in its entirety. I have to stay here where my thoughts, my feelings and my actions are revealed, constantly on watch moment by moment, passive, lucid . . . immobile.

132. *Something entirely new*

A creation is the appearance of something entirely new. It is not a projection of what already exists, coming from memory, not a repetition of something known. Creation only appears in front of the unknown. It is difficult, however, to act from the unknown, to accept not knowing. It seems that I am deprived of the capacity to "do," that is, to prove that my ordinary "I" is something important, superior to others.

I seek to distract myself from this feeling of not knowing. I search my memory for something that helps me understand. But when I can no longer escape not knowing, when I face this fact as it is and no longer try to give it a meaning that suits me, then I am no longer separated in my ordinary "I," and something new is created. This fact is truth, and truth cannot be translated. A relation appears, and this relation is an act of creation. In the face of what is unknown, what is not understood, my mind becomes silent, and in this silence I discover what is true. In the very act of seeing, there is an act of creation. To see without thought is the discovery of reality.

Under the laws, a real action is determined by two poles: the void from which it comes, and the energy and freedom of its movement. In an act of creation, the movement of interiorizing precedes the movement of exteriorization. In order for the movement inward to proceed, there must be a place that is free and felt like a "void"—void of my ego. Here is a world of finer vibrations, which can be penetrated through sensation. Sensation is the perception of these vibrations. I feel the fineness of this sensation in a state of immobility where there is no tension in my body, and I feel the fineness of the psyche when the thought becomes passive, simply a witness that registers what happens. At this moment a certain sensation of existing appears, a potential life without movement. If this sensation is perceived for even a fraction of a second, it is enough to know what happens at the moment when the "immobile" becomes "mobile," that is, at the first spontaneous vibration. This pervading sensation of existing has its own taste and brings a certainty that erases all doubt. It is the imperative return from nonbeing toward Being. The inconceivable is alive . . . until the moment I realize this and, out of fear of losing it, I give it a name and a form, and the sensation fades away.

In ordinary life we can assemble and construct with elements of the known. But in order to create, it is necessary to be liberated by voluntary death, the death of the ego. Creative vision only belongs to one who dares to look into the depths of himself as far as the void, a matrix created by the constant movement of interiorizing and manifesting, in which one is face-to-face with oneself. We are the calm center of the whirlwind of life, and the inner life is the only good. Then everything is done without attachment, as though we have nothing to do, living wherever it is necessary. Things arise by themselves brought by the current of life.

When we have a thinking that is truly free, we can face life in a new way, including challenges like disease and poverty. Instead of approaching issues as separate from the totality of existence, we can see them as particular aspects of the whole. If I understand the totality of existence in a connected world, I will see that in order to transform things outside me, I have to transform myself. As I approach a better quality in myself, I wish to participate in something higher in this one world. Then I can accept as a fact this life in which I find myself, voluntarily assuming the role given to me within it. I understand my part in the struggle within the totality of existence.

AN ATTITUDE OF VIGILANCE

🌿 *133. Meditation is not contemplation*

For thousands of years the human brain has been conditioned to act from the center to the periphery and from the periphery to the center by a continuous movement, going out and coming back. How could this movement ever stop? If it ceases, an energy will appear that is without limit, without cause, without beginning or end. To come to this, it is first necessary to make order—to clean house—a task that requires complete attention. The body must become very sensitive and the mind completely empty, without any desire. Understanding comes not by an effort to acquire or become, but only when the spirit is still.

Our true nature, an unknown that cannot be named because it has no form, can be sensed in the stop between two thoughts or two perceptions. These moments of stop constitute an opening to a Presence that is without end, eternal. Ordinarily we cannot believe in this because we think anything without form is not real. So we let pass the possibility of experiencing Being.

Our fear of being nothing is what pushes us to fill the void, to wish to acquire or become. And this fear, conscious or not, leads to the destruction of our possibility *to be*. We cannot get rid of it by an act of will or by any effort to free ourselves. Opposing one desire with another can only engender resistance, and understanding will not come from resistance. We can be liberated from this fear only by vigilance, by becoming conscious of it. We must see clearly through the contradictory desires with which we live. It is not a question of concentrating on a single desire, but of freeing oneself from the conflict engendered by avidity. With the dissolution of this conflict comes tranquillity. Reality can appear.

The highest form of intelligence is meditation, an intense vigilance that liberates the mind from its reactions, and this alone, without any willful intervention, produces a state of tranquillity. This requires an extraordinary energy, which can only appear when there is no conflict in us, when all ideals have completely disappeared, all belief, hope and fear. Then it is not contemplation that arises, but a state of attention in which there is no longer a sense of "I," someone present to participate in the experience, to identify with it. So there is no experience. Understanding this at the deepest level is important for one who wishes to know what truth is, what God is, what is beyond the constructions of the human mind.

In this state of vigilance, I do nothing, but I am present. The mind is in a state of attention in which there is lucidity, a clear observation without choice of all that one thinks, all that one feels, all that one does. The mind concentrates without boundaries. This state creates tranquillity, and when the mind is perfectly quiet, without any illusions, "something" comes into existence, not constructed by the mind, that cannot be expressed in words.

134. *Opening without fear*

The mind is my instrument of knowledge, but it will not know truth by some method or discipline, by suppressing or adding, or by changing. All it can do is be quiet, without any intention, not even to receive truth. This is so difficult because I always believe that I can experience reality by doing certain things. Yet all that matters is that my mind be free, without barriers, without conditioning. I need a state of extreme vigilance, asking nothing, expecting nothing, living the moment itself.

This vigilance is the proper activity of the mind, its power. We call it attention. In this state I become pure attention. Then truth can be revealed to me.

How do we understand the teaching of Gurdjieff?

Our existence depends on the state of being in which we live, in which our entire life is conditioned and directed by certain influences. We are subjugated, prisoners of a certain form of thinking, feeling and acting. When we realize the limitations of this state, we feel the need for change. We come to the first true inner question: Is change of being possible? This initial discernment between the true and the false itself signifies a change in consciousness.

The possibility of conscious effort is brought by self-observation. This involves a new attitude toward myself and requires a new relation between my different centers, a new inner form. I cannot observe myself without remembering myself. In one state I can observe, in another I cannot. If I have the sincerity to accept not knowing, I can observe. But if I am fooled by the lie in saying "I," I cannot. If I look with an idea of myself, my thoughts and emotions revolve around this illusion of "I." This prevents my awareness from expanding to consciousness of my whole being.

What can change in me is the awareness of myself, and self-observation only brings results if it is related to the aim of consciousness. I need to see myself living, see all of myself. This requires a certain freedom in which I begin to feel other unknown elements of my being as more real. The search is for a new order, a new state of Being, in which the body and its attributes, my functions, are subject to a higher force that animates them. It calls for a struggle between the "yes" and the "no," and requires the appearance of will. This can produce a second body, an inner form that will give a new form to my life.

Sometimes our work goes better, sometimes less well. We do not understand what happens in us. We want something to take place, and we believe it will be the result of our efforts. We believe we must force a passage toward being. But it is just the opposite. Being is always working in us, trying to break through the hard crust of our ego into the light of consciousness. The primordial impetus animating human will is the striving of being toward this light. Thus it is not our efforts that produce the experience of being. They simply prepare the way. The experience is not of our doing, but a revelation of *what is*. If we repeat unceasingly our efforts—and they need to be repeated—it is to learn to let the reality of Being emerge.

We wish to try to open without fear, to open not once or twice but constantly, until we become conscious of the power of the ego which separates us from life. We undertake this adventure of opening in order to know all the signs by which Being makes itself felt. We learn not to look at ourselves as the measure of all things and as the master of our lives. We begin to feel that we participate in a great unity, a great Whole.

135. *Watchfulness is our real aim*

We cannot change our physical, organic structure. We are conditioned in our movements and attitudes. Our feeling and thinking are also conditioned. In effect, we find ourselves imprisoned in a narrow circle by our conditioning. The only thing that could change this total lack of freedom is the act of seeing. This is the possibility of consciousness.

I can see myself with my eyes, and I can see myself with an inner look. The possibility of becoming conscious, of knowing what I am, depends on the inner look I learn to discover in myself. This look belongs to a new form, an inner body that needs to enter into relation with my physical body. It is only when this look is present, when my automatism is under its light, that a relation can be established. And it is only through this relation, which appears and disappears, that I learn what I am. This is no blind submission, but a conscious giving. There is both a seeing without getting lost and a letting go, a withdrawal without refusal, without hardening. This requires an attention that is as total as possible and, for this attention to appear, a very great tranquillity. Yet we have to remember that we cannot be without relation; we always obey a relation. Either we are related to something higher or we are taken by the lower. It is a struggle of forces.

I wish to know myself as a whole. So I try to look in myself and to be watchful. Watchfulness is our real aim. If we work alone or together without inner watchfulness, it is of no use—we will be taken by one thing or another. I have to be watchful with an intense effort, because everything depends on this. At the same time, I wish to go toward life and, in so doing, to lose myself. Yes, I wish to lose myself. But I do not know what it means. I always think that it is some evil identification that takes me, this awful life that takes me. But it is not true. I go toward it. There is something I like in it. Yet I do not know why. And I have to see that this is an essential question—it is *me* after all, not something outside. So, above all, I need this watchfulness, this way of being here all the time. When I am really able to remain in this attitude, I will become another being.

How can I live this opening to the one reality and at the same time be in front of life and live my life? What is essential is this movement of opening to the fact of being, of existing, without which there will be no awakening. The obstacle is that my mind is occupied all the time. It is not enough to notice this once and for all. I have to live it as my truth until all my thoughts, emotions and actions can be held under my attention without excluding or condemning anything. For this I need a certain inner space and an attention that is free. It is only in a state of free attention that true seeing can appear.

The continual vision of what takes place in us is the beginning of a crystallization, the formation of something indivisible, individual. The clearer the vision, the more alive the impression, and the greater the transformation of our thought and feeling. When they are related, the thinking is lucid and the feeling is clear and subtle. Then we can be open and entirely under the action of a higher force. It is necessary to feel remorse of conscience, a feeling that illuminates, that brings vision of the lack. It is only with this feeling of remorse that we begin to see clearly.

Lucidity, observation that takes place across an inner space, dissolves all forms of conditioning. To be lucid is to be conscious of the way we walk, we sit, we use our hands, and to listen to the way we speak and the words we use. It is to observe all our thoughts, emotions and reactions in a state of attention that is clear and whole, that has no limits. Lucidity is being totally conscious of oneself.

136. *A look from Above*

An attitude of vigilance leads us in the direction of a more objective life. It is difficult to accept the idea of having both an objective life and, at the same time, a personal life—that is, to be subjective, to let oneself live a personal life. It is even more difficult to accept that, in a sense, we have to pay with our personal life. Of course, we cannot be otherwise than personal—subjective, with our own body, our likes and dislikes, our personal feelings. This subjective life will always remain. Yet I must know it, I must experience it. My subjective life is what I am, it is me. At the same time, there is something in me that enables me to be objective in relation to it. If I am also to open to what is higher, my subjective life must be put in its place, sometimes given more, sometimes less. I cannot have new strength on top of all my weakness. I can never come to quietude if I do not sacrifice my agitation and my tensions. I cannot have a free attention if I do not sacrifice what keeps it enslaved. Everything I wish has to be paid for. If I wish to have a new state, I must sacrifice the old. We never get more than we give up. What we receive is proportional to what we sacrifice.

To live a more objective life would require an objective thought— a look from Above that is free, that can see. Without this look upon me, seeing me, my life is that of a blind man driven by impulse without knowing why or how. Without this look upon me, I cannot know that I exist.

I have the power to rise above myself and to see myself freely . . . to be seen. My thought has the power to be free. But for this it must rid itself of all the associations that hold it captive, passive. It must cut the threads that bind it to the world of images, of forms. It must free itself from the constant attraction of the feeling. It must *feel* its power to resist this attraction, to see it while gradually rising above it. In this movement, the thought becomes active. It becomes active in purifying itself, and acquires an aim, a unique aim: to think "I," to realize *who I am*, to enter into this mystery. This look from Above both situates me and liberates me. In the clearest moments of self-awareness, a state is given in which I am known. I feel the blessing of this look that comes down to embrace me. I feel myself under its radiance.

Each time I remember, the first step is the recognition of a lack. I feel the need for an active thought, a free thought turned toward myself, so that I might become truly conscious of my existence. So my struggle is a struggle against the passivity of my ordinary thought, a struggle to let go of the illusion of my ordinary "I." Without this struggle, a greater consciousness will not be born. Without this effort, my thinking will fall back into a sleep filled with vague and drifting thoughts, words, images and dreams, the thought of a man without intelligence. It is terrible to realize suddenly that one has been living without one's own independent thought, living without intelligence, without anything that sees what is real, and therefore without any relation with the world Above. Then I may understand that it is in my essence that I rejoin the one who sees.

This free and impartial thought, which sees and knows, belongs to what Gurdjieff called "individual." Unlike feeling and sensation, which are given by Nature, its formation requires voluntary efforts toward consciousness. It is the seat of will. With its separation from the body, which this thought sees as merely an empty container, there comes freedom, detachment. And through this detachment, we join the sensation of eternity.

A NEW WAY OF BEING

꒰꒱   *137. I must live the lack of relation*

In working in the quiet, we can have the sensation that there is a real Presence in us, something that is here, that really exists. It is here all the time even though we are not in touch with it. We do not have the attention that is required. For there to be contact with this Presence, our attention must have the same subtle quality. And it must be active, not the passive attention we have for our ordinary life. In my usual state there is no contact because whenever I manifest, my attention is taken by my functioning. The energy is chaotically and blindly taken, I know not for what. There is nobody here to know how my force is manifested.

This Presence in me cannot manifest. It has nothing, no specific properties in itself, no material with which it could manifest. It is not educated. This Presence is like a newborn child who does not know how to walk, to eat or to do anything by himself. It needs to grow by receiving impressions that are deposited in a new place in me. Without impressions of this Presence, I will never feel a need to return to it, and it will never have its own life or be able to manifest. So, first, I must really search to experience this Presence in myself and not go away, not forget all the time. When all my force is taken outside, the relation is cut, as if it did not exist. I need a capacity that I do not yet know, an attention of a new kind, without which I will never be related.

In order to feel the need for this Presence, I have to see again and again how I am taken in one or another part of myself and that my centers are not related. I must understand how they could be related and how the relation comes about. It cannot be forced. I need to understand their different lives, their different needs. Each center has a different attention whose force and duration depend on the material they have received. The part that has received more material will have more attention. The nonexistent relation between the centers is the most important thing to live. I must not be satisfied with brief moments when some relation is possible, but actually live the lack, live the incapacity and the resistance.

Can I say today that my body and my feeling are as touched by the Work as my thought is? I am interested by ideas that my body does not live and in front of which my feeling is indifferent. I wish for a change of being, a change in the state of my Presence. The thought can change easily, but not the body or the feeling. Yet, as Gurdjieff said, the power of transformation is not in the thought. It is in the body and the feeling. And our body and feeling experience no demand so long as they are contented. They live only in the present moment, and their memory is short. Until now, the greatest part of our wish, of our efforts, has come from the thought. The thought wishes to obtain, to change something. But what has to change is the state of the feeling. The wish must come from the feeling, and the power to do—the capacity—must come from the body.

With my thought I remember that I wish to be present. My thought has concluded that this would be useful and necessary for all the centers, that I should do everything I can to interest and convince the other centers. But it must be understood that the greatest part of our "I" is not interested in self-remembering. The other centers do not even suspect the existence in the thought of a wish to work in this direction. It is therefore necessary to try to put them into contact with this desire. If they can feel a wish to go in this direction, half of the work will have been accomplished.

138. Conscience

It seems that something is missing in our work, something that demands more on our part from us. We need a demand that would come not from constraint, from a sense of obligation, but from our own understanding. This would bring discipline to all the parts of ourselves solely through understanding, through the way of understanding. Since we entered the Work, we have known the idea of self-remembering, and we have tried to remember ourselves. We have accepted this idea. It has a certain place in our lives, especially in our thinking. Yet it has remained only an idea. It is not alive, it does not apply to our whole life. We do not live the teaching. The different parts of ourselves are not profoundly touched by this idea. They remain unengaged, unconcerned.

Our body, for example, is not truly involved in self-remembering. I always ignore the experience of my body on the earth, belonging to the earth, and go off into speculations or emotions that deprive me of all possibility of being unified, of being whole. This can be seen at each instant. Either my energy is concentrated in my thought—in judging, approving, disapproving, looking for arguments . . . or I am taken by my emotional reactions—in opposing, being afraid, envying, wishing to dominate. In every case, my body is isolated, apart. It tries to safeguard its appetites, all the time paying dearly for the demands of the other parts. Here there is no Being, only parts of Being.

When I feel a Presence in me, my body becomes secondary, fades away as if it did not exist, because I recognize a life—something alive—coming from a much higher level than my body. I perceive this Presence as a whole, which has its own existence and which, in a certain way, does not need my body. At the same time, this life is the life of my body. This real life is active and, in submitting, my body is passive.

This Presence could make it act, speak, listen, if my functions were available, if a connection were established between this life and my body. For example, if I were to raise an arm, I feel that this Presence could perfectly well raise it. In animating this body, this Presence would embrace all my functioning under its look and choose the action necessary to accomplish what has to be done. When I see this, I understand that being connected with this Presence is truly my work, the meaning of my life.

At the same time, I need my body in order to act, to respond to the sense of my Presence here. Without my body, the Presence cannot be determined and defined, nor can it create a certain life on the earth. Without my Presence, the body is only an animal, obliged to eat, sleep, destroy and reproduce. A close relation between them, a kind of communion, is necessary so that from this cooperation an unknown movement can appear, creating a new force, a new life. Then I feel the demand to maintain the relation, to avoid a separation that leads to bestial avidity or disembodied dreams. For example, the body belonging to the earth wants to eat and hungers for cakes set on a plate. It wants one, two, a number of them. The question is not whether to refuse the body the right to take what it wants. It is how many it can eat without impairing the relation with the Presence. Perhaps one, perhaps two, perhaps only half a cake.

When the Presence and the body are together, there is unity, with a new vision that sees the whole, a living whole. In the absolute silence, I can feel "I Am." Part of my attention is turned toward a level beyond my functions and, at the same time, I function and am related to all the functioning of life around me. If I do not maintain the attention at this depth where the energy is entirely free, I will be unable to see, to understand. I will be unable to act freely. I will be merely acted upon by forces from outside. It is here that conscience needs to appear. Then the work is to be as attentive as possible, as "one" as possible, and at the same time to act—that is, to be on two levels at the same time. Conscience awakens not by referring to a pattern, a concept, but in a way that is independent, individual. This has nothing in common with what until now we have believed conscience to be. In the effort to situate myself between forces in me, a true emotion appears—the emotion of *being*.

✎ 139. *Living two lives*

One should think seriously before deciding on the definite goal of becoming conscious and developing a relation with the higher centers. This work does not admit compromise and requires strong discipline. One must be ready to obey laws.

I can thoroughly study the system of ideas, but if I do not realize my mechanicalness and my powerlessness, this will not lead me very far. Conditions can change and I can lose all possibility. The thinking must not remain lazy. I have to understand the necessity of introducing the principles of work into my personal life. I cannot accept that one part of myself is mechanical and at the same time hope that another part is going to be conscious. I need to live the teaching with all of myself.

It is absolutely necessary to have a continual sensation, a constant relation between the mind and the body. Otherwise, I am taken by the automatism. This relation depends on a voluntary, active attention. When the relation is strong, there is a current of higher energy that passes through the head. The attention must be engaged voluntarily in maintaining the relation between the energies of the centers. We see that our centers have to be in accord, and that to do anything together they have to submit to a common master. But it is difficult for them to submit because with a master each one could no longer do what it pleases. Yet, when there is no master, there is no soul . . . neither soul nor will.

In order for the relation not to be lost, I need to maintain a collected state all the time. For this, I have to go against my own subjectivity in daily life. For example, I can do the opposite of my habits. What I usually take with the right hand, I take with the left. In sitting at the table, I do not sit in my usual way. All the time, I go against myself. I think of this relation often during the day, remembering that I wish to keep my attention, not lose it. I wish to keep it in myself, for myself, consciously. What is important in our work is inner struggle. Without it, time will pass and no change will appear. We must learn inside not to identify, and outside to play a role. One helps the other. While I do this, I identify with nothing. Without being strong outside, it is impossible to be strong inside. Without being strong inside, it is not possible to be strong outside. The struggle must be real. The more difficult the struggle is, the more it is worth.

Playing a role requires attending to what takes place around me and at the same time to what takes place within me. Two kinds of events, each of a different order—two lives, one within the other. How I live these two lives shows the extent of my power *to be*. As long as I cannot play a role in this way, there are attempts, moments of more intensity, but no power. A role is a kind of cross on which one must be nailed in order to be able to be attentive without respite. It is like being in a fixed frame or mold that constitutes my limit. I have to be conscious of this limit, to recognize it. I can then be what I am within this frame. Without the limit of this role. no concentration of force is possible. In this way, my outer life becomes like a rite, a service, for my inner life.

Voluntary suffering is the only active principle in us that can be converted into higher feeling. This is necessary for the creation of the second body. In the struggle between two octaves, the body has to refuse its automatism in order to submit to the action of the higher. Through the effort to stay in front, the energy intensifies and an active force appears that makes the passive force obey. This energy must be maintained in the face of all the situations of life. It is necessary to come to a certain state again and again, to make an effort consciously, again and again, until something has been formed that has its own life. Afterward, it will be indestructible. We work for tomorrow, for the future. We suffer consciously today in order to know real joy tomorrow.

✦ 140. To know means to Be

To know oneself is not to look from outside but to catch oneself in a moment of contact, a moment of fullness. In this there is no longer "I" and "me," or "I" and a Presence in me—no separation, no more duality. To know means *to Be*. There is no room for anything else.

When I come to unity in myself, I experience an energy, a force of another sphere, which allows me to be born to my being as part of a great Whole. I can serve. I serve this force, first by a new attitude toward it in all the parts of myself, and then by a vision—ever renewed—of what I am, of the sense of my life in the life of the Whole. This vision includes understanding the relation between my ego and my being. It opens for me the way toward free manifestation, and thus a life in the world that is more true. It leads to a wish to change my ordinary way of being, to be responsible to express truth in my attitude and in my life.

More and more I receive the impression of a mysterious force in me and, at the same time, I receive impressions of the surrounding world to which my functions respond. Is there one life and another life? Or, is it one life, a single life force? In order to have a relation between worlds of finer and coarser materiality, there has to be a current of intermediate intensity—an emotional current of purer feeling. The purification of feeling, the creation in oneself of "divine being," comes through vigilance. There can be no purity without vigilance, an extraordinary vigilance where there is no longer higher or lower, no more struggle, no more fear. There is only consciousness, joy. For this, in all circumstances I have to be the witness of myself, to withdraw from the mental functioning that gives birth to reactions, and to quiet all ambition, all avidity. Then I can see myself responding to life while something in me, something immobile, does not respond. With this vigilance comes a new valuing. I am touched by a wish, a will, that is the very essence of the feeling of "I" in all its purity. It is a will to be what I am, awakening to my true nature—"I am" and "I Am." With this consciousness there is love. But this love is impersonal, like the sun radiating energy. It illuminates, it creates, it loves. It is attached to nothing and yet draws everything to it.

The expansion comes not from "doing" something, from the ego, but from love. It signifies *being* and *becoming*, with an attention that is more and more free. This is the liberation that Gurdjieff speaks of. It is the aim of all schools, all religions. With consciousness, I see *what is*, and in the experience "I Am," I open to the divine, the infinite beyond space and time, the higher force that religions call God. My being is Being. To be one, whole in the face of life, is all that matters.

So long as I remain conscious of this, I feel a life within me and a peace that nothing else can give. I am here, alive, and around me exists the entire universe. The life that is around me is in me. I feel this universal life, the force of the universe. And I feel myself existing as part of the world that surrounds me. Here everything helps, even the cushion on which I sit. I am present, awakened to what I am. And I see that the most important thing is *to be*. I know it—now—and as I know it, I feel related to everything around me. There is no before, no after, only life itself.

I have the impression of emerging from a dream. Everything is real. I feel free, and at peace. In this state, I do not seek, I do not wish, I do not expect anything. There is only what "I am" in this moment. I know now how I am here and why I am here.

Lundi 29 mars — sitting

Je suis là, vivante et autour de moi existe l'univers entier.
La vie qui est autour de moi est en moi — Je ressens cette
vie universelle —
La force de l'univers derrière moi —
Autour de moi des forces existent et je suis une parmi elles —
Je me sens exister —
Tout m'y aide —
Même le coussin sur lequel je suis assise m'aide —
Je me sens une part du monde qui m'entoure —
Je suis là, éveillée à ce que je suis
Et je vois que c'est là la chose la plus importante : être —
Je le sais, maintenant.
Et pendant que je le sais, je reste en relation avec tout ce qui m'entoure.
Il n'y a pas avant, ni après. Il y a la vie même
J'ai l'impression de sortir d'un rêve.
Tout est réel —
Je me sens libre et calme —
Dans cet état où je ne cherche pas, je ne désire pas ... je
n'attends rien que ce que je suis « en cet instant »

Je saurai alors comment je suis là et pourquoi je suis là.

Biographical Note

George Ivanovitch Gurdjieff

Gurdjieff was born in 1866 in the Caucasus on the frontier of Russia and Turkey, the son of a Greek father and Armenian mother. From childhood he felt he had to understand the mystery of human existence, and delved deeply into religion and science to find some explanation. He found both approaches persuasive and consistent within themselves, but bound to reach contradictory conclusions given the different premises from which they began. He became convinced that neither religion nor science could separately explain the meaning of man's life and death. At the same time, Gurdjieff felt certain that a real and complete knowledge had existed in ancient times, and must have been handed down orally from generation to generation. He set out to find this knowledge over a period of some twenty years. His search led him on expeditions through the Middle East and Central Asia to the mountains of the Hindu Kush.

Gurdjieff eventually discovered elements of a forgotten knowledge of being that reconciled the great traditional beliefs. He called it "ancient science" but did not identify its origin, those who discovered and preserved it. This science viewed the world of visible matter as modern physics does, recognizing the equivalence of mass and energy, the subjective illusion of time, the general theory of relativity. But its inquiry did not stop there, accepting as real only phenomena that could be measured and proved by controlled experiment. This science also explored the mystic's world outside sense perception, the vision of another reality, infinite beyond space and time. The aim was to understand the place of man in the cosmic order, the meaning of human life on the earth, and actually to know and experience in oneself the reality of both worlds at the same time. It was a science of being.

In 1912 Gurdjieff began to gather pupils in Moscow and St. Petersburg. In 1917, the year of the Russian Revolution, he moved to the Caucasus, and eventually, in 1922, he established an institute for his work on a larger scale near Paris. During these years he brought a comprehensive system of ideas to introduce his teaching and attract followers. After a near-fatal automobile accident in 1924, Gurdjieff closed the institute and, for the next ten years, turned all his energies to writing his trilogy on the life of man, titled *All and Everything*. He stopped writing in 1935 and thereafter gave himself to intensive work with pupils principally in Paris until his death in 1949. In his later years Gurdjieff regarded the study of the original system of ideas as merely a preliminary stage of the work toward consciousness. He turned aside questions about ideas as being theoretical and presented his teaching in terms of a direct perception of reality.

Gurdjieff's magnum opus, *All and Everything*, was published in three series as *Beelzebub's Tales to his Grandson* (1950), *Meetings with Remarkable Men* (1963) and *Life Is Real Only Then, When "I Am"* (1975). The system of ideas he taught from 1914 to 1924 was faithfully recorded and published in P. D. Ouspensky's *In Search of the Miraculous* (1949) and also in notes, principally of Jeanne de Salzmann, presented in *Views from the Real World* (1974). This teaching included the following fundamental concepts:

The Law of Three Forces (the Law of Three). In Gurdjieff's teaching every phenomenon, on whatever scale, from molecular to cosmic in whatever world, results from the combination of three opposing forces—the positive (affirming), the negative (denying), and the neutralizing (reconciling) force. The possibility of unity depends on a confrontation between the *"yes"* and the *"no,"* and the appearance of a third reconciling force that can relate the two. The third force is a property of the real world—*"what is"* and what *"I am."*

The Law of Octaves (the Law of Seven). All matter in the universe consists of vibrations descending toward manifestation of form ("involution"), or ascending in a return to the formless source ("evolution"). Their development is not continuous but characterized by periodic accelerations and retardations at definite intervals. The laws governing this process are embodied in an ancient formula that divides the period in which a vibration doubles into eight unequal steps corresponding to the rate of increase in the vibrations. This period is called an "octave," that is to say, "composed of eight." This formula lies at the basis of the Biblical myth of the creation of the world, and our division of time into workdays and Sundays. Applied to music, the formula is expressed in the musical scale *do-re-mi-fa-sol-la-si-do*, with semitones missing at the intervals *mi-fa* and *si-do*. The inner movement toward consciousness requires a "conscious shock" at these two intervals in order to proceed to a higher level, that is, a new octave.

The Enneagram. The symbol on the title page—a triangle within a circle with nine equal parts—expresses the Law of Three Forces and the Law of Octaves. Gurdjieff said it is a "universal symbol," which shows the inner laws of one octave and provides a method of cognizing the essential nature of a thing examined in itself. The closed circle represents the isolated existence of the phenomenon, and symbolizes an eternally returning and uninterruptedly flowing process.

Jeanne de Salzmann

Jeanne de Salzmann was born in 1889 in Reims, France, the eldest of five children of Jules Allemand and Marie-Louise Matignon, both descendants of old French families. She was brought up in Geneva, Switzerland, in a home dominated by the interaction of the strong Protestant faith of her father and the devout Catholicism of her mother. She spent childhood hours listening to priests and ministers who often came to dine at her parents' home, where they debated theological questions. This created at an early age a compelling need to understand the truth underlying her parents' Christian faith. Jeanne's mother took her to Sunday mass until, as a little girl, in the middle of the priest's homily she whispered loudly: "He lies!" She always felt her father understood her independent spirit.

Jeanne's education was concentrated on music, for which she showed an exceptional gift as a child prodigy. She began serious study of the piano at the age of four and conducted a full orchestra by the time she was fifteen. During this period the Conservatory of Geneva included famous musicians from other countries, notably Jacques Dalcroze, an innovator widely acclaimed for his work in composition, improvisation and dance. At the age of seventeen, Jeanne was chosen, together with a handful of other gifted students, to follow him to the newly completed Dalcroze Institute at Hellerau near Dresden, Germany, and give demonstrations of his work in capitals throughout Europe. It was during her years with Dalcroze that Jeanne met Alexandre de Salzmann, a well-known Russian painter who was assisting Dalcroze in staging and lighting his demonstrations. She married de Salzmann in Geneva in 1912 and returned with him to his home in Tiflis in the Caucasus, where she began her own school of music based on the Dalcroze method.

In 1919, Gurdjieff arrived in Tiflis with a small group of followers, including the composer Thomas de Hartmann. It was through de Hartmann that the de Salzmanns met Gurdjieff, a meeting that was to change the course of their lives. Jeanne's first impression was unforgettable: "The presence of Gurdjieff, and especially his penetrating look, made an extraordinary impression. You felt that you were truly seen, exposed by a vision that left nothing in shadow, and at the same time you were not judged or condemned. A relationship was immediately established which removed all fear and at the same time brought you face to face with your own reality." In Gurdjieff and his teaching Jeanne de Salzmann found the way toward the truth she had longed for since her childhood.

Within less than a year the disruptions in Russia had extended to the Caucasus, and Gurdjieff was obliged to leave Tiflis with his followers. By this time the de Salzmanns were wholly committed to him and his work. In order to go with him, they gave up their house and other possessions, and Jeanne left behind her school of pupils. The group traveled first to Constantinople and then to Berlin, and finally settled in Fontainebleau near Paris in 1922. Jeanne de Salzmann remained close to Gurdjieff and worked at his side in groups until his death. She was among the handful of pupils included in what he called "special work" for a more conscious sensation.

Mme. de Salzmann played the principal role in Gurdjieff's introduction and practice of the dance exercises called the "Movements." In Tiflis she organized his first class with pupils from her music school. In 1923–1924 in Paris and New York she was herself a central participant in his demonstrations. And in the 1940s she assembled a class of pupils on her own and invited him once again to bring Movements. She later arranged the material in accordance with the aim and principles he had taught. After his death she made a series of films to preserve the Movements in their authentic form.

Before Gurdjieff died he charged Mme. de Salzmann to live to be "over 100" in order to establish his teaching. He left her all his rights with respect to his writings and the Movements, as well as the music that de Hartmann had composed with him. During the next forty years she arranged for publication of his books and preservation of the Movements. She also published the music written to accompany the Movements but ceded to Gurdjieff's heirs all rights to the other Gurdjieff / de Hartmann music because, as she explained, it was not part of his teaching.

Mme. de Salzmann established Gurdjieff centers in Paris, New York and London, as well as Caracas, Venezuela. There she organized groups and Movements classes, and later introduced expanded sittings for "special work" together.

Mme. de Salzmann died at the age of 101 in Paris in 1990.

Gurdjieff Centers

The centers organized by Mme. de Salzmann are:

The Gurdjieff Foundation, New York
The Gurdjieff Society, London
L'Institut Gurdjieff, Paris
Fundacion G. I. Gurdjieff, Caracas, Venezuela

For further information contact www.RealityofBeing.org.

Index

passivity, voluntary, 20, 45, 68, 139,
    141, 219–20, 248
pay/payment, 110, 203, 250, 283
peace, 172, 256, 262, 292
perception, 13, 19, 36, 40, 61, 82, 83,
    206–7, 232
    direct, 18, 42, 56–57, 163, 267
    door of, 59, 162–63
    sensation, 213
    with others, 107
permanence, 9, 251
personality, 13, 20, 37, 108, 156
place, 45, 96
    with others, 105, 114
pleasure or pain, 34–35, 98, 158, 160
poles, 64, 136, 219, 276
position. *See* posture
possess, 32, 37, 40, 44, 47, 69, 80, 239,
    251
possibilities, 19, 31, 70, 87, 88, 90, 167,
    172
posture, 49–50, 83, 84, 120, 140,
    142–44, 192, 213–15, 232
power "to be," 52, 240
prayer/praying, 26, 65, 196, 198, 211
Presence, 13, 16, 20, 31–52, 82, 132–33,
    139–40, 225–43
prison/prisoner, 12, 14, 49, 57, 64, 88,
    121, 280
progress, 15
projecting, 51, 95, 163, 168, 171, 183,
    206–7, 250, 264
promise, 93
purify, 41, 49, 51–52, 67–68, 132, 257,
    291
purity, 43, 70, 72, 73, 75, 163, 259, 291

question/questioning, 9, 20, 81, 83, 96,
    97, 109, 111, 115, 236
    and answer, 36, 56, 59
quiet, work in, 79–86, 92, 142, 148

radiate/radiations, 267–68, 292
react, 14, 34, 207, 211
reaction(s), 22, 23, 24, 26, 55, 123, 211,
    254
    with others, 109, 116, 118
reality, 94, 142, 167, 169, 254–60, 266,
    292
    inner, 25, 48, 71, 81, 82, 84, 95, 99
    of being, 135, 142
rebirth, 263
reconciling, 71, 209, 243
reference, point of, 26
reflection, 18, 253
refusal, 65, 211, 217, 240, 241
relation, 16, 19, 45, 47, 48, 71, 96–97,
    126–27, 281, 291
    centers, 37–38, 47, 48, 286
    ego-being, 44, 88, 291
    mind-body, 187, 191, 228, 289
    with higher, 14, 17, 51, 95, 240, 289
    with others, 106–9, 113, 118–19
relaxation, 68, 212, 215, 230, 250,
    254–55, 261
    See also letting go
religions, 292
remember oneself, 15–21, 34, 37, 41, 74,
    81, 83, 264
remorse, 239, 259–60, 282
repeat, 90, 115, 124, 125, 188, 281
repetition, 97, 111, 121, 188, 273, 275
resist, 42, 89, 97–98
resistance, 64, 90, 92–93, 106, 147, 240,
    278–79
resonance, 82, 106, 134, 163–65, 211
respect, 40, 141, 206, 214, 236, 252
respond/response, 31–32, 41, 87, 120,
    148, 206, 208, 291
responsibility, 5, 199, 220, 229, 238,
    291
    with others, 105, 106–8, 113, 124, 200
result(s), 20, 25, 48, 95–96, 97, 242, 274